Cambridge Academic English

An integrated skills course for EAP

Student's Book

Upper intermediate

Martin Hewings

Course consultant: Michael McCarthy

CAMBRIDGE
UNIVERSITY PRESS

CAMBRIDGE UNIVERSITY PRESS
Cambridge, New York, Melbourne, Madrid, Cape Town,
Singapore, São Paulo, Delhi, Tokyo, Mexico City

Cambridge University Press
The Edinburgh Building, Cambridge CB2 8RU, UK

www.cambridge.org
Information on this title: www.cambridge.org/9780521165204

First published 2012

Printed in the United Kingdom at the University Press, Cambridge

A catalogue record for this publication is available from the British Library

ISBN 978-0-521-1652-04 Student's Book
ISBN 978-0-521-1652-66 Teacher's Book
ISBN 978-0-521-1652-35 Class Audio CD
ISBN 978-0-521-1652-97 DVD
ISBN 978-1-107-6071-49 Audio and DVD pack

Cambridge University Press has no responsibility for the persistence or
accuracy of URLs for external or third-party internet websites referred to in
this publication, and does not guarantee that any content on such websites is,
or will remain, accurate or appropriate. Information regarding prices, travel
timetables and other factual information given in this work is correct at
the time of first printing but Cambridge University Press does not guarantee
the accuracy of such information thereafter.

Acknowledgements

Author acknowledgments

Many people have contributed in various ways to this book. My thanks go first to my editors at Cambridge University Press, especially Kate Hansford, Karen Momber and Caroline Thiriau, who have taken the book to publication with great care, professionalism, and patience. Thanks, too, to Dilys Silva and Robert Vernon for their guidance and encouragement in the early stages, to Jessica Errington for her editorial work, and to Linda Matthews for organising production schedules. Michael McCarthy has played an important role in shaping the course as a whole and also advising on the use of corpora in the material. I would also like to thank the Corpus team at Cambridge University Press for their help in accessing the academic corpus.

At home, my thanks as always to Ann, David and Suzanne for their support.

Between 1985 and 2009 I taught English for Academic Purposes in the English for International Students Unit at the University of Birmingham. Much of the material in this book began its life in handouts produced for students I had the pleasure to work with there. I would like to thank those students for their contribution.

Publisher acknowledgements

A special thanks to Dr Karen Ottewell at the University of Cambridge Language Centre for reviewing the material so thoroughly and helping us to organise the lectures and to all the lecturers who allowed us to film them delivering lectures for the book: Dr Hugh Hunt, Dr Maru Mormina, Dr Charles Moseley and Dr Prodromos Vlamis.

We'd like to thank all the reviewers who have provided valuable feedback on this project: Jane Bottomley, Anna Derelkowska, Ludmila Gorodetskaya, Chris Hilton, Sylwia Maciaszczyk, Maggie McAllinden, Marie McCullagh, Gavin McGuire, Margareth Perucci, Elaine Rowlands, Chris Sowton, Lisa Zimmermann, and members of the Cambridge ELT Adult Course Advisory Panel: Michael Carrier, Hanna Komorowska, David Larbalestier, Carlos Lizarraga, Jason Moser, Ron Schwart, Anna Shpynova and Scott Thornbury.

We would also like to thank the students who participated in the interviews which appear in the Lecture skills units: Frederike Asael; Larissa Bosso; Fei He; Cristoffer Levin; Anna Lowe; Zaneta Macko; Sithamparanathan Sabesan; Maria Silva-Grazia; Anita Thillaisundaram.

Text and photo acknowledgements

The authors and publishers acknowledge the following sources of copyright material and are grateful for the permissions granted. While every effort has been made, it has not always been possible to identify the sources of all the material used, or to trace all copyright holders. If any omissions are brought to our notice, we will be happy to include the appropriate acknowledgements on reprinting.

The Cambridge Advanced Learner's Dictionary is the world's most widely used dictionary for learners of English. Including all the words and phrases that learners are likely to come across, it also has easy-to-understand definitions and example sentences to show how the word is used in context. The Cambridge Advanced Learner's Dictionary is available online at dictionary. cambridge.org. © Cambridge University Press, Third edition & 2008, reproduced with permission.

Development of this publication has made use of the Cambridge English Corpus (CEC). The CEC is a computer database of contemporary spoken and written English, which currently stands at over one billion words. It includes British English, American English and other varieties of English. It also includes the Cambridge Learner Corpus, developed in collaboration with the University of Cambridge ESOL Examinations. Cambridge University Press has built up the CEC to provide evidence about language use that helps to produce better language teaching materials.

William S. Pearson et al for the text on p. 12, 'Analysis of Language as a Barrier to Receiving Influenza Vaccinations Among an Elderly Hispanic Population in the United States' Copyright 2011;

Duane Brown and Associates for the images on p. 14, 'Career Choice and Development' 4th Edition, published by John Wiley & Sons Ltd;
Emerald for the image on p.15, 'Career Development International' © Emerald Group Publishing Limited;
Spinnaker Leadership Associates, Inc. for the image on p. 15, 'Career Transition and Achievement';
Cambridge University Press for the adapted text on pp. 16-17, 'Solutions for the world's biggest problems' by Bjorn Lomborg 2007 © Cambridge University Press, Dr. Bjorn Lomborg, director of Copenhagen Consensus Center, www.copenhagenconsensus. com;
Cambridge University Press for the adapted text on pp. 27-28, 'Natural Hazards' by Edward Bryant, 1991, © Cambridge University Press;
Cambridge University Press for the adapted data on p. 31, 'People and the Earth - Basic Issues in the Sustainability of Resources and Environment' by Rogers and Feiss 1998 © Cambridge University Press;
World Health Organisation 2008 for the adapted material on p. 32, 'The global burden of disease' 2004;
Cambridge University Press for the adapted text on p.48, 'Communication Across Cultures - Mutual Understanding in a Global World' by Bowe and Martin, 2007 © Cambridge University Press;
Cambridge University Press for the adapted text on pp.43-44, 'The Study of Language' 3rd Edition by George Yule 2006 © Cambridge University Press;
Pearson Education for the adapted text on p. 55, 'International Business' 4th Edition by Rugman & Collinson 2006;

Brooks/Cole for the adapted text on p. 73, 'Physical Geography' 9th Edition by Gabler, Petersen, Trepasso and Sack © 2009, part of Cengage Learning, Inc. Reproduced by permission. www.cengage.com/permissions;

Wadsworth for the adapted text on pp. 83-84 'Learning and Behavior' 6th Edition. By Chance © 2009, a part of Cengage Learning, Inc. Reproduced by permission. www.cengage.com/permissions;

Cambridge University Press for the adapted text on p. 83 'Behaviour' by Dockery and Reiss 1999 © Cambridge University Press;

Families and Work Institute for the data on p. 84 'Times are changing: gender and generation at work and at home' by Galinsky, Aumann & Bond taken from Families and Work Institute Report 2009, www.familiesandwork.org;

TAYLOR & FRANCIS for the adapted text on p. 85 'Gender Development' by Owen Blakemore, Berenbaum, Liben 2009;

Wadsworth for the adapted text on p. 86 'Understanding Human Behavior and the Social Environment' 8th Edition by Zastrow, Kirst-Ashman. © 2010, a part of Cengage Learning, Inc. Reproduced by permission. www.cengage.com/permissions;

Cambridge University Press for the Definition of UNESCO noun, on p. 159 from the Cambridge Advanced Learner's Dictionary © Cambridge University Press;

Allen & Unwin Pty Limited for the adapted text and imges on pp. 98-99 'Who Cares? The changing health care system' by Lumby 2001;

McGraw Hill Companies, Inc, for the material on pp. 99-100 'Who killed health care? America's $2 trillion medical problem - and the consumer-driven cure' by Herzlinger, 2007;

Oxford University Press for the adapted text on pp. 100-102 'How to Change the World: Social entrepreneurs and the power of new ideas' by D. Bornstein, 2007;

The Poverty Site for the material on p. 110 Guy Palmer, www.poverty.org.uk;

Cengage Learning, Inc for the adapted text on pp. 111-112 'Human Development' 5E. by Kail and Cavanaugh, © 2010 Wadsworth, a part of. Reproduced by permission. www.cengage.com/permissions;

National Centre for Social Research (NatCen) for the adapted text on pp. 128-129 'British Social Attitudes: Perspectives on a changing society' by Park 2007;

The Office for National Statistics for the data on p. 135 'The Time Use Survey, 2005' licensed under the Open Government Licence v.1.0. © Crown copyright 2006;

World Health Organisation Statistics for the data on pp. 138, 140, 'Mortality and burden of disease' © World Health Statistics 2010;

OECD (2009) for the adapted text on p. 139, 'Health at a Glance 2009: OECD Indicators', OECD Publishing, http://dx.doi.org/10.1787/health_glance-2009-en;

Elsevier for the adapted text on pp. 140-142, 145-146, adapted from 'Health Promotion: Foundations for practice' by Naidoo and Wills, 2000 (Figure on p. 142 adapted from Crawford 1984), Copyright Elsevier;

For the slides in Lecture skills E, p. 153, 'David Begg, Stanley Fischer and Rudiger Dornbusch, 'Economics' © 2002, Reproduced with the kind permission of Open University Press. All rights reserved.

The publishers are grateful to the following for permission to reproduce copyright photographs and material:
Key: l = left, c = centre, r = right, t = top, b = bottom
Alamy/Simone Brandt for the unit headers, /©Denkou Images for p59(B), /©Paul Phillips/iOpeners for p63(r), /©Sami Sarkis for p63(l), /©Peter Titmuss for p72(c), /©aberCPC for p144(t); Corbis/©Anna Peisl for p59(A), ©Moodboard for p82, /©Helen King for p144(b); Fotolia/©Alexey Bannykh for p30(t), /©c#8344922 for p72(r); Getty Images/©Tom Pfeiffer/VolcanoDiscovery for p30(ct), /©Peter Dazeley for p30(cb), /©BZM Productions for p59(D); istockphoto/©Bartosz Haydniak for p59(C), /©Chris Schmidt for p144(c); Masterfile/©Asia for p59(E); Photolibrary/©Sven-erik Arndt for p63(b); Shutterstock/©George Bailey for p30(b), /©Laurence Gough for p113.
We are unable to trace the copyright of the photo on page 41 and would welcome any information enabling us to do so.

Picture Research by Hilary Luckcock.

Designed and produced by Wild Apple Design, www.wildappledesign.com
Video production by Phaebus, and Phil Johnson.
Audio production by Leon Chambers.

Introduction

Who is the course for?

Cambridge Academic English is for anyone who needs English for their academic studies.

It is an integrated skills course, which means that at each of the levels you will develop your abilities in reading, writing, listening and speaking in an academic context. In your class there will probably be students studying or hoping to go on to study many different subjects. With this in mind, *Cambridge Academic English* includes topics and texts that will be of interest to students from all disciplines (subject areas), and teaches language and skills that will be of use to students working in all subjects. However, some parts of the course also help you to develop abilities relevant to your particular area of study.

Student's Book B1 is aimed at students who need to improve their English significantly in order to guarantee success in higher education. If you are familiar with the Common European Framework of Reference (CEFR) proficiency levels, Student's Book B1 is likely to be most useful for Independent Users at level B1 and above. Student's Book B2 is aimed at students who will soon be starting undergraduate or postgraduate studies and are Independent Users at level B2 and above. Student's Book C1 is aimed at students who may already have begun their academic studies. It will also be of interest to non-native English-speaking academics who need to present and publish in English. It will be of most use to Proficient Users at level C1 and above.

How is the book organised?

The introductory unit, *Academic orientation*, introduces you to aspects of studying academic English. For example, you will learn about academic culture and consider possible differences in study methods in different countries and in different subject areas.

The Student's Book is organised into integrated skills and lecture skills units:

• Integrated skills units 1–10 (with separate Audio CD)

Ten units are organised around a broad topic of interest and help you develop your skills in reading, speaking and writing academic English. Each of these units ends with a grammar and vocabulary focus that is of particular importance in academic written and spoken communication. The cross references in the margins point to further information, strategies, or extra practice which can be found in the *Grammar and vocabulary* section of that unit.

(◀)0.0) The separate Class Audio CD includes all the recordings needed for the listening and speaking sections and gives students focused listening practice, strategies to participate in tutorials and group work.

• Lecture skills units A–E (with separate DVD)

After every two integrated skills units there is a *Lecture skills unit* to help you develop skills in listening to lectures and taking notes. For this course, a variety of lectures were recorded at the University of Cambridge and a separate DVD accompanies the Student's Book, containing clips of these lectures and of students talking about their experience of studying in English at university.

(▣ A.0) Extracts from these lectures have been used in the lecture skills units to help you understand, for example, how lecturers use language, visual information, gesture and pronunciation to present content and show how they are organising the lecture.

What kind of language does the course teach?

Cambridge Academic English uses authentic academic texts. The texts you will read are taken from the kinds of textbooks and journal articles that your subject tutors might recommend you to read. You may find these challenging at first but you will learn strategies in the course to help you to cope with them. We believe that working with authentic texts in EAP is the best way of preparing to read them during your academic course of study.

The lectures you will watch are delivered by experienced lecturers and researchers. In many colleges and universities around the world you will be taught in English by some tutors who are native English speakers and others who are non-native English speakers. To help you prepare for this, both native and non-native English-speaking lecturers have been included in this course.

The vocabulary focused on in the course has been selected for being of particular importance in academic writing, reading, lectures and seminars. In choosing what to teach we have made use of the Academic Word List compiled by Averil Coxhead (see www.victoria.ac.nz/lals/resources/ academicwordlist/ for more information). This list includes many of the words that you are likely to encounter in your academic studies.

What are the additional features?

Each unit contains the following additional features:

 The *Study tip* boxes offer practical advice on how you can improve the way you study.

 The *Information* boxes provide useful background on language or academic culture.

 The *Focus on your subject* boxes encourage you to think about how what you have learnt applies to your own subject area.

 The Corpus *research boxes* present useful findings from the CAEC.

- The *Word list* at the back of the Student's Book covers key academic words essential for development of academic vocabulary.

- For each level of the course, a full-length version of one of the lectures from the DVD is available online. This gives you the opportunity to practise, in an extended context, the listening and note-taking skills that you develop in the *Lecture Skills* units. The video and accompanying worksheets are available for students at www.cambridge.org/elt/academicenglish.

To make sure that the language we teach in the course is up-to-date and relevant, we have made extensive use of the Cambridge Academic English Corpus (CAEC) in preparing the material.

 What is the Cambridge Academic English Corpus (CAEC)?

The CAEC is a 400-million-word resource comprising two parts. One is a collection of written academic language taken from textbooks and journals written in both British and American English. The second is a collection of spoken language from academic lectures and seminars. In both parts of the corpus a wide variety of academic subject areas is covered. In addition to the CAEC, we have looked at language from a 1.7-million-word corpus of scripts written by students taking the IELTS test.

Conducting our research using these corpora has allowed us to learn more about academic language in use, and also about the common errors made by students when using academic English. Using this information, we can be sure that the material in this course is built on sound evidence of how English is used in a wide variety of academic contexts. We use the CAEC to provide authentic examples in the activities of how language is used, and to give you useful facts about how often and in what contexts certain words and phrases are used in academic writing.

We hope you enjoy using *Cambridge Academic English* and that it helps you achieve success in your academic studies.

Martin Hewings

Contents

Unit 4 **Difference and diversity** Page 54	**Reading**	**Listening and speaking**	**Writing skills**	**Grammar and vocabulary practice**
	Thinking about what you already know Reading in detail Taking notes Vocabulary building 1: word families Vocabulary building 2: adjective–noun collocations Collecting information for an essay Taking notes for essay writing	Working with colleagues: generating ideas and reporting Pronunciation: dividing speech into units	Language for writing 1: the grammar of reporting verbs Language for writing 2: comparing and contrasting Reporting what you read	Linking parts of a text: conjunctions and sentence connectors Single–word verbs and multi- word verbs Word families
Lecture skills B *Page 66*	**Preparing for lectures**	**Listening**	**Language focus**	**Follow up**
	Using preparation strategies Making predictions before a lecture starts	Making predictions during a lecture Identifying topic change Following an argument Taking notes: using symbols and abbreviation in notes	Organising questions and topic changes	Expanding your vocabulary
Unit 5 **The world we live in** *Page 70*	**Reading**	**Listening and speaking**	**Writing skills**	**Grammar and vocabulary practice**
	Recognising plagiarism Getting started Identifying the main ideas in a text Summarising what you have read Vocabulary building: single- word verbs and multi-word verbs Vocabulary in context: hedging adverbs	Reaching a consensus in group work Pronunciation: contrasts	Using paraphrases Including quotations in your writing	Articles: *zero article* and *the* Complex prepositions *Person, people, peoples*
Unit 6 **Behaving the way we do** *Page 82*	**Reading**	**Listening and speaking**	**Writing skills**	**Grammar and vocabulary practice**
	Organising information for an essay Skimming and scanning texts Taking notes and explaining what you have read Vocabulary building: collocations	Referring backwards and forwards in presentations	Writing conclusions in essays Language for writing: hedging Giving references	Avoiding repetition: expressions with *so* *Wh-* noun clauses Using viewpoint adverbs to restrict what is said Verb/adjective + preposition combinations
Lecture skills C *Page 94*	**Preparing for lectures**	**Listening**	**Language focus**	**Follow up**
	Thinking about the purposes of lectures	Understanding evaluations Understanding lists	Noticing differences in the language of lectures and academic writing Noticing prominent words	Taking notes: annotating Reconstructing your notes

Academic orientation

- Assessing your academic skills
- Thinking about academic culture
- Thinking critically
- Avoiding plagiarism
- Recognising variation across academic subjects
- Focusing on academic vocabulary

1 Assessing your academic skills

This unit introduces some key skills that you will learn about during the course. It focuses on features of academic English and issues relevant to using English in an academic context.

1.1 a **Look at the list of some of the academic skills that you will practise in this course and answer the following questions.**

   1 Which two skills do you think are the most important for your academic studies, and which two are the least important?

   2 Which two skills do you think are your strengths, and which two do you need to practise more?
   - Understanding lectures in English
   - Taking part in group work
   - Giving presentations
   - Reading academic texts
   - Finding information to include in my own writing
   - Writing essays
   - Summarising what I have read
   - Learning academic vocabulary

   b **In pairs, discuss your answers. Do you have any advice to give on how to improve these skills?**

2 Thinking about academic culture

Academic culture means the beliefs, opinions and ways of behaving shared by people working or studying in a higher education institution. If you go abroad to study, you may find that the academic culture is different from that in educational institutions in your own country.

2.1 a **In pairs, discuss whether the statements about academic culture (1–8) are true (T) or false (F) in your own country.**

   1 If you arrive late to a lecture, you shouldn't enter the room.
   2 If your mobile phone goes off in class, you should go out of the room to answer it.
   3 If your lecturer says something you don't understand, you should ask them to explain.
   4 You will get all the information you need to pass exams in the course lectures, so you only need to do extra reading if you are aiming for excellent marks.
   5 Textbooks are written by experts so you can accept what you read in them as true.
   6 If you are having difficulties writing an essay, you should go to your tutor for help.
   7 To help you understand what is needed in academic writing, you should look at the texts (e.g. essays, dissertations) of past students.
   8 You will get good marks for an essay if you can show you support your tutor's opinion on the subject.

   b **Discuss whether your answers would be different if you studied in another country.**

2.2 a  **◀) 0.1** One aspect of academic culture concerns the ways in which students and lecturers interact. Listen to Zaneta talking about her experiences in Poland and Britain. How would she address her lecturers in both countries?

b How would students normally address university lecturers in your country?

Zaneta

3 Thinking critically

In your academic studies, writers and lecturers will often present you with arguments, trying to persuade you to accept certain ideas by giving reasons why you should. Critical thinking involves judging these arguments; that is, deciding whether to accept them or not.

3.1 a You are going to discuss an extract from a student's essay on behavioural studies. Before you start, look at the words in the box which might be useful to you in your discussion. Use your dictionary to look up any words you don't know.

b Read the extract and in pairs, discuss whether you are persuaded by the argument the student makes. Why? / Why not?

> **Verbs:** distinguish identify justify provide
>
> **Nouns:** assumption claim evidence explanation fact opinion reason

> The majority of people believe that children's behaviour is worse now than it was in the past. The reason for this poor behaviour can be found in the breakdown in discipline in schools in recent years. Along with the family environment, school is an important influence on how a child develops. It follows, therefore, that it is only by improving discipline in schools that we can stop this decline in standards of behaviour.

4 Avoiding plagiarism

It is unacceptable in academic culture to plagiarise; that is, to use the ideas or words of another person and pretend that they are your own.

4.1 In pairs, make a list of reasons why plagiarism might be unacceptable. Report your ideas back to the rest of the class.

4.2 Read the extract from a textbook and the extract from a student's essay which follows. Do you think the student is guilty of plagiarism?

> ### Environmental Effects of Earth Rotation
>
> The first – and perhaps most obvious – effect of the Earth's rotation is that it imposes a daily, or *diurnal*, rhythm in daylight, air temperature, air humidity, and air motion.
>
> All surface life responds to this diurnal rhythm. Green plants receive and store solar energy during the day and consume some of it at night. The daily cycle of incoming solar energy
> 5   and the corresponding cycle of fluctuating air temperatures are topics for analysis in Chapters 2 and 3.
>
> A second environmental effect is that the flow paths of both air and water are turned consistently in a sideward direction because of the Earth's rotation. Flows in the northern hemisphere are turned toward the right and in the southern hemisphere toward the left.
> 10 This phenomenon is called the *Coriolis effect*. It is of great importance in studying the Earth's systems of winds and ocean currents and is discussed in Chapter 5.

Strahler, A. H. & Strahler, A. (2002). *Introducing Physical Geography (3rd edn.)* New York: John Wiley.

Extract from a student's essay

> The Earth's rotation has a number of effects on the environment. The first – and perhaps most obvious – effect of the Earth's rotation is that it imposes a daily, or *diurnal*, rhythm in daylight, air temperature, air humidity, and air motion. All surface life responds to this diurnal rhythm. Green plants receive and store solar energy during the day and consume some of it at night. A second effect is known as the *Coriolis effect* – the sideward movement of air and water on Earth, to the right in the northern and to the left in the southern hemisphere – which has a major impact on winds and ocean currents (Strahler and Strahler, 2002).

5 Recognising variation across academic subjects

Different academic subjects (or disciplines) are interested in different topics and consequently use different methods of working and ways of talking and writing about their work.

5.1 Read three abstracts (short summaries of the contents) from academic journal articles and in pairs answer the following questions.

1 Without reading the texts in detail, what can you say about differences in the language and the organisation of the abstracts?
2 Do these differences suggest anything to you about differences in the three subjects themselves?

Abstract 1 (from a medical journal)

Background. The Hispanic population in the United States is growing, and disparities in the receipt of healthcare services as a result of limited English proficiency have been demonstrated. We set out to determine if Spanish language preference was a barrier to receiving influenza vaccinations among Hispanic persons 65 years and older in the USA. *Methods.* Differences in the receipt of vaccinations by language preference were tested with both Chi-square analyses and adjusted logistic regression analyses. *Results.* Findings suggest that elderly Hispanic persons, 65 years of age and older, who prefer to communicate in Spanish instead of English, are significantly less likely to have received influenza vaccinations when compared to their Hispanic counterparts who prefer to communicate in English. *Conclusions.* Influenza infections can more often be fatal in older persons and may disparately affect minority populations such as Hispanic persons. Therefore, understanding barriers to the receipt of effective preventive health measures is necessary.

Pearson, W. S., Zhao, G. and Ford, E. S. (2011). An analysis of language as a barrier to receiving influenza vaccinations among an elderly Hispanic population in the United States. *Advances in Preventive Medicine.*

Abstract 2 (from a chemistry journal)

Multiconfigurational quantum chemical calculations on the R-diimines dichromium compound confirm that the Cr–Cr bond, 1.80 Å, is among the shortest Cr^I–Cr^I bonds. However, the bond between the two Cr atoms is only a quadruple bond rather than a quintuple bond. The reason why the bond is so short has to be attributed to the strain in the NCCN ligand moieties.

La Macchia, G., Aquilante, F., Veryazov, V., Roos, B. O. and Gagliardi, L. (2008). Bond length and bond order in one of the shortest Cr-Cr bonds. *Inorganic Chemistry, 47*, 11455.

Abstract 3 (from a music journal)

This article provides a brief sketch of how scholars may be actively involved in conflict transformation efforts using music or the arts beyond their purely artistic connotations. Here I will explore the ways in which music has been employed in some ethnomusicological projects based on my personal experiences, which can hopefully stimulate debate and provide some ideas for other scholars in different branches of humanities and social sciences.

Pettan, S. (2010). Applied ethnomusicology: bridging research and action. *Music and Arts in Action, 2*, 90.

5.2 **Think about two academic subjects you are familiar with (e.g. subjects you have studied at high school) and answer the following questions.**

1 What are typical topics studied in each subject, and what methods are used to research them?

2 What types of text did you read when you studied these subjects?

3 In what ways were the language and organisation different in texts in the two subjects?

6 Focusing on academic vocabulary

Academic texts include three main types of vocabulary.

1 general vocabulary – *words that are also commonly used in everyday language*

2 academic vocabulary – *words that are commonly used in many different academic subjects, but are less common in everyday language*

3 specialised vocabulary – *words that are used mainly in particular academic subject areas, but may be rare in other subjects or in everyday language*

6.1 **Look at the following words which appear in the texts in 5.1 and in pairs decide whether they are general (G), academic (A) or specialised (S). The first one has been done for you.**

analyses	_A_	Hispanic	_____
beyond	_____	likely	_____
conclusions	_____	methods	_____
debate	_____	necessary	_____
dichromium	_____	proficiency	_____
different	_____	quintuple	_____
ethnomusicological	_____	transformation	_____
growing	_____		

In this book, you will focus in particular on building your *academic* vocabulary.

1 Choices and implications

Reading

1 Researching texts for essays

1.1 You have been given an essay with the title *What factors affect people's choice of career?* and decide to use the Internet for your initial research. When you do a search for 'career choice', you get the following results (A–D).

a Match the text types (1–4) to the search results (A–D).

1 an academic textbook   3 a company website

2 a general information website   4 a research article

A Wiley: Career Choice and Development, 4th Edition
Introduction to Theories of **Career** Development and Choice: Origins, Evolution,
..Status of Theories of Career Choice and Development (Duane Brown.) …
www.wiley.com/.../produceCd-0787957410,descCd-tableOfContents.html

B What factors affect your choice of career iknow-what.com
Most people want a **career** that brings them money, security, and job satisfaction.
But what factors …
www.iknow-what.com/careers/factors.html

C Emerald Full Text Article: The factors affecting the career choice …
The results of the survey as they apply to the factors affecting **career** choice
similarities and differences are discussed in this paper. … by S Wilkinson 1996
www.emeraldinsight.com/insight/ViewContentServlet?Filename…

D Career Transition/Achievement
Other major factors affecting **career** choice are parental guidance, teacher or
professor influence and peer or social status pressures. …
www.spinnakerleadership.com/id70.html

---

b Look at the sources of information (A–D) you find after you click on the links and check your answers to 1.1a.

c Which of the sources (A–D) would it be appropriate to refer to in your essay?

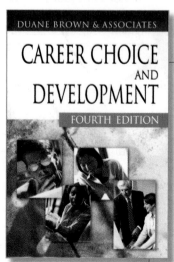

A

DUANE BROWN & ASSOCIATES

CAREER CHOICE AND DEVELOPMENT
FOURTH EDITION

Contents

Preface   xi

About the Authors   xv

Part One: Introduction and Cases

1. Introduction to Theories of Career Development
and Choice: Origins, Evolution, and Current Efforts   3
Duane Brown

2. Case Studies   24
Duane Brown

B

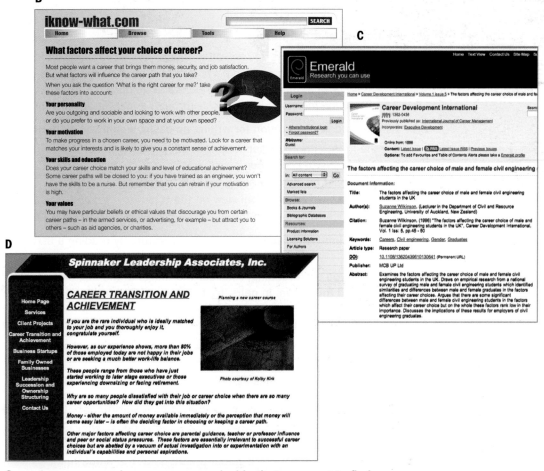

iknow-what.com

Home | Browse | Tools | Help | SEARCH

What factors affect your choice of career?

Most people want a career that brings them money, security, and job satisfaction. But what factors will influence the career path that you take?

When you ask the question 'What is the right career for me?' take these factors into account:

Your personality
Are you outgoing and sociable and looking to work with other people, or do you prefer to work in your own space and at your own speed?

Your motivation
To make progress in a chosen career, you need to be motivated. Look for a career that matches your interests and is likely to give you a constant sense of achievement.

Your skills and education
Does your career choice match your skills and level of educational achievement? Some career paths will be closed to you: if you have trained as an engineer, you won't have the skills to be a nurse. But remember that you can retrain if your motivation is high.

Your values
You may have particular beliefs or ethical values that discourage you from certain career paths – in the armed services, or advertising, for example – but attract you to others – such as aid agencies, or charities.

C

Emerald
Research you can use

Home › Career Development International › Volume 1 Issue 5 › The factors affecting the career choice of male and fe

Career Development International
ISSN: 1362-0436
Previously published as: International Journal of Career Management
Incorporates: Executive Development

The factors affecting the career choice of male and female civil engineering

Document Information:

Title: The factors affecting the career choice of male and female civil engineering students in the UK

Author(s): Suzanne Wilkinson, (Lecturer in the Department of Civil and Resource Engineering, University of Auckland, New Zealand)

Citation: Suzanne Wilkinson, (1996) "The factors affecting the career choice of male and female civil engineering students in the UK", Career Development International, Vol. 1 Iss: 5, pp.45 - 50

Keywords: Careers, Civil engineering, Gender, Graduates

Article type: Research paper

DOI: 10.1108/13620439610130641 (Permanent URL)

Publisher: MCB UP Ltd

Abstract: Examines the factors affecting the career choice of male and female civil engineering students in the UK. Draws on empirical research from a national survey of graduating male and female civil engineering students which identified similarities and differences between male and female graduates in the factors affecting their career choices. Argues that there are some significant differences between male and female civil engineering students in the factors which affect their career choice but on the whole these factors rank low in their importance. Discusses the implications of these results for employers of civil engineering graduates.

D

Spinnaker Leadership Associates, Inc.

Home Page
Services
Client Projects
Career Transition and Achievement
Business Startups
Family Owned Businesses
Leadership Succession and Ownership Structuring
Contact Us

CAREER TRANSITION AND ACHIEVEMENT

Planning a new career course

If you are the rare individual who is ideally matched to your job and you thoroughly enjoy it, congratulate yourself.

However, as our experience shows, more than 80% of those employed today are not happy in their jobs or are seeking a much better work-life balance.

These people range from those who have just started working to later stage executives or those experiencing downsizing or facing retirement.

Photo courtesy of Kolby Kirk

Why are so many people dissatisfied with their job or career choice when there are so many career opportunities? How did they get into this situation?

Money - either the amount of money available immediately or the perception that money will come easy later – is often the deciding factor in choosing or keeping a career path.

Other major factors affecting career choice are parental guidance, teacher or professor influence and peer or social status pressures. These factors are essentially irrelevant to successful career choices but are abetted by a vacuum of actual investigation into or experimentation with an individual's capabilities and personal aspirations.

1.2 a As you research your essay you decide that you want to find:

1 a summary of the current state of knowledge on the topic.
2 a number of research papers on the topic.
3 the latest statistics on the number of people in different careers in a country.
4 definitions of specialist terms.
5 reports of the most up-to-date research on the topic.
6 a personal view on why someone went into a particular career.

In which of the text types in the box would you be most likely to find these? There may be more than one answer.

> blogs   edited collections   journals   monographs   official reports
> online encyclopedia entries (e.g. Wikipedia)   textbooks

Note: An *edited collection* is a book which includes articles usually written by different authors. *Monographs* are usually short books on a specialised subject, written mainly for other academics rather than students.

b Are there any of these text types that you would not refer to in your academic writing?

1.3 a ◀1.1 **Listen to Fei He talking about the types of texts he had to read during his undergraduate studies in China and his postgraduate studies in Britain.**

1 Which of the text types in 1.2 did he read during his undergraduate studies?
2 What additional text types did he read during his postgraduate studies?

b In pairs, discuss the following questions.

1 What text types have you read in your academic studies so far?
2 What additional text types are you likely to read in your future studies?

Fei He

2 Skimming and scanning

Two reading techniques you will often use in your academic studies are skimming *and* scanning.
· *Skimming means reading parts of a text, such as the title, sub-headings and the first sentences in paragraphs, to understand its purpose, its organisation and the main ideas.*
· *Scanning means looking quickly through a text for specific information.*

2.1 **As you read in preparation for writing an essay, would you skim or scan a text to find:**

1 the most important sections to read. _____

2 definitions of key terms. _____

3 if it would be worth reading the text in detail. _____

4 what the writer's general view on the topic is. _____

5 statistics to include in the essay. _____

2.2 **Your tutor has asked you to prepare for a lecture by reading a text with the title *Why should we prioritize?***

a **Before you start reading, consider the things in the box that most national governments have to spend money on. In pairs, try to agree on their order of importance.**

| agricultural improvement | arts and culture | education | health care |
| industrial development | law and order | national security | |

b **Did you have difficulties agreeing? If so, why?**

2.3 **Skim the text and decide which sentence best summarises the main idea.**

1 National governments are good at prioritising, so they should also decide the order in which global problems are dealt with.

2 We cannot deal with all global problems at the same time, so we have to find ways of deciding the order in which they are dealt with.

3 The world's major problems are all of equal importance, so we should try to deal with them all at the same time.

Why should we prioritize?

Tremendous progress has been made in our lifetimes. People in most countries live longer, healthier lives; air and water quality in the developed world is generally getting better; and a much larger population is being adequately fed.

5 But there are still many problems to tackle. The minority of us lucky enough to have been born in the developed world take for granted universal education, an assured food supply and clean, piped water. Hundreds of millions of people are not so lucky. And although the world's problems fall disproportionately heavily on the developing world, rich countries also have their own problems, including drugs, conflicts and corruption.

10 When it comes to the globe's toughest issues, policy-makers have a huge list of spending possibilities akin to a gigantic menu at a restaurant. But this menu comes without prices or serving sizes. If an international agency spends $10m on one project instead of another, how much more good will it do? Global leaders can rarely answer that question. They need better information and so do ordinary citizens. Economics gives us the tools to look at the costs of taking effective action and measure the expected benefits. When we know the costs and benefits, it will be a lot easier to choose the best projects – the
15 projects which do the most good with the money available.

National governments prioritize all the time. Government revenues are finite and there are many competing demands for expenditure. Responsible economic management means balancing priorities between defense, education, healthcare and welfare. This prioritization is straightforward enough in

➤ Problems to tackle
G&V 3, p25

➤ Prioritize; priorities; prioritization
G&V 2, p24

20   a democratic state: although the debate may be vigorous and high-pitched, the result is an explicitly
acknowledged trade-off between different segments of society and different problem areas for a share
of a finite pot of money. There is widespread recognition that governments do not have infinite resources
and that they must satisfy important social needs without running unsustainable deficits.

But when we come to global welfare projects, the situation gets murky. We seem to believe that we can
achieve anything, that the pool of money is infinite, and that everything should be tackled at once.

25   In effect, the majority of the big decisions are made by international agencies that receive money
from rich nations and use it for the benefit of the world, especially developing countries. Each such
organization has its own remit, scope of work and funding base. But most operate as independent silos.
There is little incentive for cross-agency comparison. After all, there's little to be gained and much to
lose if one organization's work turns out to be costlier or less effective than that of another. As a result,

30   there are few attempts to contrast the work of, say, the United Nations Environment Program (UNEP)
with that of the United Nations Educational, Scientific and Cultural Organization (UNESCO), and almost
no overt efforts at comparing the outcomes achieved by development charities such as Oxfam and
Médecins Sans Frontières.

Of course, in principle we ought to deal with all the world's woes. We should win the war against hunger,

35   end conflicts, stop communicable diseases, provide clean drinking water, step up education and halt
climate change. But we don't. We live in a world with limited resources and even more limited attention
for our biggest problems.

This means we have to start asking the crucial questions: if we don't do it all, what should we do first?

Lomborg, B. (Ed.) (2007). *Solutions for the world's biggest problems: Costs and benefits.*
Cambridge: Cambridge University Press.

► That of

G&V **1, p24**

3   Identifying the sequence of ideas

*As you read an academic text it is important to understand the sequence of ideas in order to
follow the writer's argument.*

3.1   **Here are the main ideas in the text in 2.3. Read the text in detail and put the ideas in the
order that they appear.**

a   We can use economics to compare the costs and benefits of projects. _____

b   All global welfare projects should be worked on at the same time. _____

c   Both developed and developing countries still have problems. _____

d   International agencies are not motivated to compare the effectiveness of their work. _____

e   The quality of life for most people has been improving. __*1*__

f   People understand that governments have to prioritise national spending. _____

g   We need to face the problem of how to prioritise problems. _____

h   It is difficult to compare the costs and benefits of global welfare projects. _____

4   Understanding implicit meanings

4.1   a   **Read the following extracts from the text in 2.3. Is the second sentence in each extract a
reason for or a *consequence of* something described in the first sentence? How do you know?**

1   After all, there's little to be gained and much to lose if one organization's work turns out
to be costlier or less effective than that of another. As a result, there are few attempts to
contrast the work of, say, the United Nations Environment Program (UNEP) with that of the
United Nations Educational, Scientific and Cultural Organization (UNESCO).

2   National governments prioritize all the time. Government revenues are finite and there are
many competing demands for expenditure.

b **For each of the following extracts decide which of the labels in the box best describes the relationship between the second and the first sentence in each extract.**

| contrast | example | expansion | reason |

1 Tremendous progress has been made in our lifetimes. People in most countries live longer, healthier lives; air and water quality in the developed world is generally getting better; and a much larger population is being adequately fed.
2 The minority of us lucky enough to have been born in the developed world take for granted universal education, an assured food supply and clean, piped water. Hundreds of millions of people are not so lucky.
3 Global leaders can rarely answer that question. They need better information …
4 Of course, in principle we ought to deal with all the world's woes. We should win the war against hunger, end conflicts, stop communicable diseases …

5 Inferring the meaning of words

5.1 If you find a word in a text that you don't understand, you can use the context to help you. Look at this extract from the text in 2.3. Before you look up the word *woes* in a dictionary, follow steps 1–5.

Of course, in principle we ought to deal with all the world's **woes**. We should win the war against hunger, end conflicts, stop communicable diseases, provide clean drinking water, step up education and halt climate change. But we don't. We live in a world with limited resources and even more limited attention for our biggest problems.

1 Think about the wider context of a) the text and b) the paragraph.
e.g. What types of things does the writer of this text say we should prioritise?

2 Look at some of the words that come after the word. Do these words help you understand the word you don't know?
e.g. Are the words hunger, conflicts *and* diseases *positive or negative things?*

3 Look at some of the words that come before the word you don't know. What other words are often associated with the words you find? Do these associations help you understand the word you don't know?
e.g. What things do we deal with? Are they positive or negative things?

4 Can you think of a word or phrase that seems to have a similar meaning to the word you are trying to understand?

5 If you need to, check the meaning of the word in a dictionary. Try to write a new sentence including the word to help you remember what it means.
e.g.'The country's financial woes won't be solved easily.' Can you think of another example of the world's woes?

5.2 a Match the words (1–3) to the synonyms (a–c) using the strategy in 5.1.

1 akin to (line 10)   a spending
2 expenditure (line 17)   b strong
3 vigorous (line 19)   c similar

b **Can you think of a word with a similar meaning to replace these words from the text in 2.3?**
remit (line 27)   overt (line 32)

6 Vocabulary building: adjectives

6.1 a Complete the following sentences using an adjective from the box with a similar meaning to the word or phrase in brackets.

> assured   communicable   crucial   finite   infinite
>
> straightforward   universal   widespread

1 Governments have a _____ amount of money to spend. (**limited**)
2 Prioritising spending is quite _____ in democracies. (**simple**)
3 We should prevent _____ diseases. (**passed from one person to another**)
4 We need to start asking _____ questions. (**extremely important**)
5 In the developed world we take for granted _____ education and an _____ food supply. (**for everyone; guaranteed**)
6 There is _____ recognition that governments do not have _____ resources. (**among many people and in many places; unlimited**)

Listening and speaking

7 Introducing your presentation

Most students have to give presentations during their academic studies. The activities in the Listening and speaking *sections will help you prepare for these.*

7.1 ◀1.2 **You are going to listen to the beginning of two talks on choices that governments make. Listen and complete the information on slides (A and B).**

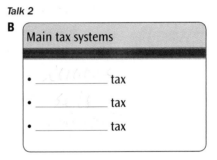

Talk 1

A

Main voting systems
• proportional _____
• _____ voting
• _____-past-the-post

Talk 2

B

Main tax systems
• _____ tax
• _____ tax
• _____ tax

8 Clarifying key terms

8.1 ◀1.3 **Complete the beginning of the first talk by writing the words in brackets in the correct order. Listen to the extract again and check your answers.**

1 *I want to begin by talking about* (by / about / want / I / to / talking / begin) the different voting systems that democracies have to choose from, and **2** _____
(focus / here / on / I'll) the three main ones. First, there's proportional representation.
3 _____ (this / when / is) the number of seats a political party wins matches the number of votes the party gets. Second, there's alternative voting.
4 _____ (this / meant / what's / that / is / by) voters rank candidates in order of preference ... Third, there's the so-called first-past-the-post system.
5 _____ (words / other / in) a candidate just has to win more votes than any of their rivals in a particular area, not a majority of the votes. Let me go on to talk about each of these in more detail, and I'll discuss the advantages and disadvantages of each.

8.2 a **Match the phrases that you wrote in 8.1 (1–5) to the functions (a–c).**

    a   to introduce a general topic   <u> *1* </u>

    b   to introduce a sub-topic <u>   </u>

    c   to introduce a clarification or explanation <u>   </u>   <u>   </u>   <u>   </u>

    b   ⏪**1.4** **Listen again to the second talk and match the phrases (6–10) to the functions (a–c).**

    6   What I'd like to do is outline ...   **8**   I'm going to highlight ...   **10**   That's to say, ...

    7   What happens here is that ...   **9**   In this case, ...

8.3 a **Prepare a short talk to accompany the following slide. Make notes on how you will introduce the general topic and the sub-topics, and explain the terms you introduce. Use the information in the three boxes to help you.**

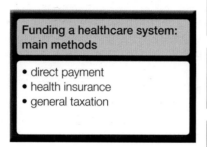

> **Funding a healthcare system: main methods**
>
> • direct payment
> • health insurance
> • general taxation

> *Direct payment:* Individuals pay for medical care at the time they receive it.

> *Health insurance:* Individuals make regular payments to a sickness insurance company that pays for all or part of the costs of any medical care received.

> *General taxation:* Health care is provided for everyone in the country and this is funded through taxation.

    b   **In pairs, give your talks. Try to use some of the phrases in 8.1 and 8.2.**

Writing

9   Understanding how essay types are organised

Students in many subjects have to write essays and there is considerable variation in what you might be expected to write. However, three main essay types are: describe, discuss and defend.

Essay type	Purpose	Example essay question
Describe	To describe a topic or aspects of the topic	Compare and contrast the position and powers of the UK Prime Minister and the US President.
Discuss	To argue the case for two or more positions on an issue and evaluate these positions. Often you will say which position you support.	Discuss the relative merits of private and state-funded education.
Defend	To put forward a particular position on a topic, or to challenge a position given in the essay question	"Governments should be able to use prisoners as a source of cheap labour." Discuss.

9.1   **Which essay type are questions 1–6: *describe*, *discuss* or *defend*?**

    1   Discuss the impact of out-of-town shopping centres on the regions in which they occur.

        <u> *discuss* </u>

    2   It has been claimed that democracy is the best form of government in the modern state. How far do you agree? <u>   </u>

    3   Discuss the ways that politeness is achieved in English and another language you are familiar with. <u>   </u>

    4   "Newspapers should not identify a person by their race, colour or religion unless this information is relevant to the news story." Discuss. <u>   </u>

    5   To what extent does the media influence how the general public views scientists and their work? <u>   </u>

    6   What factors affect people's choice of career? <u>   </u>

Each of the main essay types has a typical general structure with three main sections: introduction, body *and* conclusion.

	Describe	**Discuss**	**Defend**
Introduction	· Give background on the topic. · Say which aspects of the topic will be described.	· Give background. · Say what the different positions are (and perhaps give your view).	· Give background. · Say what your position is on the topic.
Body	· Describe each aspect in turn with supporting evidence.	· Give sub-arguments for each position with supporting evidence.	· Give sub-arguments for your position with supporting evidence.
Conclusion	· Summarise the description.	· Summarise the different positions (and perhaps reinforce your view).	· Reinforce your position.

9.2 **In which section (introduction, body or conclusion) would you be most likely to find:**

1 a statement of the writer's position on the topic? _introduction_
2 a summary of the main arguments in support of the writer's position? _____
3 a series of generalisations relevant to the topic? _____
4 an outline of how the essay is organised? _____
5 definitions of key terms used in the essay? _____
6 evidence to support each generalisation? _____
7 a restatement of the writer's position on the topic? _____
8 background information on the topic? _____

Study tip *Academic writing is generally more impersonal than everyday language. Try to avoid expressions such as* I think …, I believe … *and* In my view … .
*It is **interesting** to note that the population has risen rapidly in the last ten years.*
NOT ~~I think it's interesting that the population's gone up so quickly in the last ten years.~~

> **→** *Impersonal language*
> **Unit 3, G&V 1, p52**

9.3 **Read the opening sentence from each paragraph in the body of an essay on the social responsibility of large international companies. Which type of essay is it:** *describe*, *discuss* **or** *defend*?

The basic human rights of all people should be respected, and international companies should recognise this in their dealings with employees …

There are economic reasons, too, for prioritising social responsibility …

In addition, involvement in corruption scandals and environmental accidents can severely damage the reputation of a company …

Finally, it has been found that the provision of good working and living conditions for employees can increase levels of productivity, and therefore profits to companies …

On the other hand, some would argue that profit should take priority over social responsibility …

It has also been suggested that a company's duty to its shareholders should come first …

The motives of some companies who have implemented social-responsibility programmes have been questioned …

10 Drafting the introduction to an essay

> ⓘ *Some people refer to a sentence near the start of an essay in which the writer presents their main idea as a* thesis statement. *In this book we talk about the* writer's position *on the subject of the essay.*

10.1 Read the introduction to an essay with the title *Discuss the impact of out-of-town shopping centres on the regions in which they occur.*

> **1** Over the last twenty years out-of-town shopping centres have been built on the outskirts of many European and North American cities. **2** Typically, they contain a wide range of shops and entertainment facilities such as cinemas, and car parking is free. **3** There is widespread recognition that these centres have social, economic and environmental impacts on the region in which they occur. **4** However, there is considerable debate about whether their overall impact is positive or negative. **5** In this essay I will argue that, while there are clear advantages for consumers in having access to out-of-town shopping centres, in general they have an adverse impact on the surrounding area.

a Which sentences in the introduction are:

   a the background? _____   _____

   b a recognition of different views? _____   _____

   c a statement of the writer's position? _____

b The writer avoids repetition by using words that substitute for 'out-of-town shopping centres'. For example:

Typically, they contain … (*they* substitutes for *out-of-town shopping centres*)

Find other examples in the extract where the writer uses substitutes in this way.

10.2 Put the following sentences in order to make a first draft of an introduction to an essay with the title *To what extent does the media influence how the general public views scientists and their work?*

a In films and television, for example, scientists are often shown as being mad or out of touch with the real world. _____

b I will argue that although the media plays a part in forming people's views of scientists and their work, other factors may be equally influential in forming people's views. _____

c One reason it is important is that the general public's view of scientists and their work can affect whether young people decide to take up a career in science. _____

d For example, most people study science at school, and people's experience of science at school may have an impact. _____

e The media clearly has a significant influence on the image of scientists that is presented to people. _____

f In modern society the way that the general public views scientists and the work of scientists is important. __*1*__

g However, the media is not the only influence on people's view of scientists and their work. _____

10.3 Write a second draft of the introduction in 10.2. Avoid repetition by using substitute words (as you saw in 10.1) and by deleting unnecessary parts. For example,

In modern society the way that the general public views scientists and ~~the work of scientists~~ *their work* is important. One reason ~~it is important~~ is that ...

 Study tip *It is likely that you will need to produce a number of drafts of any academic text that you write. Make sure you give yourself enough time to do this.*

10.4 a Write an introduction to an essay with the title *To what extent should large international companies make acting in a socially responsible manner more of a priority than increasing their profits?* (You saw the opening sentences of the body of this essay in 9.3.)

b When you have written a first draft, redraft it to make sure you avoid repetition. In pairs, compare your finished introduction.

11 Language for writing: common knowledge

Common knowledge is information that general readers or readers working within your subject are likely to share. We often refer to common knowledge in essay introductions.

11.1 The following extracts (a–c) all make the same claim. In which extract does the writer:
1 give an example to support the claim? _____
2 assume that the claim is common knowledge, so no supporting evidence is needed? _____
3 support the claim by referring to a published work where the same claim is made? _____
a Out-of-town shopping centres have social, economic and environmental impacts on the region in which they occur (Johnson, 2005).
b Out-of-town shopping centres have social, economic and environmental impacts on the region in which they occur. For instance, since the building of the Merry Hall shopping centre, many small shops in the nearby town of Dudstone have been forced to close.
c There is widespread recognition that out-of-town shopping centres have social, economic and environmental impacts on the region in which they occur.

11.2 Complete the following sentences by underlining the most appropriate words in italics.
1 *It is widely accepted / No one can deny* that service quality has a direct effect on customer satisfaction.
2 *As is known by everyone, / The consensus view is that* there is no gender difference in general intelligence.
3 *Everybody now accepts / It is generally believed* that recent global climate change is the consequence of human activity.
4 *There is broad agreement / We all think* that international aid needs to increase.
5 *As is well known, / Most people know that* many types of cancer are avoidable.

> ✪ *Research shows that the most common adverbs in the written academic corpus that go in the following structures are:*
> 1 commonly, generally, now, well, widely   it is _____ accepted ...
> 2 commonly, generally, now, often, widely   it is _____ believed ...
>
> *Can you guess which is the most frequent adverb in each structure?*

11.3 Look again at the essay introduction you wrote in 10.4. Revise it so that you include at least one of the phrases in 11.2.

> 🎓 **Focus on your subject** *As you read, observe other phrases that introduce common knowledge. There may be particular ones often used in your subject. Keep a record of them and use them in your own writing.*

Grammar and vocabulary

Grammar and vocabulary
· Avoiding repetition: *that (of)* and *those (of)*
· Word families: linking parts of texts
· Verb–noun collocations

1 Avoiding repetition: *that (of)* and *those (of)*

1.1 Which previously mentioned words or ideas do *that* and *those* refer to in these examples?

1 After all, there's little to be gained and much to lose if one organization's work turns out to be costlier or less effective than **that of** another.

2 Their policy priorities differed from **those of** the Clinton administration.

1.2 Using the information in the following figures, complete the sentences by making comparisons using *that of* or *those of*.

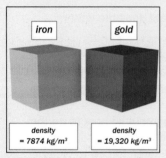

iron | gold

density = 7874 kg/m³ | density = 19,320 kg/m³

1a The density of gold is
greater than that of iron

b The density of iron is
_____

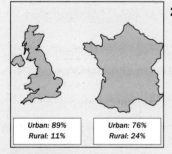

Urban: 89% Rural: 11% | Urban: 76% Rural: 24%

2a The rural population of the United Kingdom
_____

b The rural population of France is
_____

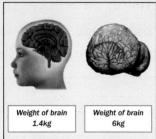

Weight of brain 1.4kg | Weight of brain 6kg

3a Human brains
_____

b Whale brains
_____

Average life expectancy: 77 years | Average life expectancy: 72 years

4a The life expectancy of an average weight male
_____

b The life expectancy of an overweight male
_____

2 Word families: linking parts of texts

2.1 Find two words from the same family in each extract.

1 Responsible economic management means balancing priorities between defense, education, healthcare and welfare. This prioritization is straightforward enough in a democratic state.

2 Early language acquisition research assumed that all classrooms are alike. However, this assumption has been shown to be too simple.

2.2 Complete this table by writing the nouns from the same family as the verbs.

verb	noun(s)	verb	noun(s)
approach		identify	
assess		indicate	
assume	assumption	interpret	
benefit		occur	
create		prioritize	priority prioritization
define		process	
distribute		require	
establish		research	
estimate		respond	
function		vary	

ⓘ *Most words can be spelt with either -ize or -ise or -ization/-isation. Use a dictionary to check for exceptions.*

ⓘ *priority = the importance given to something to be done*
prioritization = the process of putting things in order of importance

2.3 a Using words from the table in 2.2, complete the sentences with a word from the same family as an earlier word in the sentence.

1 A low turnout at a general election might be interpreted to mean that voters are satisfied with the government. However, this *interpretation* does not explain what happened in 1984.

2 Patients' reaction to the medication varied according to their age and gender. _____ was also found to result from the level of fat in their diet.

3 Patients were found to benefit from small, regular doses of aspirin. However, these _____ have yet to be evaluated in large, controlled trials.

4 The participants were asked to respond to questions about their level of physical activity and diet. Their _____ are summarised in Table 3.

b Complete the sentences using your own words. Use a dictionary where necessary to help you.

1 Coleman (1992) argued that the Romans relied on slaves for all their needs and that this _*reliance*_ inhibited technological development.

2 Nine participants were excluded from this stage of the research. Reasons for their _____ are given in Section 5 below.

3 Less than a third of the 50 teachers questioned reacted favourably to the curriculum changes. In attempting to understand this unexpected _____ I conducted a number of follow-up interviews.

4 The data were analysed using the Mann-Whitney test. From this _____, it was possible to draw conclusions on the duration of the disease.

 Study tip *When you record a new word, it can be useful to write down other words in the same word family. Use a dictionary to find these.*
For example,

(un)identifiable (adj) — *identification (n)*

identify (v) — *identity (n)*

2.4 Write a second sentence using the information in brackets. Look for a verb in the first sentence and change it to a noun in your answer.

1 The aim of the study was to analyse the impact on the regions of new government planning legislation.
A number of statistical techniques were used in the analysis.
(We analysed the impact using a number of statistical techniques.)

2 Prior to the course, students' ability in Spanish was assessed.
_____
_____
(We assessed them to determine whether learning occurred during the course.)

3 People wishing to take up an academic career are generally required to have a PhD.
_____
_____
(People are not always required to have a PhD in Business Studies.)

4 The pilot research allowed us to hypothesise about the slow improvement in reading ability in the group.
_____
_____
(We then tested each one individually.)

5 The disappointing result of the drug trial has been interpreted by some (e.g. Cales, 2008; Dwyer, 2009) as indicating that patients failed to take medication at the agreed times.
_____
_____
(White (2009) has interpreted the result differently.)

3 Verb–noun collocations

3.1 Collocations are combinations of words which commonly go together. Match the verbs in the box to the nouns to make typical verb–noun collocations. These verb–noun collocations occur in the text you read in 2.3 on pages 16–17.

achieve   make (x2)   measure
satisfy   tackle   take

1 _*tackle*_ problems   **5** _____ outcomes
2 _____ action   **6** _____ progress
3 _____ benefits   **7** _____ decisions
4 _____ needs

○ *Research shows that in the written academic corpus the ten most common verbs that collocate with* problem(s) *are:*
1 solve *2* pose *3* face *4* resolve *5* tackle *6* circumvent *7* overcome *8* raise *9* avoid *10* deal with.

3.2 Write the ten verbs from the corpus research box into the mind map according to their meaning. Use a dictionary to help you.

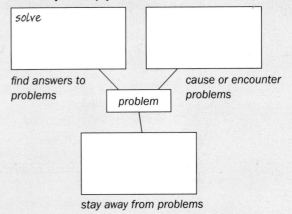

solve

find answers to problems

problem

cause or encounter problems

stay away from problems

 Study tip *Using a mind map can be a useful way to record vocabulary items.*

2 Risks and hazards

Reading

1 Selecting and prioritising what you read

Study tip *Most of the academic reading you do will be for a particular task (e.g. preparing for a written assignment, background reading before a lecture or tutorial, finding particular information to help you solve a problem). You should carefully select and prioritise your reading for each task.*

1.1 As part of a course on natural hazards, such as earthquakes and tsunamis, you have been given the essay title *Discuss the risks and impacts of weather-related natural disasters.* You have drafted an outline for your essay, which is shown below.

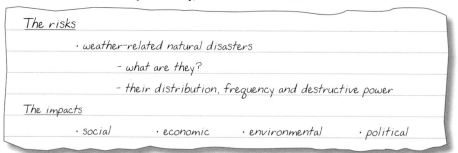

The risks
· weather-related natural disasters
  - what are they?
  - their distribution, frequency and destructive power

The impacts
· social   · economic   · environmental   · political

a Look at the course reading list below and cross out any publications which you think are unlikely to be relevant for your essay.

b Decide the order in which you will look at the remaining publications.

c In pairs or small groups, compare your answers to a and b.

Module 211: Natural hazards   Reading list

1 Alexander, D E (1985). Death and injury in earthquakes, *Disasters* 9: 57-60.
2 Benson, C and Clay, E J (2004). *Understanding the economic and financial impacts of natural disasters.* Disaster Risk Management Series No. 4. Washington, DC: World Bank Publications.
3 Bryant, E A (2005). *Natural Hazards* (2nd edn.). Cambridge: Cambridge University Press.
4 Burton, I, Kates, R W and White, G F (1978). *The Environment as Hazard.* Oxford: Oxford University Press.
5 Handmer, J W (2000). Flood hazard and sustainable development, in D Parker (ed) *Floods* (pp. 276-286). London: Routledge.
6 Health and Safety Executive. (1989). *Risk criteria for land-use planning in the vicinity of major industrial hazards.* London: HMSO.
7 Intergovernmental Panel on Climate Change. (2011). *Managing the risks of extreme events and disasters to advance climate change adaptation.* http://www.ipcc.ch/popup-managing-risks-extreme-events_sp.htm
8 Jacoby, H and Skoufias, E (1997). Risk, financial markets, and human capital in a developing country. *Review of Economic Studies* 64: 311–335.
9 Jovel, J R (1989). Natural disasters and their economic and social impact. *CEPAL Review,* 38: 133-45.
10 Kates, R W (1980). Climate and society: lessons from recent events. *Weather* 35: 17-25.
11 Takada, J (2004). *Nuclear Hazards in the World: Field studies on affected population and environments.* Berlin: Springer.

1.2 Match the publications on the reading list in **1.1** to the text types in the box.

> article in a journal   official report on a website   textbook
> official report published as a book   paper in an edited collection

2   Thinking about what you already know

 Study tip *Before you read a text, it is useful to consider how much you already know about the topic. This helps you to decide what you want to learn from the text, so that you can read selectively and more efficiently.*

2.1 a As you prepare your essay on the topic of weather-related natural hazards, you find a text on tropical cyclones. Before you read it, think about how much you already know about the topic. Work in pairs and answer these questions.

1   What is the difference between a *cyclone* and a *tropical cyclone*?
2   What other terms have a similar meaning?
3   What are the main effects of tropical cyclones?
4   Do tropical cyclones have any positive effects?
5   Can you give any examples of notable tropical cyclones?

b Scan the text to find the answers to questions 1–5.

Tropical cyclones

Introduction

Tropical cyclones are defined as intense cyclonic storms that originate over warm tropical seas. In North America, the term 'hurricane' is used because cyclone refers to an intense, counterclockwise rotating, extra-tropical storm. In Japan and south-east Asia tropical cyclones are called 'typhoons'. The hazards relating to tropical cyclones can be grouped
5 under three headings: storm surge, wind and rain effects. Storm surge is a phenomenon whereby water is physically piled up along a coastline by low pressure and strong winds. This leads to loss of life through drowning, inundation of low-lying coastal areas, erosion of coastline, loss of soil fertility due to intrusion by ocean salt-water and damage to buildings and transport networks. High-wind velocities can directly cause substantial
10 property damage and loss of life, and constitute the main agent for crop destruction. Surprisingly, strong winds – simply because they are so strong – can also exacerbate the spread of fires in urban and forested areas, even under heavy rainfall. Rainfall is responsible for loss of life, property damage and crop destruction from flooding, especially on densely populated floodplains. Contamination of water supplies can lead to
15 serious disease outbreaks weeks after the cyclone. Heavy rain in hilly or mountainous areas is also responsible for landslides or mud flows as floodwaters in stream and river channels mix with excess sediment brought down slopes. The destruction of crops and saline intrusion can also result in famine that can kill more people than the actual cyclone event. This was especially true on the Indian subcontinent during the latter part
20 of the nineteenth century.

Earthquakes are not an obvious consequence of cyclones; however, there is substantial evidence for their occurrence during cyclones. Pressure can vary dramatically in a matter

➤ *Extra-tropical*
G&V 4, p37

➤ *Loss of life; erosion of coastline*
G&V 1, p36

➤ *Serious disease outbreaks; substantial evidence*
G&V 3, p37

➤ *Occurrence*
G&V 2, p36

of hours with the passage of a cyclone, bringing about a consequentially large decrease in the weight of air above the Earth's surface. The deloading can be as much as 2–3 million tonnes km^{-2} over a matter of hours. In addition, tidal waves or surges in the order of 10–12 m in height can occur in shallow seas with a resulting increase in pressure on the Earth's surface of 7 million tonnes km^{-2}. In total the passage of a cyclone along a coast can induce a change in load on the Earth's crust of 10 million tonnes km^{-2}. In areas where the Earth's crust is already under strain, this pressure change may be sufficient to trigger an earthquake. The classic example of a cyclone-induced earthquake occurred with the Tokyo Earthquake of 1923. A typhoon swept through the Tokyo area on 1 September, and was followed by an earthquake that evening. The earthquake caused the rupture of gas lines, setting off fires that were fanned by cyclone-force winds through the city on 2 September. In all, 143,000 people lost their lives, mainly through incineration. There is also evidence that tropical cyclones have triggered earthquakes in other places along the western margin of the Pacific plate and along plate boundaries in the Caribbean Sea. In Central America the coincidence of earthquakes and cyclones has a higher probability of occurrence than the joint probability of each event separately.

Bryant, E (1991). *Natural Hazards*. Cambridge: Cambridge University Press.

2.2 Read the text in more detail and underline descriptions of any risks or impacts of tropical cyclones to use in your essay.

3 Inferring the meaning of words

➤ *Inferring the meaning of words*

Unit 1, 5.1 p18

3.1 Try to infer the meaning of the words in bold from context using the strategy introduced in Unit 1, 5.1. Use a dictionary to check your answers.

1 Tropical cyclones are defined as **intense** cyclonic storms that **originate** over warm tropical seas.
2 High-wind velocities can directly **constitute** the main agent for crop destruction.
3 Surprisingly, strong winds can also **exacerbate** the spread of fires in urban and forested areas …
4 Pressure can **vary dramatically** in a matter of hours …
5 The passage of a cyclone along a coast can induce a change in load on the Earth's crust of 10 million tonnes km^{-2}. This pressure change may be **sufficient** to **trigger** an earthquake.

4 Vocabulary building 1: collocations

4.1 Complete the expressions using the words in bold from 3.1.

1	_constitute_ an offence a threat a problem	4	_____	evidence information detail
2	_____ considerably greatly enormously	5	_____	a change a response growth
3	_____ competition pressure interest	6	_____	increase improve reduce

5 Vocabulary building 2: cause–effect markers

5.1 a Read the first paragraph of the text in 2.1 again. Find the phrases used to link the causes and effects and write them in the table.

cause	→	effect
storm surge high wind velocities strong winds rainfall contamination of water supplies heavy rain in hilly areas the destruction of crops	*leads to*	loss of life through drowning substantial property damage the spread of fires loss of life serious disease outbreaks landslides famine

b Read the second paragraph again and underline other phrases that link cause and effect.

> **Focus on your subject** *Using some of the phrases from 5.1 a and b, write three new sentences linking cause and effect relevant to your subject. For example:*
> *Management is responsible for establishing effective communication in a company.*

6 Retelling what you have read

> **Study tip** *Retelling in your own words something that you have read can be a useful way of checking your understanding of what you have read and helping you to remember it.*

6.1 Read the report in the text of the Tokyo Earthquake of 1923 (lines 30–34) again. In pairs, retell the story of the earthquake using the events and the sequencing phrases in the boxes.

Events

earthquake	fires made worse by strong winds
gas caught fire	gas lines broke
people died in fires	typhoon

Sequencing phrases

first of all ...	after that ...
next ...	then ...
at the same time ...	

Listening and speaking

7 Preparing slides for presentations

> **Study tip** *When you give presentations you may be expected to use slides. It is worth learning how to prepare slides on a computer, both for your academic studies and for your future career.*

7.1 In pairs, decide whether the following pieces of advice on preparing slides are things you should do (✓) or things you shouldn't do (✗).
   1 Use bullet points rather than continuous text. ___✓___
   2 Use different fonts within a slide. _____
   3 Use a simple font like Times New Roman or Arial. _____
   4 Use a font size of at least 24 points. _____
   5 Use phrases and key words instead of sentences. _____
   6 Use as many illustrations as possible. _____
   7 Use a light text on a dark background. _____
   8 Use a font colour that contrasts with the background. _____
   9 Use underlining or italics for emphasis rather than bold. _____
   10 Use different font sizes for main and secondary points. _____
   11 Use capital letters for all your text. _____
   12 Use three to five points per slide. _____

7.2 Identify the positive and negative features of the following slides using the advice in 7.1.

A

Main classes of volcano

- Active: regularly erupt
- Extinct: now quiet
- Dormant: haven't erupted in historical times

B

Main classes of VOLCANO

There are three main classes of volcano that are referred to as active, extinct, and dormant. ACTIVE volcanoes are ones that regularly erupt (e.g. Mount St Helens in the US). **Extinct** volcanoes are now quiet, although they have erupted in historical times (e.g. Kilimanjaro in Tanzania). *Dormant* volcanoes are ones that haven't erupted in historical times (e.g. Nisyros in Greece).

C

Main classes of volcano

- Active: regularly erupt
- Extinct: now quiet
- Dormant: haven't erupted in historical times

8 Choosing the right type of chart for a slide

8.1 In pairs, discuss which of the charts (A–F) would be particularly useful for the following purposes (1–5). There may be more than one answer.

1 Showing trends
2 Showing the steps in a process
3 Showing percentages
4 Comparing different amounts
5 Comparing multiple sets of numbers

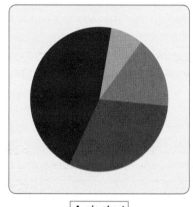

A pie chart

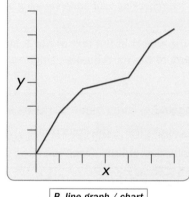

B line graph / chart

	men	women
1	88	16
2	46	35
3	28	92
4	21	28
5	79	100
6	11	62

C table

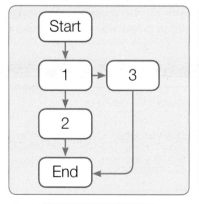

D flow chart / diagram

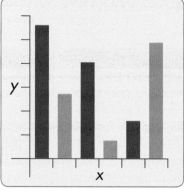

E vertical bar graph / chart

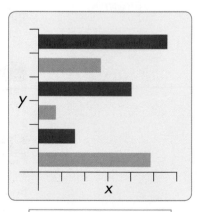

F horizontal bar graph / chart

9 Presenting charts

9.1 a You are going to hear an extract from a lecture on natural hazards, where the lecturer talks about the following chart. Before you listen, in pairs discuss which three pieces of information in the chart you think the lecturer will highlight.

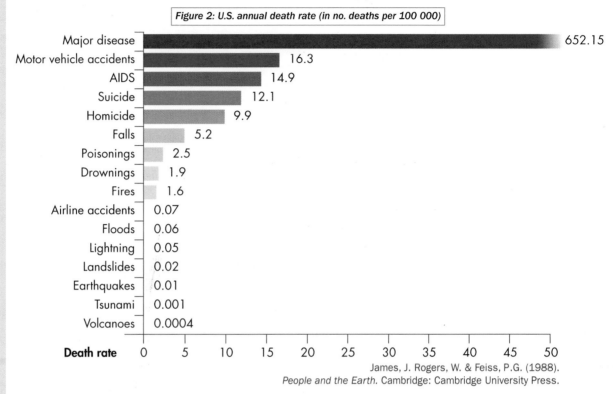

Figure 2: U.S. annual death rate (in no. deaths per 100 000)

Major disease	652.15
Motor vehicle accidents	16.3
AIDS	14.9
Suicide	12.1
Homicide	9.9
Falls	5.2
Poisonings	2.5
Drownings	1.9
Fires	1.6
Airline accidents	0.07
Floods	0.06
Lightning	0.05
Landslides	0.02
Earthquakes	0.01
Tsunami	0.001
Volcanoes	0.0004

James, J. Rogers, W. & Feiss, P.G. (1988).
People and the Earth. Cambridge: Cambridge University Press.

b (◀2.1) Listen and check your ideas.

9.2 a (◀2.2) When speakers talk about charts in their presentations they often follow the four stages shown below. Listen and complete the following extracts.

1 Tell the audience what to look for

_____ Figure 2 on the second page of your handout?

⬇

2 Explain what the chart shows

Ok, _____ the causes of death in the United States.

⬇

3 Highlight the main information

Although there's a lot here of interest, _____ three pieces of information. The first is that by far the major cause of death is disease.

⬇

4 Explain how the information relates to the rest of the talk

So, _____ is that while the risks of natural hazards can sometimes seem very serious ...

b Here are some more phrases that might be used to introduce these four stages. Which stage (1–4) are they most likely to introduce?

a   The chart gives information about ...   _____
b   What's of particular relevance here is that ...   _____
c   Could you turn to Figure 2.3?   _____
d   There are a couple of things of particular note.   _____

9.3 **a** **Prepare to present the chart below as part of a longer presentation comparing the health risks faced by males and females. Organise your talk using the four stages from 9.2a and use the phrases in 9.2a and b to introduce each stage.**

b **Give your talk to a partner.**

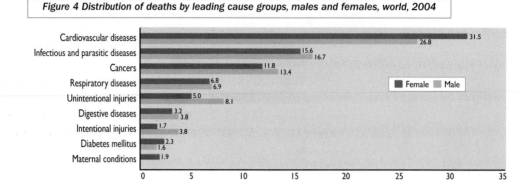

Figure 4 Distribution of deaths by leading cause groups, males and females, world, 2004

WHO (2008). *The Global Burden of Disease: 2004 Update.* Geneva: World Health Organisation.

10 Pronunciation 1: numbers

When you give a presentation with charts, it is likely that you will have to use a variety of numbers.

10.1 **a** **Decide how these groups of numbers should be pronounced.**

    1 Cardinal numbers
        a 0; 101; 466   **b** 1200; 1201; 12,245   **c** 111,456; 1,222,567
        d 100; 1000; 10,000   **e** 100,000; 1,000,000

    2 Ordinal numbers
        a 1st; 2nd; 3rd   **b** 14th; 21st; 32nd   **c** 100th; 1000th

    3 Dates
        a 1234; 1954; 1987   **b** 2008; 2012; 2020   **c** 21st May 1956; 2/9/1989

    4 Decimals and fractions
        a 0.1; 0.02; 0.009   **b** 3.4; 56.78; 39.197   **c** $\frac{1}{2}$; $\frac{1}{3}$; $\frac{3}{4}$

b (◀2.3) **Listen and check your answers, then in pairs practise saying the numbers.**

11 Pronunciation 2: inserts

In presentations, we often use inserts *(extra, non-essential information added to sentences).*
In writing, we often put dashes [–] or brackets [()] before and after inserts.
In speech, we usually pause before and after the insert. We use a fall-rising tone on the main stress in short inserts; in longer inserts there is more variety.

11.1 **a** (◀2.4) **Listen to the inserts in these extracts from the presentation you heard in 9.2a. Match each extract (1–3) to the explanation of the use (a–c).**

    1 So, for example, the death rate from homicide – *that's the **fifth*** ➘➚ *figure down* – was 9.9 per 100,000.

    2 The second is that, apart from car accidents, which kill large numbers of people, death from accidents – *in **falls**,* ➘ *drowning,* ➘ *airline crashes,* ➘➚ *and **so on*** ➘ – are relatively small in number.

    3 And the third – *and of particular* ➘➚ *relevance to this talk* – is that natural hazards kill a relatively tiny number of people.

    a The insert adds an **example**. _____

    b The speaker inserts an **opinion**. _____

    c The speaker inserts a **guide**, telling the audience where to look on the chart. _____

b **In pairs, practise saying the extracts (1–3) to each other.**

11.2 a Add the inserts in brackets to the following sentences in an appropriate position.

1 Levels of unemployment∧rose rapidly during the 1970s. (– that's the blue line –)

2 A number of grain crops need huge amounts of water to grow. (– rice, for example –)

3 Managers need to be motivated to carry out their activities, and so compensation has to be linked to performance. (– and this is key –)

4 In a number of European countries over 80 per cent of the population now lives in urban areas. (– Sweden, for instance –)

5 The results showed a considerable amount of disagreement between participants in the study. (– and this was unexpected –)

b In pairs, say the extracts using a fall-rising tone for the insert, and pausing before and after it.

c Write down three pieces of information that you might present on a topic from your subject, and then add extra information to each in the form of an insert. In pairs, say the sentences.

Writing

12 Using claims to plan essays

> ⓘ *A claim is a statement or judgement made by a writer.*
> · Writers *try to persuade the reader that the claims are true.*
> · Readers *evaluate claims: has the writer convinced us that they are true?*

➤ Essay types
Unit 1, 9 p20

12.1 a You have been asked to write an essay with the title *Natural disasters have a greater impact on less economically developed countries (LEDCs) than more economically developed countries (MEDCs). How far do you agree with this statement?* What type of essay is it: describe, discuss, or defend?

b After some initial reading, you listed the following claims made by writers. Which claims support the statement in the essay (✓) and which ones don't (✗)?

1   Healthcare facilities in LEDCs are often less able to cope with demand after a natural disaster. ✓

2   Poorer people may have to risk living in disaster-prone areas, where land is cheap, in order to make a living. _____

3   Factors other than the level of national development influence how severe the impact of a natural disaster on a country is. _____

4   Disasters have a greater social impact on poorer people than better-off people.

_____

5   Infrastructure (e.g. roads, airports, electricity and gas supply) in LEDCs is often of poorer quality, and can easily be damaged or destroyed in natural disasters. _____

6   While MEDCs may be better placed than LEDCs to face natural disasters, there may be variation within MEDCs. _____

7   In some LEDCs there are only basic water and sewage facilities, which can easily be damaged by natural disasters. _____

8   Most people who die as a result of natural disasters are in LEDCs. _____

9   Tourism, which is an important part of the economy in many LEDCs, can be particularly badly hit by damage to infrastructure. _____

10 MEDCs have more developed infrastructure, which is very expensive to replace or repair if it is damaged. _____

11 Fewer people in LEDCs have insurance against property damage. _____

12.2 Match the claims you ticked in 12.1 to the types of impact they relate to.

Number of lives lost   __2__   _____

Social impact   _____   _____

Economic impact   _____   _____

Health impact   _____   _____

Study tip As you do research for an essay, note down general points (or claims) that you want to make. Then try to organise these claims as the skeleton of the body of the essay in a way that is relevant to the question.

12.3 Complete the following skeleton of the body of an essay using the claims in 12.1. Two of the answers have been written for you.

Natural disasters have a greater impact on LEDCs than MEDCs in a number of different ways. In terms of the number of lives lost, <u>most people who die as a result of natural disasters are in LEDCs.</u>

In addition, _____

_____

As far as economic impact is concerned, _____

_____

In particular, tourism, _____

_____

With respect to social impact, _____

_____

It is also the case that _____

_____

From the point of view of health, _____

_____

This can be made worse by the fact that _____

_____ .

However, in some respects natural disasters may have a greater impact on MEDCs.

For example, <u>MEDCs have more developed infrastructure, which is very expensive to replace or repair if it is damaged.</u>

It may also be that _____

_____

Finally, _____

_____ .

13 Supporting claims with evidence

Study tip *Unless they are 'common knowledge' (see Unit 1, section 11), most claims that you make in your writing should be supported with evidence.*

13.1 a As you read more on the topic, you find evidence to support some of the claims in 12.1. Match the pieces of evidence (1–5) to the claims (a–e).

1 Research has shown that the United States and Japan suffered the most economic damage from natural disasters between 1991 and 2005 (Wills, 2009).	**a** Most people who die as a result of natural disasters are in LEDCs.
2 Between 1991 and 2005, 630,000 people were killed by natural disasters in LEDCs compared with 72,000 in MEDCs (International Strategy for Disaster Reduction, 2010).	**b** Disasters have a greater social impact on poorer people than better-off people.
3 When I did voluntary work in Haiti after the 2010 earthquake, the medical services there were clearly unable to deal with the huge number injured.	**c** MEDCs have more developed infrastructure, which is very expensive to replace or repair if it is damaged.
4 For example, most of the farming population of Bangladesh live in low-lying parts of the country where severe floods occur regularly.	**d** Healthcare facilities in LEDCs are often less able to cope with demand after a natural disaster.
5 "Although a household on a lower income may spend less in total terms than a wealthier household, they are likely to spend a higher proportion of their income on recovery" (Adams, 2008).	**e** Poorer people may have to risk living in disaster-prone areas in order to make a living.

b Match the pieces of evidence (1–5) to the following types of evidence (a–e).

A quotation _____   An example _____   Statistics _____
Personal experience _____   Research findings _____

> *Some useful phrases for introducing supporting evidence are:*
> [Author] ([date]) has argued/claimed that …
> In my personal experience …
> *Research shows that in the written academic corpus the most common verb that goes in the structure* It has been + *reporting verb +* that *is* suggested.
> *What do you think are the next most common verbs?*
>
> 1 s *uggested*   2 sh_____   3 ar_____   4 pr_____
> 5 re_____   6 de_____   7 fo_____   8 es_____
> 9 ob_____   10 as_____

13.2 Revise the first draft that you wrote in 12.3. Write a second draft, adding the evidence from 13.1 and using the structure *It has been* + verb + *that* where possible. Try to find evidence to support other claims made, and include this in your new draft.

Example

In terms of the number of lives lost, most people who die as a result of natural disasters are in LEDCs. It has been reported, for example, that between 1991 and 2005, 630,000 people were killed by natural disasters in LEDCs compared with 72,000 in MEDCs (International Strategy for Disaster Reduction, 2010).

Grammar and vocabulary

Grammar and vocabulary
· Complex noun phrases
· Countable and uncountable nouns
· Adjectives meaning *large* or *important*
· Prefixes

1 Complex noun phrases

Academic texts contain many examples of complex noun phrases. Often these take the form of a noun followed by a prepositional phrase beginning with of. Compare the following two sentences, where the second one uses a complex noun phrase with of to express the idea more efficiently.

> Hansen (2008) focuses on the way in which second-language pronunciation is acquired.
>
> Hansen (2008) focuses on the acquisition of second-language pronunciation.

Notice how the structure of the sentence changes.

· *The verb becomes a noun:*
  is acquired $\longrightarrow$ the acquisition of

· *Some words are now not necessary:*
  ~~the way in which~~

1.1 Rewrite the underlined parts of the following sentences using a noun phrase with *of*. Find the main verb in the underlined part of each sentence and replace it with a related noun. Make any other changes necessary.

1 It has been argued that <u>if wealth is distributed unequally, this</u> can cause social unrest in any country (Johnson, 2010).
the unequal distribution of wealth

2 The next section will consider <u>the ways in which foreign languages are assessed in schools</u>.

3 <u>Water supplies can be contaminated, and this</u> can lead to serious disease outbreaks weeks after the cyclone.

4 <u>If a woman consumes alcohol during pregnancy, this</u> can affect the developing baby.

5 It has been found that a positive emotional state can reduce <u>the pain that someone experiences</u>.

6 When it was announced that <u>the top rate of tax would increase to 80 percent, this</u> led to multinational companies moving their offices out of the country.

Study tip When you record a new verb, make sure you also make a note of any related nouns e.g. distribute (v), distribution (n). *This will help you when you try to write complex noun phrases. (See also Unit 1, G&V 2.3, p 24.)*

1.2 Look at a piece of writing that you have done recently. Can you find any places where you could express yourself more efficiently using a noun phrase with *of*?

2 Countable and uncountable nouns

Study tip Some nouns can be used either countably or uncountably. A good dictionary will tell you if a word can be used in both ways. When you come across a new noun, make a note of whether it is countable, uncountable, or both, and indicate this in your notes.
e.g. requirement (C), research (U), analysis (C/U)

2.1 a In pairs, write the following nouns in the correct column in the table. Use a dictionary to check your answers.

coincidence consequence damage decrease disease erosion evidence margin occurrence phenomenon transport weight

countable	uncountable	countable and uncountable
coincidence		

b The words that you have written in the third column come from the text in 2.1 on pages 27–28. Are they used countably or uncountably in that text?

ⓘ As research *is an uncountable noun, it is only very rarely used as a plural and does not follow a number, or a quantifier used with countable nouns. For example:*
· a recent piece of research *NOT* ~~a recent research~~
· two research studies *NOT* ~~two researches~~
· much research *NOT* ~~many researches~~

3 Adjectives meaning *large* or *important*

> ❷ *Research shows that the following nouns occur frequently after the adjectives* considerable, serious, significant, *and* substantial.

considerable	amount attention number interest	significant	reduction effect increase change
serious	consideration implications consequences challenge	substantial	number amount increase part

3.1 Write four sentences related to your subject using the adjective + noun combinations in the corpus research box. For example (from Business Studies):

- *In the past few years there has been considerable interest in Total Quality Management (TQM).*
- *Recruitment of CEOs can present a serious challenge to large firms.*
- *A reduction in labour costs can lead to a significant increase in a company's profits.*
- *Improvements in IT can save a company substantial amounts of money.*

4 Prefixes

4.1 a Match the prefixes (1–10), which are commonly used in academic vocabulary, to the definitions (a–j).

1	*sub-*	e.g. subheading, subsonic	_e_
2	*intra-*	e.g. intrafamily, intracompany	___
3	*pro-*	e.g. pro-American, pro-life	___
4	*post-*	e.g. postgraduate, post-industrial	___
5	*under-*	e.g. underfunded, underrate	___
6	*super-*	e.g. super-virus, superabundance	___
7	*extra-*	e.g. extra-tropical, extraordinary	___
8	*anti-*	e.g. anti-racist, anticlockwise	___
9	*pre-*	e.g. prerequisite, prerecord	___
10	*over-*	e.g. over-ambitious, overheat	___

- **a** before
- **b** too much / more than / on / above / on top of
- **c** within / into
- **d** supporting / approving
- **e** under / below / less important / smaller part
- **f** more than usual / over / above
- **g** after / later than
- **h** not enough / below / less important
- **i** opposed to / against / opposite of / preventing
- **j** outside / in addition to / beyond

b Find pairs of prefixes with opposite meanings, e.g. *over/under*.

4.2 a Read the definitions and complete the words using the prefixes (1–10) in 4.1.

1 _pro_____-European
(*adj*) in favour of European unification

2 _____pay
(*v*) to pay someone too little for their work

3 _____section
(*n*) one of the smaller parts into which a text is divided

4 _____-terrestrial
(*adj*) outside of planet Earth

5 _____-operative
(*adj*) the time after a medical operation

b Read the definitions and add word endings to the following prefixes.

1 over_____
(*v*) to extend beyond a safe or reasonable limit

2 intra_____
(*adj*) within the same culture

3 pre_____
(*v*) to have existed before another thing

4 super_____
(*n*) a country with great political and military strength

5 anti_____
(*n*) a medicine that can kill harmful bacteria

> 🎓 **Focus on your subject** *Can you find terms commonly used in your own subject that use these prefixes? If you are unsure of their meaning, check them in a dictionary or (if available) an online glossary.*

Lecture skills A

Preparing for lectures

1 Lecturing styles

1.1 **(A.1) During your academic studies you will hear many different styles of lecturing. Watch three lecture extracts that illustrate a reading style, a conversational style, and an interactive style. What differences do you notice?**

1 Reading style

2 Conversational style

3 Interactive style

1.2 a **In pairs, discuss the following questions.**

1 Which style do you find easiest to understand, and why?
2 Is there a style of lecturing that is common in your subject?

2 Revising basic information

 Study tip *A lecturer will assume that you already know certain information and build on this in the lecture. It is helpful to prepare for a lecture by making sure you understand key terms and concepts that your lecturer may use.*

2.1 a **You are going to watch extracts from a lecture given by Dr Maru Mormina with the title *The origins of human diversity*. Read the notes from a previous lecture on her course.**

- DNA = material inside the core (= nucleus) of each cell in the body; it carries genetic information in genes (= sections of the DNA)
- genetic information controls the cell's chemistry → gives the body its characteristics & influences how the body works
- genetic variation = differences between individuals that are inherited (e.g. eye colour is inherited from parents)
- genome = total set of genetic information of a living thing (human, plant, etc.); located in chromosomes (in centre of cells; control what living thing is like)

Dr Maru Mormina is a Research Fellow at the Leverhulme Centre for Human Evolutionary Studies, within the Department of Biological Anthropology, Cambridge University.

b **In pairs, take it in turns to explain the following key terms without looking back at the notes.**

DNA   genetic information   genetic variation   genome

Listening

3 Understanding lecture aims

3.1 a (A.2) **As Dr Mormina introduces her lecture, she shows the following slide. Read the slide, and then watch the extract and answer the questions.**

1 What *evolutionary mechanisms* will Dr Mormina talk about in her lecture?
2 What word does Dr Mormina use to describe the biological diversity of human populations? Does she mean that the diversity is *large* or *small*?
3 Which of the three topics on the slide will Dr Mormina talk about most?

b **In pairs, try to predict what Dr Mormina might say about each of the three headings on the slide.**

> **The purpose of this talk**
>
> • To explore some of the evolutionary mechanisms responsible for the diversity of human populations, mostly from a biological perspective but with some reference to cultural diversity.
>   • Migration
>   • Adaptation
>   • Culture

4 Understanding outlines

4.1 a **You are going to listen to Dr Mormina talk in more detail about how she will organise the lecture. Before you listen, in pairs discuss which of the headings (a–f) are likely to follow each of the two main section headings.**

a Gene flow (= migrations)
b Culture
c Geography and migrations in human prehistory
d Selection and environmental adaptation
e Natural selection
f Mutation

> **Outline**
>
> • <u>Biological mechanisms generating diversity: general background</u>
>   • _____
>   • _____
>   • _____
>
> • <u>The structuring of human biological and cultural diversity</u>
>   • _____
>   • _____
>   • _____

b (A.3) **Watch the extract and complete the rest of the slide by writing in headings (a–f).**

c **What do you think Dr Mormina will talk about next?**

5 Identifying main and secondary points

5.1 a (A.4) **Watch the beginning of the next section of Dr Mormina's talk and answer the following questions.**

1 What question does she ask at the end of the clip to indicate what she is going to say next?
2 In pairs, discuss possible answers to her question.

 Study tip *Many lecturers use questions to help them organise what they say and to indicate to the audience what they are going to talk about. If the lecturer asks questions, main points usually answer these questions directly.*

➤ *Making predictions during a lecture*

Unit B, 3 p67

b (A.5) **Watch the rest of the section and read the transcript to check your predictions.**

> Well, certainly because over, over many, many years we have had to adapt to different environments so the challenges that our ancestors encountered in Africa are very different from an environmental perspective, from the challenges that they might have found in Siberia. So the, the body has adapted in different ways to respond to these different challenges. But also the fact that, er, after their origin in, in Africa humans spread all over the world and from that moment on, populations became isolated and therefore they evolved independently, er, finding different ways, different solutions to the different environments. So migrations, human dispersals, have played a role in generating this, erm, array of biological diversity. But also culture contributes to, er, our differences, and the reason why I like this picture so much is because the differences you see between these different faces has not only to do with the way they look, but also with the way they dress. So culture also contributes, and particularly language, also contributes to generate … to generating diversity.

5.2 a **Look at some of the points Dr Mormina makes and decide which are main points (MP) and which are secondary or supporting points (SP).**

1   People adapt to their environments. _____
2   The environments of Africa and Siberia are different. _____
3   People migrated to different environments. _____
4   Culture is important in creating diversity. _____
5   Language plays a part in creating diversity. _____

b **What language does Dr Mormina use in this section to highlight that there are three main points?**

6 Taking notes: annotating slides 1

Many lecturers today use slides to illustrate their lectures and give out copies of these slides on a handout for students. However, there will be more information in the lecture than appears on the slides, so it is important to annotate slides on a handout during the lecture.

6.1 a **You are going to watch Dr Mormina explain how gene flow plays a role in generating diversity. Before you watch, in pairs discuss what you think the slide and notes mean.**

b (A.6) **Watch the extract and annotate the slide with the notes (1–5) in the appropriate place (a–e).**

1   have different characteristics
2   populations intermix
3   migration in one direction
4   many more different forms
5   subset with new characteristics moves to new region

a   _____
    (= gene flow)

b   _____
    (e.g. yellow and green)

c   _____
    (= polymorphic)

d   _____
    (= genetic bottleneck)

e   _____
    (= diversity is changed)

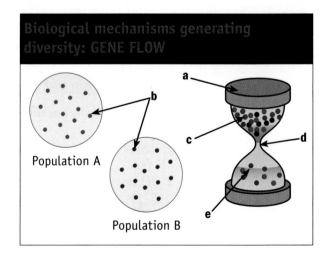

Language focus

7 Repetition and rephrasing

Lecturers often repeat information, particularly in conversational and interactive styles, if it is important or if they think it may be difficult for you to understand. They may rephrase or repeat information in order to give you a second opportunity to understand, and it is important to listen carefully for this. For example, in the lecture extract in 6.1 'different characteristics' is rephrased as 'look different'.

> These are two different populations. Erm, one could think individuals in these populations **have different characteristics, look different.**

7.1 **⬛A.7 Listen and complete the following extracts from Dr Mormina's lecture. Underline the words that are rephrased.**

1 So I spoke about mutations because at the <u>heart</u> of, at the _____*centre*_____ of it all, there's the process of mutation. Mutation is what generates diversity.

2 However, at about ten thousand years, the agricultural populations, _____, that were, developing, or that were domesticating species were only in these pockets.

3 … and therefore they evolved independently finding different ways, different solutions to the different environments. So migrations, _____ have played a role in generating this, erm, array of biological diversity.

4 But then the weather changes again and at around twelve thousand years we enter into the Holocene. And the Holocene is the period, the _____, we're living in now.

5 It is around this time that some species like, er, begin to dwindle, begin to, erm, _____.

6 But we can also use indirect evidence, which is the distribution of genetic diversity today, and from that we infer back, we look back and _____, how this diversity might have been generated.

Follow up

8 Taking notes: annotating slides 2

8.1 **⬛A.8 Listen to another extract from Dr Mormina's lecture and add your own notes to the following slide. In pairs, compare your notes.**

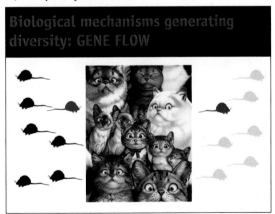

Biological mechanisms generating diversity: GENE FLOW

Study tip If you have time, review your notes a day or two after a lecture. This will help you to remember the information in the lecture, and also identify any gaps in your understanding.

9 Reviewing your notes

9.1 **In pairs, look back at the two slides you annotated in this unit and take it in turns to explain each slide.**

3 Language and communication

Reading
- Predicting the content of a text
- Reading for detail
- Scanning for information
- Understanding implicit meanings
- Vocabulary building: adjectives
- Thinking about ways of taking notes

Listening and speaking
- Making suggestions in group work
- Pronunciation: stress in adjectives ending in –ic and –ical

Writing
- Referring to other people's work with in-text references and reporting verbs

Reading

1 Predicting the content of a text

1.1 **a** You have been asked to prepare for a tutorial on the question *How are language choices influenced by the context in which communication takes place?* You need to decide which books on your reading list will contain relevant information. Use the strategy below to assess the first book on the list.

1 Read the title of the book. What does the main title tell you about the topic of the book? What does the subtitle tell you? What do you know about the topic already?	*Communicating Across Cultures: Understanding in a global world*
2 Read the title of Chapter 2. What do you know about these topics already? How does this relate to the title of the book? Does this title tell you anything about how the chapter will be organised?	*2 Speech acts, politeness and misunderstanding*
3 Read the title of section 2.5. What do you think the section is about?	*2.5 The gender factor*
4 Read the opening sentence of the first paragraph of section 2.5. What do you think follows in the paragraph?	Some sociolinguistic research suggests that women are more likely than men to use politeness strategies in their speech.
5 Read the opening sentence of the second paragraph. What do you think follows in the paragraph?	Hobbs (2003) argues that it is important that studies in gender variation should examine the relationship between situation and language use.

b How might the text in 1.1a be relevant for the tutorial question *How are language choices influenced by the context in which communication takes place?*

1.2 **In pairs, discuss whether you agree or disagree with the following statements about making predictions before and while you read.**

1 It helps me decide whether I want to carry on reading the text.
2 It makes me evaluate what the writer is saying.
3 It helps me understand vocabulary in the text.
4 It is more important when reading some texts than others.
5 It improves my reading speed.
6 It helps me find the information I need in a text.

Study tip *You can improve your reading efficiency by predicting what is to come and then checking your predictions against what you find in the text.*

1.3 **You are going to read an extract from a book with the title *The Study of Language*, taken from a chapter with the title *On the development of writing*. What do you already know about writing and its development? In pairs, complete the following statements by underlining the correct words in italics.**

1 Most alphabets contain *20 to 30 / 30 to 40* symbols.
2 The earliest known alphabet developed around 1700BC in *the Middle East / North America*.
3 The earliest remaining examples of written symbols are on pieces of *wood / clay*.
4 The earliest writing systems used *letters / pictures*.
5 Some of the earliest Chinese writing was done on *paper / bones*.
6 The largest alphabet is Khmer, with *74 / 54* letters.

1.4 **Before you start reading, look at the title *Pictograms and ideograms* and predict what the text will be about.**

1 Do you know what *pictograms* and *ideograms* are?
2 Do you know any other words beginning *pict-* and *ide-* that might give you a clue?

2 Reading for detail

2.1 **Read the text and decide where the following pictures (A–F) should be inserted in the text (1–6).**

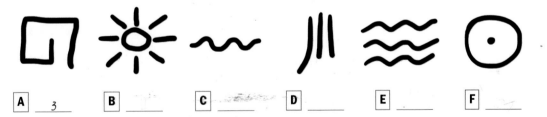

A   3   B   _____   C   _____   D   _____   E   _____   F   _____

Pictograms and ideograms
Cave drawings may serve to record some event (e.g. Humans 3, Buffaloes 1), but they are not usually thought of as any type of specifically linguistic message. They are usually treated as part of a tradition of pictorial art. When some of the 'pictures' came to represent particular images in a consistent way, we can begin to describe the product as a form of picture-writing, or pictograms. In this way, a form such as **1** might come to be used for the sun. An essential part of this use of a representative symbol is that everyone should use a similar form to convey a roughly similar meaning. That is, a conventional relationship must exist between the symbol and its interpretation.

➤ *Symbolic, ideographic*

G&V **3, p53**

10 In time, this picture might develop into a more fixed symbolic form, such as **2**, and come to be used for 'heat' and 'daytime', as well as for 'sun'. Note that as the symbol extends from 'sun' to 'heat', it is moving from something visible to something conceptual (and no longer a picture). This type of symbol is then considered to be part of a system of idea-writing, or ideograms. The distinction between pictograms and ideograms is essentially a difference in the relationship between the symbol and the entity it represents. The more 'picture-like' forms

15 are pictograms and the more abstract derived forms are ideograms.

A key property of both pictograms and ideograms is that they do not represent words or sounds in a particular language. Modern pictograms, such as those represented in the accompanying illustration [Figure 1], are language-independent and can be understood with much the same basic conventional meaning in a lot of different places where a number of

20 different languages are spoken.

It is generally thought that there were pictographic and ideographic origins for a large number of symbols that turn up in later writing systems. For example, in Egyptian hieroglyphics, the symbol **3** was used to refer to a house and derived from the diagrammatic representation of the floor-plan of a house. In Chinese writing, the character **4** was used for a river, and had

25 its origins in the pictorial representation of a stream flowing between two banks. However, it is important to note that neither the Egyptian nor the Chinese written symbols are actually 'pictures' of a house or a river. They are more abstract. When we create symbols in a writing system, there is always an abstraction away from the physical world.

When the relationship between the symbol and the entity or idea becomes sufficiently

30 abstract, we can be more confident that the symbol is probably being used to represent words in a language. In early Egyptian writing, the ideogram for water was **5**. Much later, the derived symbol **6** came to be used for the actual word meaning 'water'. When symbols are used to represent words in a language, they are described as examples of word-writing, or 'logograms'.

➤ *It is important to note: it-clause*

G&V **1, p52**

Figure 1

Yule, G. (2006). *The Study of Language.* (3rd edn). Cambridge: Cambridge University Press.

3 Scanning for information

3.1 **Read the text again and decide which of the characteristics (a–f) apply to each of the following terms (1–4). Some characteristics apply to more than one term.**

1 Pictograms ___a___ _____ _____
2 Ideograms ___b___ ___f___ ___c___
3 Modern pictograms ___d___
4 Logograms ___e___

a A picture that represents an image
b The source of symbols in later writing systems
c Doesn't stand for particular words or sounds
d Independent of any language
e Used as words in a language
f An abstract form, not a picture

4 Understanding implicit meanings

The relationship between sentences may be signalled with a sentence connector (e.g. For instance). Where it is not, the relationship is implicit and you need to work out the connection.

4.1 **What is the relationship between the second and the first sentence? Is it an *explanation*, a *contrast* or an *example*?**

1 Cave drawings may serve to record some event (e.g. Humans 3, Buffaloes 1), but they are not usually thought of as any type of specifically linguistic message. They are usually treated as part of a tradition of pictorial art. _____

2 The distinction between pictograms and ideograms is essentially a difference in the relationship between the symbol and the entity it represents. The more 'picture-like' forms are pictograms and the more abstract derived forms are ideograms. _____

3 … it is important to note that neither the Egyptian nor the Chinese written symbols are actually 'pictures' of a house or a river. They are more abstract. _____

4 When the relationship between the symbol and the entity or idea becomes sufficiently abstract, we can be more confident that the symbol is probably being used to represent words in a language. In early Egyptian writing, the ideogram for water was [5]. _____

5 Vocabulary building: adjectives

5.1 a **In pairs, try to replace the words in bold with adjectives from the text in 2.1. Look back at the text to check your answers.**

1 When some of the 'pictures' come to represent particular images in a **way that doesn't change**, we can begin to describe the result as a form of 'pictogram'. (line 4) _____

2 As the symbol extends from 'sun' to 'heat', it moves from something **that can be seen** to something **based on ideas**, and no longer a picture. (line 11) _____; _____

3 Modern pictograms are language-independent and can be understood with much the same basic **generally accepted** meaning in many different places. (line 19) _____

4 When the relationship between the symbol and the entity or idea becomes **unconnected with real objects**, it is fairly certain that the symbol is being used to represent words in a language. (line 30) _____

b **Complete these sentences using the adjectives you wrote in 5.1a.**

1 Some doctors advocate an integrated approach to medicine, using both _____ and alternative medicine, such as homeopathy.

2 Ursa Major is a constellation _____ throughout the year in large parts of the northern hemisphere.

3 A study in 2000 has revealed that the percentage of the population belonging to religious groups has remained _____.

4 Scientists have been criticised for ignoring practical applications of science in preference to more _____ and theoretical issues.

5 The test aims to assess both the factual and _____ knowledge of students.

6 Thinking about ways of taking notes

6.1 a **In pairs, think about possible strengths and weaknesses of each of the following note type.**

1 Tabular notes: notes are organised in a table

2 Diagrammatic notes: notes are connected by lines; key words may be put in boxes

3 Highlighting notes: the most important words in the text are highlighted or underlined.

4 Margin notes: notes are written in the margin of the book, article, etc.

5 Linear notes (handwritten / word processed): notes are handwritten, or typed, as normal text; line spacing and underlining may be used to show text organisation, key words, etc.

b **Discuss when one note type would be more useful than another and then decide which of the note types you would use to make notes on the text in 2.1 to prepare for a presentation of *writing systems*.**

Listening and speaking

7 Making suggestions in group work

At university you may be asked to work in groups during seminars or tutorials to discuss issues or solve problems, or to prepare a presentation. In group work it can be important to make and ask for suggestions, and to make alternative suggestions.

7.1 **⏺3.1 Listen to six extracts from group work where students are preparing a presentation of a business case study. In which extracts do you hear the following expressions?**

Note: A business case study involves reading about and discussing a problematic situation a company has faced and suggesting courses of action.

a	I see what you mean, but what about ...?	_3_
b	Maybe we could ...?	_____
c	That's a possibility – or we could ...	_____
d	How do you feel about ...?	_____
e	How are we going to do that?	_____
f	How about if we ...?	_____

7.2 **Write the expressions (a–f) in the correct column in the table.**

Making a suggestion	Acknowledging an idea and making an alternative suggestion	Asking for suggestions

7.3 **In a tutorial during a course on *Technology and society* your tutor gave you a handout with a task to prepare.**

a You are going to prepare for the task in small groups. Before you begin, in pairs discuss the following questions:

1 How can you make sure that you work well as a team?

2 How can you support each other?

3 How can you resolve problems?

b In small groups, begin by sharing ideas on the topic to add to the notes below. As you work together, try to use some of the phrases you wrote in the table in 7.2.

Tutorial 2   Wednesday 2nd February

Next week's topic: The socio-economic impacts of the mobile phone

Prepare a talk of 2–3 minutes about some aspect of this topic and then we'll have an open discussion. You'll need to meet as a group before the end of this week to decide what areas you're going to cover, who will talk about what, what order you'll talk in, and so on.

economic

+ do business 24/7
– people can be overworked/exploited

SOCIO-ECONOMIC IMPACTS OF MOBILE PHONE USE

health & safety

environmental

the way we communicate

c **3.1** **Listen again to the extracts you heard in 7.1 and write useful expressions for:**

· asking for a volunteer to do something. _____

_____

· asking a particular person to do something. _____

_____

· offering to do something. _____

_____

d **Assign roles to decide who will present each topic, using some of the expressions in 7.3c where possible.**

8 Pronunciation: stress in adjectives ending in *-ic* and *-ical*

8.1 a **3.2** **Listen to extracts from a student discussion of the socio-economic impacts of the mobile phone. Which of the two words do you hear, the noun (a) or the adjective (b)? Circle the correct letter.**

1	**a** tech.nol.o.gy	**(b)** tech.no.log.i.cal	**7**	**a** mag.net	**b** mag.net.ic
2	**a** e.co.no.my	**b** e.co.no.mic	**8**	**a** ca.tas.tro.phe	**b** cat.a.stroph.ic
3	**a** the.ory	**b** the.or.et.i.cal	**9**	**a** e.co.no.my	**b** e.co.no.mic
4	**a** psy.chol.o.gy	**b** psy.cho.log.i.cal	**10**	**a** the.ory	**b** the.or.et.i.cal
5	**a** mag.net	**b** mag.net.ic	**11**	**a** psy.chol.o.gy	**b** psy.cho.log.i.cal
6	**a** ca.tas.tro.phe	**b** cat.a.stroph.ic	**12**	**a** tech.nol.o.gy	**b** tech.no.log.i.cal

b **Listen again and underline the syllable with the main stress in this word.**

c **Compare the position of the main stress in the adjectives which end in *-ic* or *-ical*, and in the related noun. What do you notice?**

8.2 a **Complete the sentences using the noun–adjective pairs in 8.1.**

1 For your essay you should read ___*Economy*___ and Society: a study of _____ and social theory.
2 The tsunami was a _____ for southern Thailand. In fact, it was _____ for many countries around the Indian Ocean.
3 I'm doing a course on _____ innovation at the University of _____ .
4 Essentially, the experiment involves placing a _____ into a _____ field.
5 The American _____ Association is the main organisation for _____ and psychologists in the United States.

b **Check your answers then, in pairs, say the sentences to each other. Pay particular attention to stress in the words you have written.**

> 🎓 Focus on your subject *Keep a note of adjectives ending in -ic and -ical which are commonly used in your subject. These may be specialised terms. Note also any related noun(s) and the main stress on both adjectives and nouns. For example:* genome – genomic; gene – genetic; isotope – isotopic; asymmetry – asymmetrical; analysis – analytical *(Biochemistry)*

Writing

9 Referring to other people's work

9.1 **The words and phrases in the box are often used when reporting what others have said or written. In pairs, see if you know the meaning of all of them. Check your answers in a dictionary.**

an in-text reference	the literature	to paraphrase	plagiarism	a primary source
a reference	a reference list	referencing conventions	a secondary source	

➤ *Common knowledge*
Unit 1, 11 p23

In academic writing you should provide references to all your information sources unless the information is common knowledge. Compare these extracts from students' essays in the field of Applied Linguistics.

Unless they have some learning disability, the vast majority of children become fluent speakers of their native language.

Our experience tells us that this is true. It is common knowledge, so it doesn't need a reference.

It is easier for children than adults to learn a foreign language.

Some research evidence is needed to support this claim. A reference to this evidence should be given.

9.2 **Which of the following extracts do you think are common knowledge (CK), and which do you think need references (R) to information sources?**

1   Learning a second language as an adult is different from learning a first language as a child.   _CK_
2   There are around 375 million speakers of English as a first language in the world.   _____
3   Communicative language teaching has not been a success in teaching adults.   _____
4   English is currently the most important language for international communication.   _____
5   A collocation is a sequence of two or more words that regularly occur together.   _____
6   Not every language teaching method works well in every teaching context.   _____
7   Languages change over time.   _____
8   It has been shown that men interrupt in conversations more frequently than women.   _____

10 Using in-text references

➤ *References*
Unit 6, 8 p91
Appendix 1 p167

10.1 Many of the academic texts that you read and write will have *in-text references* within the text and a *reference list* at the end of the text. Underline all the in-text references in the following textbook extracts.

A

Some sociolinguistic research suggests that women are more likely than men to use politeness strategies in their speech, and that the extent of the difference between men's and women's speech may vary from culture to culture. Hobbs (2003) points out that such research suggests that women pay more compliments than men (Herbert 1990; Holmes 1988, 1998; Johnson & Roen 1992), and that women in talk with same-sex peers use a large number of positive-politeness strategies while men in analogous situations do not (Johnstone, et al. 1992). He also indicates that research has shown that women are more likely to apologise, soften criticism or express thanks than men (Tannen 1994). Similar findings have been observed in other cultures, for example Brown (1998) studying Tzeltal (Mayan) speakers in Chiapas, Mexico, where it was found that there was a greater use of both positive and negative politeness by women than men.

Bowe, H. & Martin, K. (2007). *Communicating across cultures: understanding in a global world.*
Cambridge: Cambridge University Press.

B

Both service and manufacturing firms experience similar problems in managing the introduction of IT[1], and many companies have been disappointed by their failure to achieve the benefits they sought from their investment. Porter has suggested that firms should identify all the technologies in their value chain, and then determine which technologies and potential technological changes have the most significance for reinforcing competitive advantage. He noted that 'in choosing among technologies to invest in, a firm must base its decision on a thorough understanding of each important technology in its value chain…'[2].

[1] Senker, J. and Senker, P., *Technical Change in the 1990s. Implications for Skills, Training and Employment*, Science Policy Research Unit, University of Sussex, 1990.
[2] Porter, M. 'Technology and Competitive Advantage', *The Journal of Business Studies*, Winter, 1985, pp. 60-78.

Senker, J. & Senker, P. (1992). Gaining competitive advantage from information technology.
Journal of General Management, 17, 31–43

10.2 Look at the following advice on referencing systems from a university website. Fill in the gaps using the words in the box. Use the examples you underlined in 10.1 to help you.

alphabetical	brackets	et al.	four	integral	non-integral
numerical	publication	semi-colons	subject	superscript	surname

Referencing systems

The author-date system

- In the author-date (or Harvard) system, in-text references can be either integral or non-integral to the sentence. In an **1** _____ reference, the **2** _____ of the author is used as an element of the sentence (often as the **3** _____ of the sentence). It is followed by the date of **4** _____ in brackets. For example:

  > **Hobbs (2003)** points out that such research suggests …

- In a **5** _____ reference, the surname of the author and the date of publication are put in **6** _____ at the end of the sentence. For example:

  > … women are more likely to apologise, soften criticism or express thanks than men **(Tannen 1994)**.

  Integral references focus more attention on the author.

  In a non-integral reference, you can list a number of sources by different authors. For example:

  > … women pay more compliments than men (**Herbert** 1990; **Holmes** 1988, 1998; **Johnson & Roen** 1992) …

  In this example **7** _____ sources are given: one written by Herbert, one by Johnson and Roen, and two by Holmes. Items in the list are separated by **8** _____ and usually given in **9** _____ order (He-, Ho-, J-).

- When a publication has more than two authors, only the surname of the first author is given, followed by a comma and the words **10** _____ (= and others). For example:

  > … while men in analogous situations do not (Johnstone, **et al.** 1992)

- All the sources mentioned in a text are listed alphabetically (using the surname of the author) in a reference list at the end. For example:

  > **References**
  > **Hobbs**, P (2003). The medium is the message: politeness strategies in men's and women's voice mail messages. *Journal of Pragmatics, 35, 243-262.*
  > **Tannen**, D (1994). *Talking from 9 to 5. Women and men in the workplace: language, sex and power.* New York: Avon Books.

The numeric or endnote system

- Another method of referencing is often called the numeric or endnote system. For example:

  > Both service and manufacturing firms experience similar problems in managing the introduction of IT[1] …

  A number is placed in the text, usually in **11** _____ or sometimes in square brackets, which links to a source in the reference list. These sources are listed in **12** _____ order.

> ⊙ *Research shows that in the written academic corpus 71% of references are integral and 29% are non-integral.*

10.3 **Look at the following extracts from students' essays. Identify problems with the in-text referencing and suggest improvements.**

1 To take an obvious case, there are discernible differences between sections of research articles, Hopkins & Dudley-Evans, 1988. (Hopkins & Dudley-Evans, 1988)
2 Folkes 1984 extends this line of research.
3 Useful part characterizations of this variety are provided by Widdowson ('79).
4 A number of researchers (e.g. Krishnan & Valle 1979, Valle & Wallendorf 1977) have examined the textual properties of research articles.
5 Design departments have problems communicating with senior management [Payne, 5].
6 Tyler, Caine, Hirschman and Katz (1981) suggest that case studies offer participants the opportunity to make sense of theory.
7 The methodology developed by John Kelly (1996) involves negotiating the syllabus with students and sponsors.
8 Media rankings show that management development programmes have become increasingly important for business schools 4.

> 🎓 **Focus on your subject** *Discover and practise using the usual referencing conventions in your subject, as they may vary from subject to subject. You may be told about these on your course. If not, follow the conventions used in a leading journal in your subject.*

10.4 **As a follow-up to a writing seminar on the features of different text types or genres, you have been asked to write one or two paragraphs on *How teaching different genres improves academic writing*.**

a **Before you start writing, in pairs identify the advantages and disadvantages of teaching genres mentioned in the following notes taken from a number of sources.**

Hammond, J. and Macken-Horarick, M. (1999). Critical literacy: Challenges and questions for ESL classrooms, *TESOL Quarterly*, 33: 528–44.
- *observed that teaching different genres helps students to understand texts and be more successful writers*

Luke, A. (1996). Genres of power? Literacy education and the production of capital, in Hasan, R. and Williams, G. (eds.), *Literacy in Society*. London: Longman, pp. 303–38.
- *claimed that teaching academic genres (e.g. essays, dissertations) can lead students to produce formulaic writing – they reproduce the model texts they are taught without thinking about (= critically evaluating) them*

Christie, F. (1993). The 'received' tradition of literacy teaching: The decline of rhetoric and the corruption of grammar, in Green, B. (ed.), *The Insistence of the Letter: Literary Studies and Curriculum Theorizing*. London: Falmer Press, pp. 75–106.

Martin, J. R. (1993). Genre and literacy – modelling context in educational linguistics, *Annual Review of Applied Linguistics*, 13: 141–72.
- *both agreed that disadvantaged students (e.g. from poor backgrounds) in particular need to be taught academic genres in order to be successful at school and university*

Swales, J. M. (2000). Languages for specific purposes. *Annual Review of Applied Linguistics*, 20: 59–76.
- *in favour of teaching genres; but argued that students need to be given ways of bringing their own ideas to academic texts*

Hyon, S. (2001). Long term effects of genre-based instruction: A follow-up study of an EAP reading course, *English for Specific Purposes*, 20: 417–38.
- *warned that students need to be careful not to overgeneralise about genres i.e. to apply what they have learnt about one genre (e.g. an essay) to another (e.g. a dissertation)*

Kay, H. and Dudley-Evans, T. (1998). Genre: What teachers think, *ELT Journal*, 52: 308–14.
- *researched teachers' views; found that most said a genre approach provided useful framework for teaching, but discovered that many concerned that it was too prescriptive (little room for creativity)*

b Make a skeleton plan for your writing using the notes in 10.4a.

c Using the notes, write a paragraph or two (about 200 words in total) with appropriate in-text references. Try to include examples of both integral and non-integral references. Start with the following sentence:

A number of writers have discussed the advantages and disadvantages of teaching genre analysis for academic writing. Hammond and Macken-Horarick (1999), for example, ...

d In pairs, compare your paragraph(s) and make any improvements you think necessary.

11 Language for writing: reporting verbs

➤ Reporting verbs
Unit 4, 10.2 p61

A reporting verb is often used when we refer to the work of other writers in academic text. For example:

- *Diamond (2002) **points out** that only a small number of plant and animal species have been exploited for food.*
- *A number of studies **have shown** that a dietary intake of 10% canola oil significantly shortened the life span of laboratory rats [17, 18, 19].*

Reporting verbs have one of three general functions. They indicate what other writers:

> 1 **did** in their research (e.g. *study, measure, use*).

> 2 **found** in their research (e.g. *find, observe, show*).

> 3 **thought** or **said** in their writing (e.g. *think, believe; write, state*).

11.1 Find the reporting verbs in this extract from a research article looking at variation in writing in different academic subjects. Write the verbs in the appropriate group (1–3) above.

> In a preliminary investigation, Dudley-Evans (1984) focused on dissertation titles. Recently, Dietz (1995) conducted an extensive analysis on titles of scientific texts. Finally, Berkenkotter and Huckin (1995) and Busch-Lauer (1997) analysed the conventions of title writing in scientific research articles. They revealed in their studies that newer titles are semantically richer and are characterised by an increasing syntactic fullness. In connection with this, Berkenkotter and Huckin commented that stating the results of an investigation in the title of the article is becoming very common.

Fortanet, I. et al. (1998). Disciplinary variations in the writing of research articles in English. In Fortanet, I. et al. (Eds.) *Genre Studies in English for Academic Purposes*, (pp. 59–78). Collecció Summa Sèria Filologia 9, Universitat Jaume

11.2 In pairs, add the reporting verbs in the box to the group (1–3) above.

➤ Reporting verbs
G&V 4, p53

> argue   carry out   claim   consider   demonstrate
> discover   establish   examine   explore   investigate
> note   point out   prove   show   suggest

> 🎓 **Focus on your subject** *You should consider carefully which reporting verbs to use in your writing, and try to use a variety of them. As you read textbooks and journal articles in your subject, keep a record of the most commonly used reporting verbs in the three groups and try to use them in your own writing.*

Grammar and vocabulary

Grammar and vocabulary
· Impersonal *it*-clauses
· Word families
· Nouns with related adjectives ending in *-ic* and *-ical*
· Reporting verbs

1 Impersonal *it*-clauses: saying that something is important, interesting, etc.

In academic writing, we often use a sentence with an it-clause to draw the reader's attention to a point that we think is particularly important or interesting. The following structures (a–c) show the main ways of doing this.

a   it is + adjective + (to-infinitive) + that _____ _____
b   it + modal + passive verb + that __1__ _____
c   it is + (other structures) _____ _____

1.1   Match the examples (1–6) to the structures (a–c).

1   It should be noted that most snakes grow larger the longer they live.
2   It is essential to recognise that there are individual differences between learners.
3   It is worth pointing out that these words can have multiple meanings.
4   It is noteworthy that in general well-managed and successful firms have very few problems with their labour force.
5   It is important to note that neither the Egyptian nor the Chinese written symbols are actually 'pictures' of a house or a river.
6   It must be emphasised that these conclusions are based on only limited data.

1.2   In pairs, add an *it*-clause to each of the following extracts.

· **Choose a suitable *it*-clause from 1.1.**
· **Decide the best place (1, 2 or 3) to insert the *it*-clause in each extract.**

A   **1** In 2007 it was estimated that nearly 6 million South Africans had HIV/AIDS, more than any other country. **2** This means that nearly one in six people in the world with HIV/AIDS was South African. **3** The other top five countries with the highest occurrence of HIV/AIDS are all neighbours of South Africa.
B   As well as looking at short-term trends, **1** it is always important to look at the longer term. **2** For example, although unemployment was rising in the period covered in Table 3.1, **3** the number of people in work in September 1992 was 1.3 million higher than in March 1983.

1.3

> ❷ *Research shows that in the written academic corpus the most common adjective used in the structure It is + adj + to-infinitive is easy. Which are the next most common? Use the clues to help you guess.*
> 1 eas*y*____   2 im____   3 re____   4 en____
> 5 po____   6 in____
> *What are the next most common adjectives used with it is + adjective + that*
> 1 cl*ear*____   2 po____   3 li____   4 un____
> 5 tr____   6 ev____

1.4   Look back at an academic text you have written recently (for example, for 10.4c, page 51). Try to revise it by including one of the *it*-clauses from this section.

2 Word families

2.1   a Write the words in the box from the text in 2.1, pages 43–44, in the correct place in the table.

> ~~accompanying~~   create   derived   distinction
> illustration   interpretation   specifically
> sufficiently   symbol   tradition

	Noun	Verb	Adjective	Adverb
1			accompanying	
2				
3				
4				
5				
6				
7				
8				
9				
10				

b In pairs, complete the table with words from the same family in the other columns where possible. Use a dictionary to check your answers.

3 Nouns with related adjectives ending in -ic and -ical

Some nouns have a related adjective ending:
- -ic   symbol – symbol**ic**
- -ical   method – method**ical**
- -ic *or* -ical   alphabet – alphabet**ic**/alphabet**ical**

3.1 a Look at the nouns in the box. Write the related adjectives in the appropriate column of the table. When you have finished, use a dictionary to check your answers.

~~analysis~~ ~~base~~ ~~biography~~ catastrophe
chronology   climate   cycle   democracy
economy   ethics   geography   history
hypothesis   ideology   irony   microscope
philosophy   problem   psychology   scheme
science   strategy   technology   theory

-ic	-ical	-ic *or* -ical
basic	*biographical*	*analytic/ analytical*

> (i) *Some other adjectives which end in* -ic *and* -ical *don't have related nouns, e.g.* automati**c**, domesti**c**, technica**l**.

b The pairs of adjectives *economic/economical* and *historic/historical* have different meanings. Write sentences which demonstrate the difference between them. Use a dictionary to help you.

3.2 Find and correct five mistakes with adjectives ending in -ic and -ical in these extracts from students' writing.

1. The region is subjected to western climatical influences.
2. Table 3 shows average income by geographical area.
3. It was shown to be a hereditary disease rather than a psychologic disturbance.
4. Strategic planning is a cyclical process with several related stages.
5. Section 2 includes some basical information about the software.
6. There is always a risk of a catastrophical event such as a forest fire or flood.
7. Of course, this is only a hypothetic question.
8. Holmes (2009) demonstrates why online health advice can be problematic.

3.3 Complete these sentences using adjectives in 3.1a.

1. Every moment there are m *icroscopic* changes in our brain.
2. Before describing the methodology, I will outline the t_____ framework used in the research.
3. Ultraviolet fluorescence spectroscopy is a useful a_____ technique for the measurement of many hazardous materials.
4. The importance of h_____ evidence such as coins is that they are primary sources.
5. Watkins (2009) considers the e_____ impact of climate change.
6. The third category to be described here is the b_____ novel.
7. S_____ planning requires information gathering, an exploration of alternatives, and a focus on the implications of decisions.
8. This h_____ meeting between Roosevelt and Churchill was held in Casablanca.
9. Because I was working with young children in the study, there were various e_____ issues to be considered.
10. Four experiments were conducted to identify the most e_____ method of purifying the polluted water.

4 Reporting verbs

4.1 In pairs, underline the correct reporting verbs. Use a dictionary to help you where necessary. When you have finished, check your answers in 11.1, page 51.

> ### Disciplinary variations in the writing of research articles in English
>
> In a preliminary investigation, Dudley-Evans (1984) **1** *focused on / established* dissertation titles. Recently, Dietz (1995) **2** *considered / conducted* an extensive analysis on titles of scientific texts. Finally, Berkenkotter and Huckin (1995) and Busch-Lauer (1997) **3** *claimed / analysed* the conventions of title writing in scientific research articles. They **4** *revealed / investigated* in their studies that newer titles are semantically richer and are characterised by an increasing syntactic fullness. In connection with this, Berkenkotter and Huckin **5** *commented / examined* that stating the results of an investigation in the title of the article is becoming very common.

4 Difference and diversity

Reading

1 Thinking about what you already know

1.1 You have been asked to give a ten-minute presentation in a tutorial on the topic *The importance of cultural awareness in international business*. In preparation, you are going to read extracts from a book, *International Business*, which looks at how people behave in business across different cultures.

Before you read, in pairs think of three differences in how people behave in cultures you are familiar with. Discuss how these differences might have an effect on how people from these cultures do business with each other.

2 Reading in detail

2.1 Read the first extract, *Culture at two levels*, and decide whether the following statements accurately report what the writer says (✓) or not (✗). If they are not accurate reports, explain why they are wrong.

1 The approaches to looking at culture that are described are old.   **✗**
   The writer says that there are traditionally two different approaches. In this context, 'traditionally' does not mean 'old', but instead the 'usual way of doing things'.
2 Psychic distance measures the differences between two cultures.   _____
3 The institutional level looks at how institutions differ in different countries.   _____
4 All people who were born or grew up in a country share cultural characteristics.   _____
5 It is simple to create national stereotypes.   _____
6 Studies have looked at how the national characteristics of managers and employees influence company performance.   _____

> ➤ *Multi-word verbs: focus on; look at*
> G&V **2, p65**

International Business

Culture at two levels

There are traditionally two different approaches to looking at culture:

- The psychic or psychological level, which focuses on the internalized norms, attitudes, and behaviour of individuals from a particular culture (psychic distance is a measure of differences between groups).

- The institutional level, which looks at national (or group) culture embodied in institutions (government, education, and economic institutions as well as business organizations).

In this chapter we will mainly discuss the first, culture as shared psychology, with a brief reference to national institutional differences at the end.

People who are born in, or grew up in, the same country tend to share similar cultural characteristics. Nationality and culture tend to coincide, although nations encompass a wide variety of institutions, religions, beliefs, and patterns of behavior, and distinct subcultures can always be found within individual countries. The only way to make sense of this wide diversity is to characterize distinct cultural groups through simplified national stereotypes.

Many studies have attempted to create these stereotypes by mapping and comparing the shared characteristics of managers and employees in different countries. Researchers then examine the effects of key differences on business behavior, organization, structure, and ultimately the performance of companies from different countries. The following describes the milestone studies of this kind in the management field.

54

2.2 Read the second extract and match Hofstede's four dimensions of culture (1–4) to the summaries (A–D) which follow.

Hofstede's four dimensions of culture

Geert Hofstede is a Dutch psychologist who conducted one of the earliest and best-known cultural studies in management, on IBM's operations in 70 countries around the world. Getting answers to 32 statements from over 116,000 questionnaires, he mapped key cultural characteristics of these countries according to four value dimensions:

5

1 **Power distance** is the extent to which a culture accepts that power in organizations is distributed unequally. High power distance equates with steep organizational hierarchies, with more autocratic leadership and less employee participation in decision making (see Figure 5.2 for examples).

2 **Uncertainty avoidance** is the degree to which members of society feel uncomfortable with risk and uncertainty. High uncertainty avoidance (Japan, Argentina, France) will be reflected in the

10 high priority placed on rituals, routines, and procedures in organizations and society in general. Countries with low uncertainty avoidance (Denmark, UK, India, US) tend to emphasize flexibility and informality rather than bureaucracy.

3 **Individualism** is the extent to which people are supposed to take care of themselves and be emotionally independent from others (see Figure 5.2 for examples).

15

4 **Masculinity** is the value attributed to achievement, assertiveness, and material success (Japan, Mexico, Germany, UK) as opposed to the stereotypical feminine values of relationships, modesty, caring, and the quality of life (Sweden, the Netherlands, Denmark), according to Hofstede.

Figure 5.2 illustrates some of Hofstede's findings using two of the most useful dimensions, power distance

20 against the degree of individualism / collectivism.

It reflects some general stereotypes of the countries included, with clear grouping of the UK, Australia, and US as highly individualistic and less hierarchical (small power-distance) cultures against Mexico, Thailand, and

25 Panama at the other extreme.

There are numerous problems with the methodology used by Hofstede in his most famous study, not least because the survey covered employees from just one firm, IBM. IBM's own, strong corporate culture arguably biased the

30 cross-cultural comparisons.

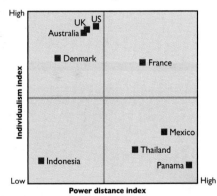

Based on: Figure 5.2 Hofstede's power distance against individualism for 20 countries

---

Rugman, A. M. & Collinson, S. (2006). *International business* (4th edn). Harlow: Pearson.

Summary A

Hofstede's value dimension _____
The tendency of people to look after themselves and their immediate family only

Summary B

Hofstede's value dimension _____
The degree to which the dominant values of a society are success, money and material things

Summary C

Hofstede's value dimension _____
The extent to which people feel threatened by ambiguous situations and have created institutions and beliefs for minimising or avoiding these uncertainties

Summary D

Hofstede's value dimension _____
The degree to which less powerful members of organisations and institutions accept the fact that power is not distributed equally

2.3 Is your home country shown in the chart in Figure 5.2? If it is, do you agree with where it is positioned? If not, where would you place it?

3   Taking notes

3.1 Look at the following reasons for taking notes from written texts. In pairs, decide whether you think each reason is not important (NI), important (I) or very important (VI).

1   To help me concentrate on the text _____
2   To help me understand the content of the text _____
3   To help me see how the text is organised _____
4   To help me identify the points that are most relevant to my studies _____
5   To help me improve my academic writing _____
6   To help me remember the content of the text _____
7   To act as a store of information that I can revise from _____
8   To show me how much I have learned _____
9   To help me understand new words _____
10 To record information that I can use in essays and presentations _____

3.2 Look again at the extracts in 2.1 and 2.2 and complete the following notes for your presentation on *The importance of cultural awareness in international business*. In pairs, compare your notes.

Approaches to looking at culture

Two different approaches:
1) Psychic / psychological level (looks at individuals from particular culture)
2) **a** _____

Psychic / psychological level
Assumptions of this approach: **b** _____

Studies: **c** _____

Hofstede's study was conducted: **d** _____

e.g. Hofstede's 4 value dimensions:

	Characteristics	
	High (+)	Low (−)
1 Power distance = acceptance of unequal power	= **e** _____	= **f** _____
2 Uncertainty avoidance = **g** _____	priority given to rituals, routines, procedures, bureaucracy	= **h** _____
3 Individualism = **i** _____	= **j** _____	take care of others
4 Masculinity = **k** _____	= **l** _____	= **m** _____

Problems with Hofstede's study? **n**
_____
_____

3.3 In pairs, decide what other information you would need to look for in further reading to add to your notes for your presentation.

4 Vocabulary building 1: word families

4.1 a The following nouns are all used in the extracts in 2.1 and 2.2. Scan the extracts to find other words in the same word family and decide if it is a noun (n), adjective (adj) or adverb (adv).

1 individuals (n)   *individualism (n)*
                      individual (adj)
                      individualistic (adj)

2 culture (n)   _____
3 institution (n)   _____
4 hierarchies (n)   _____
5 stereotype (n)   _____

b Add other words to complete the word families. Use your dictionary if necessary.

5 Vocabulary building 2: adjective–noun collocations

5.1 Complete the following collocations using adjectives from 4.1.

1 *institutional*   environment   4 _____   image
                      investor   role
                      framework   view

2 _____   classification   5 _____   diversity
                      organisation   identity
                      structure   tradition

3 _____   choice
                      freedom
                      liberty

6 Collecting information for an essay

6.1 After attending a lecture on biodiversity you were asked to write a 500-word essay with the title *Discuss the benefits to humans of biodiversity, and outline with examples the most important current threats to biodiversity*. As you research how biodiversity is beneficial to humans, you find the following sources. Skim the extracts (A–E) and decide which of the headings (1–4) they relate to. Underline key words in the extracts which give you the answers.

1 Health   _____   3 Business and industry   _____
2 Agriculture   _____   4 Leisure, culture and aesthetics   _____

A All ecosystems and human societies depend on a healthy and productive natural environment that contains diverse plant and animal species. The earth's biota is composed of an estimated 10 million species of plants, animals, and microbes (Pimm et al. 1995). Although approximately 60% of the world's food supply comes from rice, wheat, and corn (Wilson 1988), as many as 20,000 other plant species have been used by humans as food. Some plants and animals provide humans with essential medicines and other diverse, useful products. For instance, some plants and microbes help to degrade chemical pollutants and organic wastes and recycle nutrients throughout the ecosystem.

Pimentel, D et al. (1997). Economic and environmental benefits of biodiversity, *BioScience*, 47: 747–757.

B Biodiversity is an issue of strategic importance for business. Biodiversity supports the world we live in, providing the raw materials and natural assets for many businesses. Many businesses, including amongst others, farming, food processing, retail, brewing and distilling, pharmaceuticals and petrochemicals, derive direct economic benefit from biodiversity and are dependent on biodiversity as a resource. A healthy and stable environment, where biodiversity is used in an efficient and sustainable fashion, is crucial if these businesses are to continue to succeed.

Scottish Diversity Forum (2010). *Why does conserving Biodiversity matter to business?* www.biodiversityscotland.gov.uk

➤ *However; although*

G&V **1, p64**

C | Of the 300,000 or more species of flowering plants, about 12,500 are considered to be edible to humans (Rapoport & Drausal 2001). Around 200 plant species have been domesticated for food. However, at present more than 75% of the food supply (in terms of energy intake) of the human population is obtained, directly or indirectly, from just 12 kinds of plants (bananas/plantains, beans, cassava, maize, millet, potatoes, rice, sorghum, soybean, sugar cane, sweet potatoes, wheat).

…

D | Ecotourism is by definition founded on biodiversity, and has developed into a massive industry. Indeed, tourism as a whole is one of the fastest growing industries in the world. In 1988 an estimated 157–236 million people took part in international ecotourism (i.e. in countries of which they were not national), contributing between US$93 and US$233 billion to national incomes (Filion et al. 1994). However, international tourism is also estimated to account for perhaps only 9% of global tourism receipts (the rest is domestic), suggesting that these figures represent only a fraction of the scale and economic impact of ecotourism (Filion et al. 1994). In 1998, an estimated 9 million people went whale-watching alone, with expenditures on just this activity of US$1 billion (Hoyt 2000).

…

E | As well as providing sustenance, biodiversity plays other vital direct roles in maintaining the health of the human population. Natural products have long been recognized as an important source of therapeutically effective medicines, and more than 60% of the world's human population relies almost entirely on plant medicine for primary health care (Harvey 2000). Of 520 new drugs approved between 1983 and 1994, 39% were natural products or were derived from them.

Gaston, K. J. and Spicer, J. I. (2004). *Biodiversity: an introduction*. Oxford: Wiley/Blackwell.

6.2 a **Scan the extracts again and make notes for the first part of the essay *Discuss the benefits to humans of biodiversity* … Use the four headings in 6.1 to structure your notes. For example:**

· *Agriculture* ——————— *300k plant species: but 12.5k edible,*
     200 species for food: 12 (e.g. beans, rice, wheat) > 75% food supply

b **In pairs, compare your notes. Discuss whether there are any other topics in the extracts that would be relevant to the first part of the essay.**

c **Look back at your notes and identify any gaps. What additional information would you now look for before you start writing the first part of the essay?**

7 Taking notes for essay writing

7.1 **Here are some of the stages in writing an essay. Based on your experience of doing the activities in 6.1 and 6.2, draw arrows to show what order they are most likely to come in.**

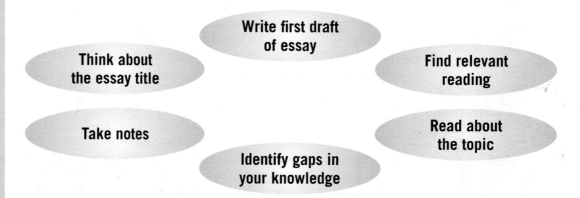

7.2 **Using your notes in 6.2, write a draft of 200–250 words for the first part of the essay *Discuss the benefits to humans of biodiversity* …**

Listening and speaking

8 Working with colleagues: generating ideas and reporting

Most students will need to work in groups during their academic studies. The activities in the Listening and speaking sections will help you prepare for this.

8.1 a **In a tutorial on the topic of *Cultural differences in behaviour*, your tutor gave you the following handout. In small groups, choose one person who will take notes and report back to the class afterwards. Then discuss the questions on the handout.**

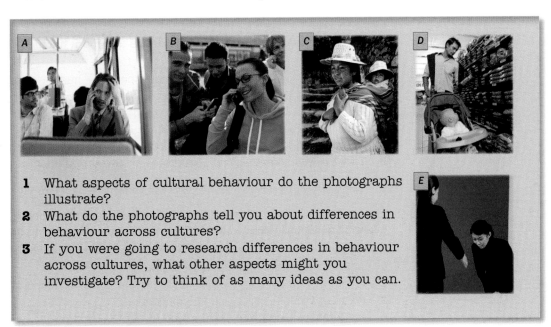

1 What aspects of cultural behaviour do the photographs illustrate?
2 What do the photographs tell you about differences in behaviour across cultures?
3 If you were going to research differences in behaviour across cultures, what other aspects might you investigate? Try to think of as many ideas as you can.

b **Report back to the class on the discussions.**

8.2 a (◀))4.1) **Listen to a student reporting back on the same activity and answer the following questions.**

1 Which photographs were the group discussing?
2 Did they answer all of the questions on the handout in 8.1?

b (◀))4.2) **Listen and complete the following extracts.**

Expressions for reporting back
1 Right. Well, **we** _thought_ _that_ _this_ picture was showing that people …
2 … and might just bow. _____ **also the** _____ _____ gender here.
3 … childcare, household tasks. _____ _____ **of the** _____ _____ **that** in some cultures …
4 … greet each other in different ways. So Zubaidah _____ _____ for most groups in Indonesia …
5 _____ _____ **to the third question, we** _____ _____ _____ a number of other aspects that could be investigated.

Expressions for referring to what people in other groups have said
6 … how young people treat their elders. Kerry **said** _____ _____ **for** _____ **one.**
7 We also talked about attitudes to punctuality. **This was** _____ _____ **group two** _____ _____ **as well.**

8.3 a **In new groups, choose one person to take notes and report back to the class afterwards. Then discuss different ways you could research *Cultural differences in behaviour*. For example, how might you do research on greetings by people from different cultures?**

b **Report back to the class on your discussion. Try to use some of the expressions in 8.2.**

9 Pronunciation: dividing speech into units

> ⓘ *As we speak, we divide what we say into* speech units *– groups of words that are separate units of information – depending on meaning and emphasis. Words within speech units are usually linked together smoothly.*

9.1 a (◄»4.3) **Listen and notice how the speaker divides up what she is saying. A break between speech units is marked with //.**

Okay Steve // do you want to tell us // what you discussed?

b (◄»4.4) **Listen to the following lecture extracts and mark the break between speech units with //.**

1 So   in some   cultures   people shake   hands   for example. ...
2 ... while others   avoid   contact   and might   just bow.
3 There's also   the question of   gender   here   which prompted us to talk about   the different   behaviour   of men and women.
4 One possibility   would be to   look at   how young people   treat their   elders.
5 This   was something   that group   two talked about   as well.

c **In pairs, read the extracts aloud with the same breaks between speech units.**

9.2 **In groups, think about cultural differences in behaviour in academic contexts and discuss the following questions about lectures. Try to divide your speech into appropriate speech units.**

Do you think it is appropriate or normal behaviour in your country to:
1 walk into a lecture late and leave before the end?
2 record the lecture without asking the lecturer's permission first?
3 interrupt the lecturer to ask for clarification?
4 interrupt the lecturer to say that you disagree with them?
5 call the lecturer by their first name?
6 ask the lecturer questions after the lecture?
7 talk to other students while the lecture is going on?

Writing

10 Language for writing 1: the grammar of reporting verbs

10.1 **Look at the examples of how the verbs** *agree*, *analyse* **and** *demonstrate* **are used. Complete the rules (A–C) using the correct verb.**

1 Johnson (1958) agreed that currency devaluation would have little effect in these circumstances.
NOT Johnson (1958) ~~agreed the ineffectiveness of currency evaluation in these circumstances~~.

2 Roberts (2004) analysed postgraduate internships and found that the average duration was six months.
NOT Roberts (2004) ~~analysed that the average duration of postgraduate internships was six months~~.

3 Henderson (1985) demonstrates the metaphoric use of words like 'door', 'gate' and 'fire' in the play.
Henderson (1985) demonstrates that the words 'door', 'gate' and 'fire' are used metaphorically in the play.

Rules
Some reporting verbs:
A may be followed by a noun phrase but not by a *that*-clause. e.g. _____
B may be followed either by a noun phrase or a *that*-clause. e.g. _____
C may be followed by a *that*-clause but not usually by a noun phrase. e.g. _____

10.2 In pairs, put the verbs in the box in the correct column in the table.

~~agree~~   ~~analyse~~   argue   believe   call for   claim   comment   compare   conclude   conduct   consider   define   ~~demonstrate~~   describe   discuss   examine   explain   investigate   note   outline   point out   question   reject   say   show   state   suggest   think   write

A-pattern verbs (V+ NP/ ~~V + that~~)	B-pattern verbs (V + NP or V + *that*)	C-pattern verbs (~~V + NP~~/ V + *that*)
analyse	demonstrate	agree

10.3 Complete the following sentences with the verbs in the boxes.

~~conducted~~   investigated   pointed out

1 According to the survey __conducted__ by Ambosa et al. [21], expecting medical staff to learn new software while caring for a full load of patients is a common reason for failure.
2 It has been _____ that even moderate storms can have an impact on coastal development (Steers, 1965).
3 Carman (1956) _____ the way in which insectivorous plants catch and digest insects.

carried out   compared   concluded

4 Dundee et al. (1994) _____ the use of acupuncture and paracetamol in pain relief.
5 Collins (2008) _____ that mental illness is twice as common in lower socioeconomic classes.
6 They _____ an investigation into employer attitudes towards the continuing professional development of their employees.

agreed   called for   examined

7 A number of studies have _____ the reasons for the slow pace of reform (e.g. Smythe, 1999; Trevor, 2008).
8 Bygrave (1989) _____ that chaos theory cannot be supported by data.
9 Other writers have _____ a change in planning policy (e.g. Lim, 2005; Newton, 2008).

🎓 **Focus on your subject** *When you make a note of reporting verbs commonly used in your subject, make sure you know the correct grammatical structures which follow them.*

11 Language for writing 2: comparing and contrasting

In academic writing we often compare or contrast two or more definitions, situations, events, etc., or what two writers do, find, or think.

➤ *Linking parts of a text: conjunctions and sentence connectors*

G&V **1.1, p64**

11.1 Match the examples (1–6) to the ways of comparing and contrasting (a–c).

a Similarities and differences are signalled using linking expressions (e.g. *similarly, whereas*). _____ _____

b Differences are highlighted using comparative adjective or adverb phrases (with *more / less / -er ... than*) or the words *more* or *less*. __1__ _____

c Similarities and differences are not highlighted with any particular words or phrases. In this case, clauses or sentences often contain the same phrases or have the same structure. _____ _____

1 The current level of crime in the country is much less than accounts in the popular press might lead us to believe.

2 Some cultures believe that suicide might be permissible under some circumstances. Other cultures may regard it as a sin or even as a crime.

3 In North America and northwest Europe business relationships are typically instrumental and all about achieving objectives. But further south and in many other cultures, business is a human affair and the whole range of emotions are deemed appropriate.

4 Although approximately 60% of the world's food supply comes from rice, wheat, and corn (Wilson 1988), as many as 20,000 other plant species have been used as food.

5 Achievement means that you are judged on what you have recently accomplished and on your record. Ascription means that status is attributed to you by birth, kinship, gender or age, and also by your connections and your educational record.

6 The universalist approach is roughly: "What is good and right can be defined and always applies." In particularist cultures far greater attention is given to the obligations of relationships and unique circumstances.

> ✪ *Research shows that in the written academic corpus the five most frequent adjectives that go in the structure* more ... than *are: 1 important 2 likely 3 complex 4 effective 5 efficient. Which of these adjectives is not as frequent in the structure* less ... than?

11.2 Write short texts with the following notes using some of the ways of comparing and contrasting you saw in 11.1. There may be more than one possible answer.

1 • Common glow-worm females up to 25 mm in length; no wings
• Common glow-worm males up to 12.5 mm in length; have wings

Female common glow worms have no wings and grow up to 25 mm long. Males, on the other hand, have wings but grow only up to half this size.

2 • soldier: refers to a member of a country's armed forces
• mercenary: a soldier hired for service in a foreign army

3 • United States, Ireland, etc. – 'college' and 'university' more or less interchangeable
• United Kingdom, Australia, etc. – 'college' usually institution between school and university

4 Forms of government include –
• constitutional monarchy: monarch is head of state, but legally bound by constitution
• absolute monarchy: monarch is sole source of political power in the state; not legally bound by any constitution.

5 • Publicity campaigns can spread knowledge about diet.
• Health education programmes in schools can provide knowledge and develop a responsible attitude towards diet.

12 Reporting what you read

12.1 a In 6.1 and 6.2 you looked at the benefits to humans of biodiversity. In pairs, discuss what threats to biodiversity are shown in the following photographs.

b In pairs, think of three other current threats to biodiversity. Try to agree on which threat is the most important.

➤ *Referencing conventions*

Unit 3, 10 p48

➤ *Reporting verbs*

Unit 3, 11 p51

12.2 Look at the notes in the table taken from four research studies on biodiversity. Use the information in the notes to write a draft of 200–250 words for the second part of the essay (*Discuss the benefits to humans of biodiversity, and) outline, with examples, the most important current threats to biodiversity.*

Use the author-date system for in-text references and try to use a variety of reporting verbs from 10.2.

Author(s)	Year	Threat	General examples	Specific examples
Ray Harris	2002	Destruction of habitat	· Building cities on farmland	· Nearly half of prime main agricultural land in California = built on
Gary Pearce and Tony Williams	2008	Pollution	· Oil spilled in the sea; kills animals and plants	· Amoco Cadiz spilled about 0.25 million tonnes of crude oil; France, 1978; major damage to environment
		Destruction of habitat	· Clearing forests for timber	· Large areas of Brazilian rainforest have been destroyed
Li Chen, Val Arle, Kim Dressler, and Mark Petrovsky	2009	Over-exploitation of animal or plant species	· Over-fishing; can eliminate species	· Cod disappeared off Newfoundland, Canada in 20th century
		Pollution	· Using pesticides on farmland	· Vulture population in India in decline (it's thought that cows take up pesticides from grass; vultures eat dead cows)
Lars Alvin	2010	Climate change	· Higher temperatures can kill animal and plant species	· Hibernating animals may wake early because of warmth; but no food, so starve

Grammar and vocabulary

Grammar and vocabulary
· Linking parts of a text: conjunctions and sentence connectors
· Single-word verbs and multi-word verbs
· Word families

1 Linking parts of a text: conjunctions and sentence connectors

1.1 Complete the following descriptions using the words in bold in the extracts (1–4).

- Conjunctions (e.g. _____ and _____) link clauses within a sentence
- Sentence connectors (e.g. _____ and _____) link two sentences.

1 **Although** approximately 60% of the world's food supply comes from rice, wheat and corn, as many as 20,000 other plant species have been used by humans as food.

2 Mental labour has usually been valued more highly than physical labour. **In addition**, work performed outside the home is judged to be more valuable than work done in the home.

3 Around 200 plant species have been domesticated for food. **However**, at present more than 75% of the food supply of the human population is obtained, directly or indirectly, from just 12 kinds of plants.

4 You should provide a reference to the source **whenever** you quote or paraphrase another writer.

1.2 Write the following conjunctions and sentence connectors in the box in the correct place in the table. Use a dictionary to check your answers.

> as soon as   at the same time   because   even so
> even though   furthermore   hence   if so
> insofar as   later   meanwhile (x2)   on the other hand
> otherwise   provided (that)   since (x2)   subsequently
> therefore   too   unless   when   while (x2)   yet

Type of link	Conjunctions	Sentence connectors
Comparison, contrast, and indicating that something is unexpected	although whereas	however on the contrary
Reasons and results	as so that	as a consequence as a result
Adding information	and	above all in addition
Condition	as long as if	if not
Time: one event at the same time as another	as whenever	at that time
Time: one event before or after another	after before as soon as	afterwards earlier

1.3 Match the beginnings (1–10) to the endings (a–j) and connect them using the words in the box. Sometimes more than one answer is possible.

> after   As a consequence   As a result
> as long as   If not   Otherwise   provided
> that   so that   Subsequently   whereas

1 The speakers were positioned in the classroom ___so that___ ___b___

2 The Industrial Revolution refers to the transformation in Britain from a predominantly agricultural to industrial society, beginning around 1750. _____, ___i___

3 A BSc degree takes three years in England, _____ ___f___

4 The population explosion will continue _____ ___j___

5 The company paid below-average wages. _____, ___e___

6 Through films and television, children are exposed to violence in the form of entertainment. _____, ___a___

7 All the subjects in the experiment had to be between the ages of 20 and 30. _____, ___d___

8 Anyone can stand for parliament, _____ ___c___

9 Climbers need to acclimatise gradually. _____, ___h___

10 Many Koreans entered the United States in the late 1960s _____ ___g___

a they grow up believing that aggression is acceptable.
b everyone could hear clearly.
c they were excluded from the research.
d they are over 18 years of age.
e employee motivation was low.
f in Scotland it usually takes four.
g changes to the immigration laws in 1965.
h they run the risk of suffering from altitude sickness.
i other nations went through a similar change.
j death rates are significantly lower than birth rates.

2 Single-word verbs and multi-word verbs

Some single-word verbs and multi-word verbs express the same meaning (e.g. discuss and talk about).

ⓘ *In general, where there is a choice, the single-word verb is preferred in academic writing, and the multi-word verb equivalent is often preferred in informal writing and speech. For example: In this chapter we will mainly **discuss** culture as shared psychology. (NOT talk about) However, some multi-word verbs are common in academic writing. For example: account for, be associated with, be based on, carry out, consist of, focus on, look at, result in.*

2.1 Match the academic single-word verbs in the box to the informal multi-word verbs (1–10). Use a dictionary to help you.

> ~~arise~~ begin calculate coincide consider delay discover experience investigate remove

1 come up → _arise_
2 come up against → _experience_
3 cut out → _remove_
4 find out → _discover_
5 go together → _coincide_
6 look into → _investigate_
7 put off → _delay_
8 start off → _begin_
9 think about → _consider_
10 work out → _calculate_

2.2 a Underline the multi-word verbs in the following extracts from academic writing.

1 Teachers should be alert to problems that might come up. _arise_
2 The experimental population consisted of 110 senior undergraduate students (78 women and 32 men). _✓_
3 The analysis is based on 2855 subject respondents. _____
4 It is rarely the case that linguistic and international borders go together exactly. _____
5 There are many factors to be thought about in determining the success of the project. _____
6 A survey carried out in 2001 showed a dramatic increase in the number of people reaching the age of 100. _____
7 Some students have found out that their learning styles make online courses unworkable for them. _____
8 Their investigation looked at a large population of school-aged children. _____

9 We worked out that software alone accounted for about one-third of the overall cost of the project. _____
10 The business came up against a number of difficulties in the following year. _____

b Replace the words you have underlined with single-word verbs if they are not normally used in academic writing. Tick the sentences which do not need changing. Use a dictionary to help you.

3 Word families

3.1 Complete the following sentences using the nouns in the box, or an adjective, verb or adverb from the same word family. Use words from the same family in each a and b pair.

> culture ~~hierarchy~~ individual institution stereotype

1a Scandinavian companies have a reputation for being somewhat more collegial and less _hierarchical_ than American ones.
b Texts are _hierarchically_ organised into paragraphs, paragraphs into sentences, and sentences into words.
2a In _individualism_ societies, the needs, values and goals of the individual take precedence over the needs, values and goals of the group.
b One-to-one marketing depends strongly on an effective dialogue with _individual_ customers.
3a To talk about the 'first' (most developed), 'second' and 'third' (least developed) world, creates the impression that parts of the Earth are _stereotypical_ and economically entirely separate.
b Organisational _stereotype_ is typically defined as 'shared values', and commonly understood as 'the way the organisation does things'.
4a As many sectors of the economy faced serious losses several major financial _institutions_ went into bankruptcy.
b Davies (2006) examined the effects of _institutional_ change on employee motivation in the car industry.
5a Ageism means that a negative _culture_ is applied towards the entire population of elderly adults.
b Pairs of students – one male and one female – were asked to divide _cultural_ feminine tasks (e.g. decorating a cake) and masculine tasks (e.g. changing a car tyre).

Lecture skills B

Preparing for lectures

1 Using preparation strategies

1.1 In pairs, discuss how you prepare for lectures and what you do to follow up after the lecture. Report back to the class your ideas about preparation and follow-up strategies.

1.2 **a** B.1 Anitha and Anna studied at university in the UK. Listen to them talking about lectures and answer the following questions.

1 How did Anitha prepare for lectures, and what did she do after her lectures?
2 Did Anna use the same techniques as Anitha?

b Do Anitha and Anna prepare for and follow up lectures in a similar way to you?

Anitha

Anna

2 Making predictions before a lecture starts

 Study tip *Predicting the content of a lecture – both before the lecture starts and during the lecture itself – is an important strategy that can help you in a number of ways. For example, it can help you to activate what you already know about the topic, to understand how the lecture is organised, and to concentrate on what is said.*

2.1 **a** You are going to watch extracts from a lecture given by Dr Hugh Hunt with the title *Boomerangs, bouncing balls and other spinning things*. Before watching the lecture, in pairs look at Dr Hunt's page from his university's website and answer the following questions

1 What do you think the lecture will be about.
2 What do you already know about the topic of the lecture?

DEPARTMENT OF ENGINEERING

Gyroscopes and Boomerangs
Dr Hugh Hunt

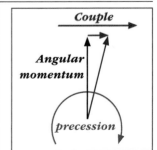

side-on view showing velocities

- *Senior Lecturer Cambridge University, Fellow of Trinity College Cambridge.*
- *Bachelor of Engineering (Mech.) Melbourne University, Ph.D. (Engineering) Cambridge University.*

---

b B.2 Watch the beginning of the lecture and check your predictions.

Listening

3 Making predictions during a lecture

Sometimes lecturers help you to make predictions by asking questions. You can predict what answers the lecturer will go on to give.

3.1 a (B.3) **Listen to and read the following extract from Dr Hunt's lecture.**

> And we know from lift, that the faster you go, the more lift you get. So for instance, if you're in a car and you stick your hand out the window and you tilt your hand, we know that if you're going pretty slowly you don't feel very much, but if you're going fast, your hand gets moved around much more. So we know that from experience. So what's that got to do with boomerangs?

b **In pairs, use the question that Dr Hunt asks at the end of the clip to predict what he will talk about next.**

c (B.4) **Watch the next section and check your predictions.**

Lecturers do not always use questions to indicate what they are going to talk about. Sometimes the content of the talk so far will help you make predictions.

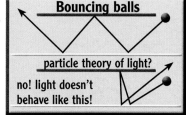

3.2 a (B.5) **Look at the slide and watch the extract from Dr Hunt's lecture. At the end of the extract, predict what he will talk about next.**

b (B.6) **Watch the next extract and check your predictions.**

4 Identifying topic change

4.1 a (B.7) **Lecturers often mark *topic change* (the ending of one section in the lecture and the beginning of the next). Watch three extracts from Dr Mormina's lecture, *The origins of human diversity*, and underline the places where she changes topic.**

> *Extract 1*
>
> In particular I want to focus on three of these mechanisms – migration, adaptation and culture – but I have to say that I'm going to focus mostly on migration. Right. Erm, this is the outline of this talk. I'm going to spend a little bit of time giving you the science behind [it] so you won't escape there is a bit of scientific talk.

> *Extract 2*
>
> I'm going to be talking a little bit about natural selection and adaptation to different environments and the role of culture in all this process. Okay, so let's start with this first part. I like using this picture because to me it represents the diversity of our human species.

> *Extract 3*
>
> And in the case of humans these barriers are not, erm, hungry cats but are geographic barriers, for example, mountains or rivers, climatical, er, barriers or cultural barriers. If you think of the caste system in India, for example, it's a tremendous, cultural barrier. Okay. Up to here, the scientific background. And I'd like now to spend some time talking about how these different, er, mechanisms of gene flow and natural selection have acted over the course of human evolution to create the pattern of biological diversity that we see today.

b **In pairs, compare your answers. What markers does Dr Mormina use to show that she is changing topic?**

4.2 In pairs, think of some more topic markers that lecturers might use and report back your ideas to the class.

4.3 **B.8** Watch an extract from a lecture given by Dr Charles Moseley with the title *Why we read Shakespeare*. Which topic markers does he use?

Study tip When a number of these markers occur together, it is usually an indication of topic change. If you can recognise topic changes, it can help you understand how the lecture is organised, and also help you organise your notes.

5 Following an argument

5.1 a Dr Mormina argues that modern humans (*Homo sapiens*) evolved in Africa for environmental reasons. In pairs, look at the following steps in her argument and put them in order.

_____ Some species die out during drought.
_____ A species with a slender body shape survives better when food resources are scarce.
_____ Bodies adapt when there are fewer resources.
___1___ About 200,000 years ago the Earth went through a cold period.
_____ Homo sapiens evolved a more slender body shape than Neanderthals.
_____ There are fewer resources for surviving species during a drought.
_____ In the tropics (e.g. much of Africa) a cold period produces drought.

b **B.9** Watch the extract from her lecture and check your answers.

6 Taking notes: using symbols and abbreviation in notes

6.1 When you take notes in a lecture, you can save time by using abbreviations and symbols. In pairs, look at the following tables of some commonly used abbreviations and symbols. Are there any others you use? Add your ideas to the tables.

Abbreviation	Meaning
cf.	compare (with)
e.g.	for example
esp.	especially
et al.	and others
etc.	etcetera; and so on
i.e.	that is; that means
imp.	important
lg.	large
max.	maximum
min.	minimum
no.	number
re.	regarding; on the subject of

Symbol	Meaning
=	equals; is the same as
≠	is not equal to; is different from
→	leads to; results in; causes
←	results from; is caused by
↑	high; increase
↓	low; decrease
@	at
&	and
>	is greater than
<	is less than
∴ (or *so*)	therefore
b/c (or *bec.*)	because
C20th	20th century

6.2 (B.10) **Watch an extract from Dr Mormina's lecture where she is talking about how natural selection influences diversity, and look at the following notes made by a student. In pairs, suggest other abbreviations and symbols that the student might have used to make their note-taking more efficient.**

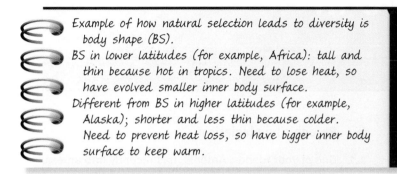

Example of how natural selection leads to diversity is body shape (BS).
BS in lower latitudes (for example, Africa): tall and thin because hot in tropics. Need to lose heat, so have evolved smaller inner body surface.
Different from BS in higher latitudes (for example, Alaska); shorter and less thin because colder. Need to prevent heat loss, so have bigger inner body surface to keep warm.

6.3 a **You are going to watch the next section of Dr Mormina's lecture. Before you listen, check that you know the meaning of the following phrases. Use a dictionary to help you.**

digest milk   the age of weaning   mutation in the gene

b (B.11) **Watch and take notes. Use symbols and abbreviations where you can. In pairs, compare your notes.**

Language focus

7 Organising questions and topic changes

7.1 **You are going to watch an extract from a lecture given by Dr Prodromos Vlamis with the title *Introduction to macroeconomics*.**

a **In pairs, look at the following key terms which are used in the extract and discuss what you already know about them. Use a dictionary to help you if necessary.**

inflation   inflation rate   macroeconomics   microeconomics

b (B.12) **Watch the extract and notice when Dr Vlamis uses organising questions and when he changes topic.**

c **Watch again and take notes. In pairs, compare your notes.**

Dr Prodromos Vlamis Associate, Department of Land Economy, University of Cambridge and Visiting Fellow, Hellenic Observatory, London School of Economics.

Follow-up

8 Expanding your vocabulary

8.1 **Look at the following notes that a student made during Dr Hunt's lecture. In pairs, try to explain what the underlined words mean. Use a dictionary to help you.**

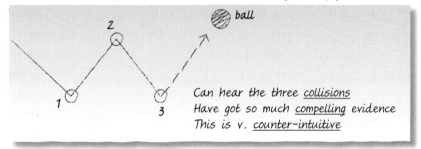

ball

Can hear the three <u>collisions</u>
Have got so much <u>compelling</u> evidence
This is v. <u>counter-intuitive</u>

Study tip *During any lecture there are likely to be words and phrases that you don't know. Use this as an opportunity to expand your vocabulary by writing down a few words and phrases each lecture that you hear but don't understand. After the lecture, look them up in a dictionary or ask a friend or teacher what they mean.*

5 The world we live in

Reading
- Recognising plagiarism
- Identifying the main ideas in a text
- Summarising what you have read
- Vocabulary building: single-word verbs and multi-word verbs
- Vocabulary in context: hedging adverbs

Listening and speaking
- Reaching a consensus in group work
- Pronunciation: contrasts

Writing
- Using paraphrases
- Including quotations in your writing

Reading

1 Recognising plagiarism

1.1 One of your friends, Antonia, has recently had an essay on how coastlines change marked and returned by her tutor. She thinks some of the comments made by her tutor were unfair. Look at an extract from her essay with the tutor's comments, and the textbook extracts. In pairs, discuss whether you agree with Antonia that her tutor's comments were unfair.

Extract from Antonia's essay

Some coastlines have changed little over the past 6000 years, but most have advanced or retreated. Some have alternated between advance and retreat. A coastline advances when the amount of sediment deposited is bigger than the rate of erosion, or where there is emergence because of uplift of the land or a fall in sea level. It retreats when erosion is bigger than deposition, or when there is submergence due to land subsidence or a rise in sea level.

Did you write this yourself? It looks like it might be copied from somewhere. You mustn't copy other people's work without saying where it's taken from.

The processes of coastline change are usually quite slow, but in some cases are very rapid indeed. An example of this is the Mississippi River, which drains an enormous area of the United States. Its waters are thick with mud that is washed downstream by rains in spring. The sediment amounts to about 360 million tons (330 million t) each year. Around the mouth of the river, the mud has built up into a marshy delta with many different channels. These empty into the Gulf of Mexico, a shallow sea without any big tides or strong currents to flush away the sediment. As a result, the coastline advances into the sea by about two-thirds of a mile (1 km) every ten years (Steele, 2003). An example of a retreating coastline is found in Oamaru, North ...

You've given the source of this information, but it's too close to the original. You need to put it into your own words more.

Extracts from textbooks

Changing coastlines

While some coastlines have changed little over the past 6000 years, most have advanced or retreated, and some have shown alternations of advance and retreat. A coastline advances where the deposition of sediment exceeds the rate of erosion, or where there is emergence due to uplift of the land or a fall in sea level, and retreats as the result of erosion exceeding deposition, or where there is submergence due to land subsidence or a sea level rise. (Figure 1.3).

Bird, E. C. F. (2008). *Coastal geomorphology: an introduction* (2nd edn). Chichester, UK: Wiley.

70

> **Case study: Mississippi River**
> The Mississippi River drains a vast area of the US. Its waters are thick with mud that is washed downstream by spring rains. The sediment amounts to about 360 million tons (330 million t) each year.
>
> **Advancing into the sea**
> Around the mouth of the river, the mud has built up into a marshy delta with many different channels. These empty into the Gulf of Mexico, a shallow sea without any big tides or strong currents to flush away the sediment. For that reason, the coastline advances into the sea by about two-thirds of a mile (1 km) every ten years.

Steele, P. (2003). *Changing Coastlines*. London: Franklin Watts.

1.2 a **5.1 Listen to an extract from a conversation between Antonia and her tutor about her essay. Complete the notes in the table summarising her tutor's view on plagiarism.**

The most common forms of plagiarism	Why plagiarism is wrong and how it can affect your grades	How to avoid plagiarism
· copying material _____	· saying that ideas or words _____	· acknowledge _____
· cutting and _____		· try to _____
· copying the work of _____	· in assessed work _____	· where exact words _____

b Her tutor is talking about views of plagiarism in British academic life. In pairs, discuss whether these are the same in your own country.

 Study tip *Most academic institutions (universities and colleges) include their policy on plagiarism on their website. Read the policy of the institution you attend or hope to attend to learn more about plagiarism.*

1.3 In the *Academic orientation* unit, 4.2, page 11 you read an extract from a textbook with the title *Environmental effects of Earth rotation*. Read it again, and the two extracts (A and B) from students' essays. In pairs, discuss the following questions.

1 Do you think either of these students is guilty of plagiarism?

2 If so, what suggestions would you make to the student to help them avoid plagiarism in the future?

A

The Earth's rotation has a number of impacts on the environment. The first impact is that it produces a daily rhythm in daylight, air temperature, air humidity, and air motion. All surface life responds to this daily rhythm. Green plants receive and store solar energy during the day and use up some of it at night.

A second environmental impact is that the flow paths of both air and water are always turned in a sideward direction because of the Earth's rotation. In the northern hemisphere flows are turned right and in the southern hemisphere toward the left. This phenomenon is called the Coriolis effect. It is very important in studying the Earth's winds and ocean currents.

B

The Earth's rotation has a number of effects on the environment. Strahler and Strahler (2002) note two of these. First, the rotation produces a daily (or diurnal) rhythm in daylight, air temperature, air humidity, and air motion. This has an impact on all life on the Earth's surface. Plants, for example, store solar energy during the day and consume some of this at night. Second, the rotation affects the flow of air and water, turning it toward the right in the northern and toward the left in the southern hemisphere. This influences the Earth's winds and ocean currents.

2 Getting started

2.1 **We use maps to represent the world we live in. In pairs, discuss the following questions and report back to the class.**

1 What do these maps represent?
2 What maps do you use regularly? Why do you use them?
3 How do maps affect the way you view the world?

● Malaria risk
● No malaria

2.2 **In preparation for a tutorial on the subject of *How maps influence our perception of the world*, your tutor has asked you to read an extract from a textbook on physical geography. Before you read, check your understanding of the key vocabulary in the box. Use a dictionary to help you.**

direction	globe	landmark	landscape	location	navigation	spatial

3 Identifying the main ideas in a text

3.1 **Skim the following text and decide which note (a or b) best summarises the main idea in each section (A–G).**

1 a People 1st needed to describe location when they started sailing across oceans
   b Language to describe location = used since people started to communicate ✓

2 a Maps developed only after invention of paper
   b Maps drawn since early human history

3 a People need to know what symbols represent so they can understand maps
   b Maps = locations on Earth vs. globes = locations elsewhere

4 a Geographers make maps
   b Cartographers make maps

5 a Mapmakers now use advanced computational techniques
   b Mapmakers use computational techniques to experiment with map design

6 a Technological changes ⟶ dramatically changed how maps made
   b Need to gather more information ⟶ slowed down mapmaking

7 a Today, main purpose of maps = no longer to represent location
   b Maps & related technologies today used for wide variety of purposes

Location on Earth

A Perhaps as soon as people began to communicate with each other, they also began to develop a language of location, using landscape features as directional cues. Today, we still use landmarks to help us find our way. When ancient peoples began to sail the oceans, they recognized the need for ways of finding directions and describing locations. Long before the first compass was developed, humans understood that the positions of the sun and the stars – rising, setting, or circling the sky – could provide accurate locational information. Observing relationships between the sun and the stars to find a position on Earth is a basic skill in **navigation**, the science of location and wayfinding. Navigation is basically the process of getting from where you are to where you want to go.

5

Maps and Mapmaking

B The first maps were probably made by early humans who drew locational diagrams on rocks or in the soil. Ancient maps were fundamental to the beginnings of geography as they helped humans communicate spatial thinking and were useful in finding directions. The earliest known maps were constructed of sticks or were drawn on clay tablets, stone slabs, metal plates, papyrus, linen, or silk. Throughout history maps have become increasingly more common, as a result of the appearance of paper, followed by the printing press, and then the computer. Today, we encounter maps nearly everywhere.

10

15

C Maps and globes convey spatial information through graphic symbols, a "language of location," that must be understood to appreciate and comprehend the rich store of information that they display. Although we typically think of maps as being representations of Earth or a part of its surface, maps and globes have now been made to show extraterrestrial features such as the moon and some of the planets.

20

D **Cartography** is the science and profession of mapmaking. Geographers who specialize in cartography supervise the development of maps and globes to ensure that mapped information and data are accurate and effectively presented. Most cartographers would agree that the primary purpose of a map is to communicate spatial information. In recent years, computer technology has revolutionized cartography.

25

E Cartographers can now gather spatial data and make maps faster than ever before – within hours – and the accuracy of these maps is excellent. Moreover, digital mapping enables mapmakers to experiment with a map's basic characteristics (for example, scale, projections), to combine and manipulate map data, to transmit entire maps electronically, and to produce unique maps on demand.

30

United States Geological Survey (USGS) *Exploring Maps,* page 1

F The changes in map data collection and display that have occurred through the use of computers and digital techniques are dramatic. Information that was once collected manually from ground observations and surveys can now be collected instantly by orbiting satellites that send recorded data back to Earth at the speed of light. Maps that once had to be hand-drawn can now be created on a computer and printed in a relatively short amount of time. Although artistic talent is still an advantage, today's cartographers must also be highly skilled users of computer mapping systems, and of course understand the principles of geography, cartography, and map design.

35

G We can all think of reasons why maps are important for conveying spatial information in navigation, recreation, political science, community planning, surveying, history, meteorology, and geology. Many high-tech locational and mapping technologies are now in widespread use by the public, through the Internet and also satellite-based systems that display locations for use in hiking, traveling, and direction finding for all means of transportation.

40

Person, people, peoples
G&V **3, p81**

Articles; Ancient maps … (not The ancient maps …)
G&V **1, p80**

As a result; such as
G&V **2, pp80–81**

Gabler, R. E. et al. (2009). *Physical geography* (9th edn.). Belmont, CA: Brooks/Cole.

4 Summarising what you have read

 Study tip *You may need to summarise information you have read in preparation for an essay or a presentation. Summarising also helps you to focus on the main parts of a text, and allows you to check your understanding of what you have read.*

4.1 **As part of a presentation on the influence of maps on our lives you have to talk for a minute about *Changes in how maps are made*. Make notes for the presentation from text in 3.1. Use your notes to give a one-minute talk to your partner.**

► *Single-word verbs and multi-word verbs*

Unit 4, G&V 2, p65

5 Vocabulary building: single-word verbs and multi-word verbs

5.1 a **In pairs, complete the following extracts using the correct form of the verbs in the box with a similar meaning to the words in brackets.**

combine	communicate	create	~~develop~~
display	encounter	observe	occur	transmit

1 Perhaps as soon as people began to communicate with each other, they also began to
   ___*develop*___ a language of location … (**build up**)
2 … humans understood that … _____ relationships between the sun and the stars … is a basic skill in navigation. (**looking at**)
3 Ancient maps … helped humans _____ spatial thinking. (**put across**)
4 Today, we _____ maps nearly everywhere. (**come across**)
5 … digital mapping enables mapmakers … to _____ and manipulate map data, to _____ entire maps electronically … (**join up; send out**)
6 The changes in map data collection and display that have _____ through the use of computers … (**come about**)
7 Maps that once had to be hand-drawn can now be _____ on a computer … (**put together**)
8 … satellite-based systems that _____ locations for use in hiking …(**lay out**)

b **Look back at text 3.1 to check your answers.**

6 Vocabulary in context: hedging adverbs

6.1 a *Hedging* **is an important process in academic communication. Complete the explanation of hedging using the words in the box.**

~~confident~~	facts	partially	possibilities	some

In academic communication we frequently avoid making statements that are too direct or too
1 ___*confident*___. This is because in the academic world we often talk about theories and
2 _____ rather than certain 3 _____. We can avoid directness by using hedges;
that is, language which indicates that something may be true, is 4 _____ true, is true in
5 _____ cases, and so on.

b **Compare the following statements. Which one is hedged?**
1 We think of maps as being representations of Earth.
2 We typically think of maps as being representations of Earth.

6.2 **a** **In pairs, decide which of the following statements from the text in 3.1 should be hedged and give reasons.**

1 As soon as people began to communicate with each other, they also began to develop a language of location ...
We don't know definitely that this happened, so the statement needs to be hedged.

2 When ancient peoples began to sail the oceans, they recognized the need for ways of finding directions.

3 The first maps were made by early humans who drew locational diagrams on rocks or in the soil.

4 Today, we encounter maps everywhere.

5 In recent years, computer technology has revolutionized cartography.

6 Maps that once had to be hand-drawn can now be created on a computer and printed in a short amount of time.

b **Add the adverbs in the box to the sentences in 6.2a that need to be hedged, and make any other necessary changes.**

nearly	~~perhaps~~	probably	relatively

1 Perhaps∧ as soon as people began to communicate with each other ...

c **Look back at the text in 3.1 to check your answers.**

> 🎓 **Focus on your subject** *Find a text from your subject. What hedging adverbs can you find in it? Are there any different ones from those you saw in the text in this unit?*

Listening and speaking

7 **Reaching a consensus in group work**

7.1 **Your tutor has asked your group to give a presentation on the subject of malaria. In small groups, decide who will take notes and report back to the class. Share what you already know about malaria.**

7.2 **You have agreed that you will talk about the following topics.**

a the future prevention and treatment of malaria _____
b the geography of malaria _____
c the prevention of malaria through history _____
d the impacts of malaria on health _____
e the economic and social effects of malaria _____
f the causes of malaria _____

a **Working alone, decide on your preferred order for these topics in the presentation and why you think this order is best. Write the order next to the topics (a–f).**

b **Now discuss the order as a group and try to reach a consensus.**

7.3 **(◄)5.2) Listen to the last part of a discussion in which students are deciding how to order topics in a presentation on antibiotics. By the end of the discussion, in what order do they agree to present these topics? Write the final order next to the topics.**

Antibiotics:
· side-effects _____   · how they work _____   · impact on public health _____
· problems of resistance _____   · discovery _____

7.4 a **Complete the following extracts from the discussion by writing the words in brackets in the correct order.**

Giving reasons for a preferred order

1 _It's sensible to put_____ (to / sensible / It's / put) how antibiotics work first.
2 Well, that's possible, but **it** _____ (to / logical / seems / talk / more) **about** their discovery _____ (before / saying) how they work. We can start with how …
3 Well, _____ (introduce / can't / really / we) side-effects _____ (about / we've / before / talked) how antibiotics work. So we need to do side-effects later.
4 … I think **the** _____ (would / better / presentation / flow) if we had impacts …

Reaching a consensus

5 We _____ (time / left / haven't / much / got) and _____ (need / we / agree / to) an order for presenting these.
6 Okay, **most** _____ (are / agreement / that / people / in) we start with …
7 Right, _____ (consensus / be / to / the / that / seems) we **talk about** how antibiotics work …
8 Right, **that's** _____ (agreed / order / then. / it / Our) is …

b (◄)5.3) **Listen again and check your answers.**

7.5 **Change groups so that you are working with different students, and repeat the activity in 7.2b. Try to use some of the useful expressions you heard in 7.4.**

8 Pronunciation: contrasts

8.1 (◄)5.4) **Listen to these extracts from 7.3. Notice how the speaker steps up to a relatively high pitch. This emphasis makes it easier for listeners to notice the contrasts that the speaker thinks are particularly important.**

1 So we talk first about the PAST, and then about the ⬆FUture.
2 We'd be going from the speCIFic to the more ⬆GENeral effects of antibiotics.

8.2 a (◄)5.5) **In pairs, complete the following sentences with contrasting words from the box. Listen and check your answers.**

abstract ~~contracted~~ contradict mental national permanent qualitative unexpected

1 We'd expected the material to expand, but in fact it _contracted_ .
2 Some of the results were expected, but others were totally _____ .
3 Rather than being temporary, as we'd anticipated, the effects were _____ .
4 We collected a lot of quantitative data, but more interesting was the _____ data.
5 Having outlined the situation in the regions, I'll now look at the _____ position.
6 I first counted the concrete nouns in the text, and then the _____ nouns.
7 While some of our results support previous findings, others _____ them.
8 I've outlined the results of our physical health survey, and now Stephan will look at _____ health.

b **Practise saying the sentences to each other with a step up on the words you have written.**

Writing **9 Using paraphrases**

🎓 **Focus on your subject** *Some academic subjects, particularly in the sciences, rarely use quotations. Look at a few textbooks and journal articles to find out whether quotations are used in your subject or not.*

9.1 a The following information comes from a university website where information is given about paraphrasing. In pairs, think of three advantages of using paraphrases as opposed to quotations in your academic writing.

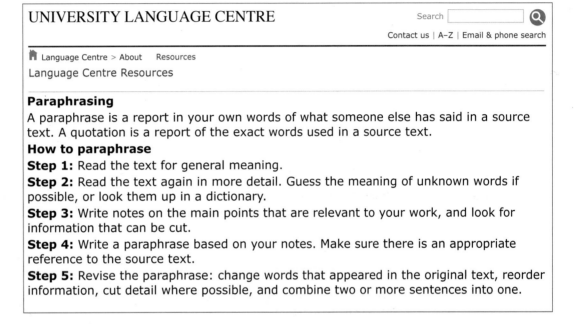

UNIVERSITY LANGUAGE CENTRE

Search 🔍

Contact us | A–Z | Email & phone search

🏠 Language Centre > About   Resources

Language Centre Resources

Paraphrasing
A paraphrase is a report in your own words of what someone else has said in a source text. A quotation is a report of the exact words used in a source text.
How to paraphrase
Step 1: Read the text for general meaning.
Step 2: Read the text again in more detail. Guess the meaning of unknown words if possible, or look them up in a dictionary.
Step 3: Write notes on the main points that are relevant to your work, and look for information that can be cut.
Step 4: Write a paraphrase based on your notes. Make sure there is an appropriate reference to the source text.
Step 5: Revise the paraphrase: change words that appeared in the original text, reorder information, cut detail where possible, and combine two or more sentences into one.

b You have been given an essay with the title *How can countries achieve sustainable development? Discuss this with reference to one country you are familiar with*. As you research the essay, you find the following text and decide that you want to use some of the information it contains. Make notes on the text using Steps 1–3 in the website to write a successful paraphrase of the extract.

Note: Sustainable development is development that uses nature's resources at a rate at which they can be replaced naturally, and so does less damage to the environment.

Role of information

Information is the foundation of sustainable development and is fundamental to successful planning and decision making. If decisions are made without sound data and information, they will be little better than best guesses and are likely to be wrong. Economic and social data are widely available and are relatively reliable and well understood. The situation with environmental data and information is somewhat different. High quality, comprehensive and timely information on the environment remains a scarce resource, and finding the 'right' information can pose problems: data are more difficult and expensive to obtain. It is also difficult to find indicators that capture and reflect the complexity of the environment and human vulnerability to environmental change. Environmental data acquisition remains a basic need in all countries.

United Nations Environment Programme (2002). *Global Environment Outlook 3*. London: Earthscan

c Look at the following notes on the text in 9.1b and answer the questions.
1 Were your notes in b different? Add to or edit your notes in any way you find useful.
2 Why didn't the student comment on sentence 2?

Info. essential for successful planning and decision making.

Reliable, well understood, economic and social data widely available.

However, little high quality, comprehensive & timely environmental data available because difficult and expensive to obtain; also difficult to find indicators of complexity of environmental change and human vulnerability.

But basic need in all countries.

d Read the following paraphrase of the text in 9.1b. Then, using the notes you made in b and c, write your own paraphrase using the guidelines in Step 4.

It has been pointed out (United Nations Environment Programme, 2002) that information is fundamental to successful planning and decision making for sustainable development. Reliable and well understood economic and social data are widely available. However, there is little high quality, comprehensive and timely environmental data available. This is because it can be difficult and expensive to obtain. It is also difficult to find indicators of the complexity of environmental change and human vulnerability to it. Nevertheless, it is a basic need in all countries.

e Read another possible paraphrase of the text in 9.1b. Compare it with the paraphrase in 9.1 d. What differences do you notice?

It has been pointed out (United Nations Environment Programme, 2002) that information is a basic requirement in successful planning and decision making for sustainable development. Although economic and social data are widely available, there is relatively limited environmental data because of its complexity and the fact that it can be expensive and difficult to produce. However, environmental data is essential.

f Look again at the paraphrase you wrote in 9.1d. Revise it using the guidelines in Step 5.

9.2 You have been given an essay with the title *Show how humans have had an impact on their environment using examples from one country with which you are familiar.* Use the five steps in 9.1 to write a paraphrase of the following text.

We can recognize certain trends in human manipulation of the environment during the modern era. Firstly, the number of ways in which humans are affecting the environment is growing rapidly. For example, nearly all the powerful pesticides post-date the Second World War. The same applies to the increasing construction of nuclear reactors, to the use of jet aircraft and to
5 many aspects of biotechnology. Secondly, environmental issues that once affected only particular local areas have become regional or even global problems. An instance of this is the appearance of substances such as DDT (a major pesticide), lead and sulphates at the North and South Poles, far removed from the industrial societies that produced them. Thirdly, the complexity, magnitude and frequency of impacts are probably increasing. For instance, a massive modern
10 dam like that at Aswan in Egypt has a very different impact from a small Roman dam.

Goudie, A. and Viles, H. A. (1997). *The Earth Transformed: An introduction to human impacts on the environment.* Oxford: Blackwell.

➤ *Using quotations*

Appendix 2, page 167

10 Including quotations in your writing

10.1 Read the conventions for including quotations in your writing in Appendix 2, page 167 and then revise the following extracts from student essays to include the quotations.

1

> One of the indicators of a country's level of development is the general health of its population. However, there are difficulties in objectively measuring some aspects of health.

"… health is a complete physical, mental and social well being and not merely the absence of disease or infirmity." (World Health Organisation, 1985, p 8)

One of the indicators of a country's level of development is the general health of its population. According to the World Health Organisation (1985: 8): 'health is a complete physical, mental and social well being and not merely the absence of disease or infirmity'. However, there are difficulties in objectively measuring some aspects of health.

2

> Children growing up in the modern world face problems never encountered before: the demands of a consumer society, a changing climate, and limited resources. It is the job of teachers and parents to give guidance to children as they try to adapt to this new world.

"The solution to adult problems tomorrow depends on how our children grow up today" (Mead, 1980, p 35)

3

> There is dispute among researchers about whether infectious diseases will cause more deaths in the future or fewer. Pimentel (1999), for example, argues that the growth in disease is expected to continue. Other researchers disagree with this view.

"… infectious disease has been decreasing since 1970 … infectious disease is expected to decrease in the future, at least until 2020" (Lomborg, 2001, p 26)

4

> Culture is shared by a group of people. The group may be very large in number, such as those sharing a Western culture, or just a few hundred, such as the inhabitants of some small Pacific islands.

"The culture of a group consists of its shared, socially learned knowledge and patterns of behaviour" (Stevens, 1987, p 3)

10.2 In pairs, read the revised extracts your partner wrote in 10.1. Check that they have followed the conventions for quotation you saw in the Appendix and suggest improvements where necessary.

Grammar and vocabulary

Grammar and vocabulary
· Articles: *zero article* and *the*
· Complex prepositions
· *Person, people, peoples*

1 Articles: *zero article* and *the*

1.1 Read the following explanations of how we use *zero article* (no article) and the definite article (*the*). In pairs, match the examples (a–k) to the explanations (1–11).

*We use **zero article** with plural and uncountable nouns when we talk generally about people or things, without definite people or things in mind. For example, we might talk about a whole class of things in a general way (**1** b), or about an indefinite number (**2** i, j) or indefinite amount (**3** ___).*

*We use **the** with singular, plural or uncountable nouns when we expect the reader to be able to identify the thing or person we are referring to in the following noun. This may be because:*
· *it is clear from the context (**4** ___).*
· *it is identified by information after the noun, often in an of-phrase (**5** ___).*
· *it is identified using a superlative adjective (**6** ___).*
· *it is identified using an adjective such as first, main or primary (**7** ___).*
· *there is only one of a particular thing or person (**8** ___).*
· *there is only one group of these things or people (**9** ___).*

*When we make generalisations about classes of things we can use either **the** with a singular noun (**10** ___) or **zero article** with a plural noun (**11** ___).*

a … the **primary purpose** of a map …
b Throughout history **maps** have become increasingly common …
c … followed by **the printing press**, and then **the computer**.
d … are now in widespread use by the public, through **the Internet** …
e … navigation, **the science** of location and wayfinding.
f When ancient peoples began to sail **the oceans** …
g **The earliest** known **maps** were constructed of sticks …
h This view shows detail of stags crossing a river, and experts suggest that some of **the artwork** represents a rudimentary map …
i **Geographers** who specialize in cartography …
j **Computers** have dramatically changed map data collection and display.
k **Information** that was once collected manually …

1.2 Add *the* before the noun or noun phrase in bold in one of each of the following pairs of sentences (a or b).

1 **a** World War I was a turning point in **history**.
  b He was a major figure in **history** of science.
2 **a** I begin by describing **most significant risks** associated with outsourcing.
  b All people taking part in sport know that **risks** are unavoidable.
3 **a** Fish is probably main **food** for most people living in coastal settlements.
  b **Food** that can be prepared and served quickly is referred to as 'fast food'.
4 **a** In the 20th century there were many innovations in the material used in **painting**.
  b *Mona Lisa* is a 16th-century portrait now in the Louvre in Paris. **Painting** shows a woman whose facial expression is often described as 'mysterious'.

2 Complex prepositions

Prepositions are words like of, in and with that come in front of a noun phrase or an -ing form. Complex prepositions consist of two or more words. For example:
  *… maps and globes have now been made to show extraterrestrial features **such as** the moon …*
  *… maps have become increasingly more common, **as a result of** the appearance of paper …*
Many complex prepositions like these are common in academic writing.

2.1 Underline the three complex prepositions in each of the following extracts.

1 A residential area is one in which housing predominates, as opposed to industry or commerce. As well as single family housing, residential areas may include multiple family housing such as apartment blocks.
2 With the exception of the new railway line linking the capital to the south coast, all the major infrastructure projects of the 1980s were completed ahead of schedule, in spite of the difficult economic conditions at the time.
3 Non-verbal communication (NVC) refers to communication by means of gestures and facial expressions, as distinct from speech. Some NVC is universal in that it is understood regardless of the culture in which it occurs.

2.2 Match the complex prepositions you underlined in 2.1 to the following descriptions.

1 something not included in what you are saying
   with the exception of

2 something that contrasts with what you have just mentioned and when you want to emphasise the first one _____ and
_____

3 something in addition to what you have just mentioned _____

4 the way or method of doing something
_____

5 an event that is more important or occurring before one you have just mentioned
_____

6 something that doesn't affect or influence an event you have just mentioned
_____

7 more examples of a type of thing you have just mentioned _____

8 a fact that makes something you have mentioned surprising _____

2.3 Complete the following sentences using one of the complex prepositions in 2.1 and an ending in the box.

> age   ~~friends~~   Malawi   rotating blades
> social responsibility
> the researchers conducting the study
> using a search engine   wealth

1 Harris (2000) studied social support from family members _as distinct from friends_ .

2 The lower a person's social class, the lower their life expectancy, _____ .

3 A wind turbine converts wind energy to electrical energy _____ .

4 Children were asked about their computing experience, _____ .

5 Nobody will be allowed to see individual responses, _____ .

6 In today's society people tend to put their own interests _____ .

7 The class system involves differences of power _____ .

8 All African countries were represented at the meeting, _____ .

Study tip *Make a note of new complex prepositions as you find them. It may help you to remember them if you group complex prepositions according to their general meaning. For example:*

DIFFERENCE   EXCEPTION
as opposed to   with the exception of
as distinct from

⊙ *Research shows that the most frequent two-word preposition in the written academic corpus is such as. What do you think are the next most common? Complete the list by writing the second part of each preposition.*

1 such ___as___	2 rather _____
3 according _____	4 due _____
5 because _____	6 up _____
7 prior _____	8 together _____
9 close _____	10 as _____

Use a dictionary to check how each one is used.

3 *Person, people, peoples*

- *The usual plural form of* person *is* people.
  e.g. Perhaps as soon as **people** began to communicate with each other ...

- *In academic writing, either* people *or* persons *can be used when referring to particular categories of people.* Persons *is preferred in American English.*
  e.g. elderly **persons/people**; **persons/people** with severe mental illness

- *The singular noun* people *refers to a nation or race.*
  e.g. Culture can be defined as the way of life of a **people**.

- *Its plural form is* peoples, *although the singular form can usually be used instead.*
  e.g. When ancient **peoples** began to sail the oceans ... (*or* When ancient **people** ...; *the plural form emphasises that there were a number of different groups*)

3.1 Complete the following sentences using the words in the box. There may be more than one possible answer.

> people   peoples   person   persons   a people

1 There are now more _____ living in urban than in rural areas.

2 Tobacco was first used thousands of years ago by native _____ in South America in religious ceremonies.

3 Providing effective primary care for homeless _____ is a difficult task.

4 There are more than 5000 _____ in the world over 100 years old.

5 The Medes were _____ who occupied the mountainous area of north-western Iran and north-eastern Iraq.

6 Their research looked at the indigenous _____ of northern Australia.

7 The subjects of the study were 200 _____ aged 65 or over.

8 In general, _____ earn more as they get older.

6 Behaving the way we do

Reading
· Organising information for an essay
· Skimming and scanning texts
· Taking notes and explaining what you have read
· Vocabulary building: collocations

Listening and speaking
· Referring backwards and forwards in presentations

Writing
· Writing conclusions in essays
· Language for writing: hedging
· Giving references

Reading

1 Organising information for an essay

1.1 During a tutorial on human behaviour, you hear two students express the following points of view. In small groups, discuss which student you agree with, and why.

Student 1
Everyone is born the same, and then as we grow up we're taught to behave the way we do.

We're all born with different characteristics – it's in our genes – and these control how we behave in our lives.
Student 2

➤ *Essay types*
Unit 1, 9, p20

1.2 a After the tutorial you were given an essay with the title *'Do we, as individuals, behave in a certain way because we were "born that way," or do we behave that way because our environment "taught" us to behave that way?' (Chance, 2009)* Discuss this *'nature'* vs. *'nurture'* debate.

Do you think it is a *describe*, *discuss* or *defend* type of essay?

b You have found the following texts which may be useful to you as you write the essay. Skim read the texts to identify the main points relevant to the essay title.
In pairs, read the texts: Student A, read texts 1–4 and Student B, read texts 5–9.
Make brief notes so that you can report back to your partner what you have read.

➤ *Ways of taking notes*
Unit 3, 6, p45

A texts

Extract 1

> … children learn to behave as boys or girls by observing and imitating the behavior of others. Considerable research suggests that children are most likely to imitate people who are powerful, nurturing, and who control rewards in their lives (Bandura & Huston, 1961; Bandura, Ross, & Ross, 1963; Mischel & Grusec, 1966). Parents fit the bill on all of these dimensions. This leads to the obvious prediction that boys are particularly likely to imitate their fathers and girls are particularly likely to imitate their mothers.

Lippa, R. A. (2005). *Gender, Nature and Nurture.* (2nd edn.). Mahwah, N.J.: Lawrence Erlbaum Associates.

Extract 2

> The concept here is that each baby is programmed in some way to take greater account of certain kinds of information, or respond in particular ways to certain objects. These are usually described as inborn biases or constraints. The linguist Noam Chomsky proposed that all children are born with a Language Acquisition Device (LAD), which enables them to learn to talk seemingly effortlessly.

Leather, N. (2004). Attachment. In Wyse, D. (Ed.) *Childhood Studies: An introduction.* Oxford: Blackwell.

Extract 3

The trouble with the nature–nurture debate is that it creates an artificial division between the contributions of heredity and experience. The debate wrongly implies that the answer must be one or the other [Kuo, 1967; Midgley, 1987]. In fact, nature and nurture are inextricably interwoven in a kind of Gordian knot. The two strands cannot be separated. As William Verplanck [1955] put it long ago, "learned behavior is innate, and vice versa" [see also Schneider, 2003].

Chance, P. (2009) *Learning and Behavior* (6th edn.). Belmont, CA: Wadsworth Cengage Learning.

Extract 4

Some behaviours, especially those associated with the very early stages of an individual's life, develop without any apparent influence of the environment or the experience of the organism – the behaviour develops due to the nature of the organism. This means that the behaviour is set in train at the appropriate time by some internal mechanism and that the conditions in which the organism is growing are not influential. This implies that the behaviour arises from inherited characteristics – that is, the
5 behaviour is innate and is already built into the organism at fertilisation. On the other hand, some behaviour is environmentally determined – that is, the organism behaves in an appropriate manner as a result of its experience in the environment in which it lives. Such behaviours are said to be due to nurture. An organism's experience might be gained through interacting with its parents and sibs, others
10 in the group, with predatory animals, with the food available in the environment, and so on.

Dockery, M. and Reiss, M. (1999). *Behaviour*. Cambridge: Cambridge University Press

B texts

Extract 5

Few would dispute that hair colour is the result of genetic inheritance, or that the ability to speak Slovenian is a product of environment. No one is born with the ability to speak Slovenian. The ability is acquired either by growing up in a Slovenian-speaking environment, or by being taught Slovenian by someone else who speaks it. On the other hand the ability to acquire language as such would seem to be the product of genetic inheritance.

Beckett, C. (2002). *Human Growth and Development*. London: Sage.

Extract 6

Richard Herrnstein and Charles Murray's *The Bell Curve: Intelligence and Class Structure in American Life* has revived the ongoing debate over the appropriateness and usefulness of IQ as an explanatory variable in models predicting behaviour. The work's main thesis is that an individual's intelligence – no less than 40% and no more than 80% of which is inherited genetically from his or her parents – has more effect than socioeconomic background on future life experiences, including criminal actions.

Manolakes, L. A. (1997). Cognitive Ability, Environmental Factors, and Crime: Predicting Frequent Criminal Activity. In B. Devlin, S.E. Fienberg, & K. Roeder (Eds.). *Intelligence, Genes, and Success: Scientists respond to The Bell Curve.* New York: Springer

Extract 7

It is too simplistic to reduce the various factors that make people what they are to 'nature' and 'nurture'. In reality a whole range of different factors contributes to making us what we are, some of which could be described as nature, some as nurture, some of which could be assigned to either category. In many cases, a complex interplay between inherited and environmental factors is at work.

Beckett, C. (2002). *Human Growth and Development.* London: Sage.

Extract 8

Consider the question, Are humans naturally aggressive? Wilson (1978) reports that among the !Kung San, an aboriginal people of Africa, violence against their fellows was almost unknown. But Wilson points out that several decades earlier, when the population density among these people was greater and when there was less governmental control over their behavior, their per capita murder rate rivaled that of America's most dangerous cities.

Chance, P. (2009) *Learning and Behavior* (6th edn.). Belmont, CA: Wadsworth Cengage Learning.

Extract 9

Although there is no clear way of knowing what the percentage of nature and nurture mix is, Debra Nicholl (1999), a Johns Hopkins-educated neuroscientist and biomedical communications professional, reports a 40- to 60-percent variation in temperament and personality traits that can be attributed to genetic factors. She maintains that nature is revealed in personality and learning style beginning at birth "in the form of individual variation in responsiveness, intensity, ability to adapt to change, reactions to novelty – traits that collectively define the characteristic approach to the world known as temperament and that are demonstrably sensitive to genetic influence" (p. 45).

Given, B. K. (2002). *Teaching to the brain's natural learning systems.* Alexander, VA: Association for Supervision and Curriculum Development, USA.

c In pairs, summarise what you have read and produce a list of the main points from all nine texts that are relevant to the essay in 1.2a. Organise the main points so that they form the outline of the introduction and body of an essay.

d Decide what additional information you should look for in your reading before you begin to write the essay.

1.3 Compare the outline you have produced with other pairs of students and report back to the class any differences.

2 Skimming and scanning texts.

2.1 a You are going to read two texts about gender roles in different cultures. Before you read, look at the results from a survey of the working population in the United States. In pairs, discuss what they tell you about gender roles and changes in gender roles between 1992 and 2008.

Who takes most responsibility for ...

Gender		... child care? (%)		... cooking? (%)		... house cleaning? (%)	
		1992	2008	1992	2008	1992	2008
Men	I do or share equally	41	49	34	56	49	53
	My spouse/partner does	58	48	56	38	51	39
	Others do	1	4	9	7	9	8
Women	I do	73	67	75	70	73	73
	My spouse/partner does or share equally	21	31	15	25	18	20
	Others do	6	3	9	6	9	7

Galinsky, E., Aumann, K. & Bond, J. T. (2009). *Times are changing: gender and generation at work and at home.* Families and Work Institute.

b Discuss whether you think results from your country would be similar or different.

2.2 You have found the following texts for an essay with the title *Discuss differences in gender roles in different cultures*.

  a Skim both texts to identify the main points relevant to the essay title.

  b Make brief notes so that you can report back to your partner what you have read.

Text 1

Gender development

1 Social scientists including sociologists, anthropologists, and psychologists have also examined gender roles across cultures (Best, 2001; Best & Williams, 1997; Gibbons, 2000; Williams, Satterwhite, & Best, 1999). Although all cultures make distinctions between male and female roles, the particular content of what is assigned to men and women can vary from culture to culture (Wade & Tavris, 1999). For example, in some cultures women may do the marketing or weaving, whereas men do so in other cultures. Cultures vary in how much emotion men and women are expected to show, whether women in particular are expected to remain sexually chaste before marriage, and how much contact men and women can have on a daily basis. Cultures also vary in the extent to which the genders are expected to be different at all. Wade and Tavris (1999) give the example of Tahiti as one of the least gender-differentiated cultures; there are few differential expectations for the behaviors of men and women. Even their language lacks gender pronouns, and most names are used for either males or females.

2 Although certain aspects of gender roles vary greatly from culture to culture, other aspects are often similar. Williams and Best and their colleagues (Williams & Best, 1990; Williams et al., 1999) have studied university students' attitudes about gender-related personality traits in 25 countries from all over the world. They have found a remarkable degree of consistency in the traits assigned to males and females in these 25 countries. For example, in these various countries, males were consistently seen as active, adventurous, aggressive, independent, strong, logical, and unemotional. Women, on the other hand, were consistently seen as affectionate, emotional, fearful, submissive, talkative, timid, weak, and whiny.

3 There is also cross-cultural similarity among the genders in aspects of production tasks. In many societies men are more likely to hunt large animals, do metalworking, and do lumbering, whereas women are more often found carrying water, cooking, laundering, and gathering vegetables (Eagly et al., 2000; Wood & Eagly, 2002). These differences seem to arise, in part, from women's reproductive roles and men's greater physical strength. Of course, one of the most consistent differences between males and females cross-culturally is that women participate in more childcare (Geary, 2000; Kenrick & Luce, 2000).

4 There are also cross-cultural similarities in gender roles related to dating and mating, with men choosing younger women, less powerful partners, and more partners than women (Buss, 2000; Kenrick & Luce, 2000); and in interpersonal violence in that men engage in more violence against other males than females do against other females, and partner violence is typically related to males' attempts to control their female partners (Smuts, 1995; Wilson & Daly, 1996).

5 In childhood, there is a great deal of cross-cultural consistency in rough and tumble play, with boys doing more, and in the phenomenon of gender segregation in which children play predominantly with children of their own sex (Best & Williams, 1997; Geary & Bjorklund, 2000). In these groups, boys are more concerned with dominance and social status, whereas girls are more intimate and communal. In addition, across many cultures, but not all, boys are also more aggressive than girls, and girls are more likely to care for younger children (Best, 2001; Edwards, 2000; Munroe, Hulefeld, Rodgers, Tomeo, & Yamazaki, 2000).

Owen Blakemore, J. E., Bernebaum, S. A. and Liben, L. S. (2009). *Gender Development.* Psychology Press. Taylor and Francis.

what is; wh- noun clauses G&V 2, p92

do so G&V 1, p92

participate in; verb/ adjective + preposition G&V 4, p93

Text 2

Cross-Cultural Perspectives on Gender-Role Development

1 Gender-role socialization varies depending on one's cultural background. Differences in roles between men and women are exaggerated in some cultures and diminished in others.

2 Traditionally, Asian American families are patriarchal, with status and power determined by age, generation, and gender (Balgopal, 2008, p. 156; Lu, 2008). Huang and Ying (1998) describe the values associated with a Chinese heritage:

3 Gender and birth positions were … associated with certain duties and privileges. Sons were more highly valued than daughters; family lineage was passed through the male, while females were absorbed into the families of their husbands. The first-born son, the most valued child, received preferential treatment as well as more familial responsibilities. The prescriptive roles for daughters were less rewarding; females often did not come into positions of authority or respect until they assumed the role of mother-in-law. (p. 38)

4 A son's primary responsibility is to be a "good son" throughout life, including caring for aging parents (Balgopal, 2008, p. 156; Lu, 2008). This does not apply to daughters. Although gender roles are changing somewhat for Mexican Americans, as they are for Americans in general, traditional Mexican American families adhere to strict separation of gender roles; men are to be heads of the household and women should submit themselves to their husbands, devoting their attention to caring for the family (Longres & Aisenberg, 2008; McCammon & Knox, 2007). Ramirez (1998) describes the gender-role socialization of many Mexican Americans:

5 Differences in sex-role socialization are clearly evident in this culture and become especially prominent at adolescence. The adolescent female is likely to remain much closer to the home than the male and to be protected and guarded in her contacts with others beyond the family, so as to preserve her femininity and innocence. The adolescent male, following the model of his father, is given much more freedom to come and go as he chooses and is encouraged to gain worldly knowledge outside the home in preparation for the time when he will assume the role of husband and father. (p. 220)

6 African Americans, on the other hand, are often taught to assume more egalitarian roles (Moore, 2008). Hines and Boyd-Franklin (1996) describe the gender roles characterizing many African American women: "African American women, who are often more actively religious than their mates, tend to be regarded as 'all sacrificing' and the 'strength of the family'. Their identity often is tied to their role as mothers. … Historically, they have worked outside the home, sometimes as the sole wage earners, particularly in times of high unemployment" (p. 69).

➤ *Historically; viewpoint adjectives*

G&V 3, p93

Zastrow, C. and Kirst-Ashman, K. K. (2010). *Understanding Human Behavior and the Social Environment* (8th edn). Belmont, CA: Brooks/Cole, Cengage Learning.

2.3 **Scan the texts and identify the text and section where you can find the following examples. Summarise the information you find in a brief note.**

1 A society where gender-role differences are relatively limited
   Text 1, section 1 – Tahiti: few differences in expected behaviour men vs women
2 Gender-related characteristics found to be similar across societies
3 The effects of physical differences on gender roles
4 How boys and girls play differently in same-sex groups
5 A society where men take responsibility for their ageing parents
6 A society where traditionally a woman becomes part of the husband's family when she marries

7 A society where female teenagers' contacts with people outside the family are carefully controlled

8 A society where gender roles traditionally are clearly differentiated

9 A society where wives have a more important role than husbands in holding the family together

10 A society where women traditionally have gone out to work

3 Taking notes and explaining what you have read

3.1 a Student A, look at text 1 and Student B, look at text 2. Underline any words and phrases used in the text to compare and contrast roles.
For example: *Sons were more highly valued than daughters*

b Make brief notes on the following topics.
Text 1: production tasks, personal relationships and childhood play
Text 2: traditional Chinese, traditional Mexican-American and African-American families

c In pairs, use your notes to explain to your partner what you have learnt from your reading.

4 Vocabulary building: collocations

The words from the texts in 2.2 in the box are used to refer to similarity and difference. In academic writing, we often indicate whether these similarities and differences are big or small.

difference	~~different~~	distinction	similar	similarity	vary

4.1 Complete the following expressions using the words in the box.

1 completely
quite
radically   *different* (from)
somewhat

2 _____ enormously
greatly
considerably
slightly

3 substantial
major _____ (in)
considerable
small

4 striking
a strong _____ (to)
close
weak

5 sharp
a clear _____
clear-cut
fine

6 remarkably
very _____ (to)
broadly
somewhat

4.2 Write sentences using the following notes and the expressions in 4.1. There may be more than one possible answer.

1 Life expectancy at birth: Japan 82.12 years; Swaziland 31.88
Life expectancy at birth in Japan and Swaziland is radically different.

2 Life expectancy at birth: Sweden 80.86 years; Norway 79.95 years

3 Percentage of people in UK who smoke: single people = 28%; married people = 18%

4 Common cold symptoms: sneezing, runny nose, sore throat, cough
Flu symptoms: sneezing, runny nose, fever, sore throat, cough

5 Course fees ($ per annum): North University (1,000), South University (15,000), East University (9,000), West University (5,000)

5 Referring backwards and forwards in presentations

During presentations it can help the audience understand the organisation of the talk if you refer back to what you said earlier, or refer forward to what you are going to say next or in a later part of the presentation.

5.1 a The following extracts are from a presentation on *The impact of tourism on society and culture in developing countries*. Put the words in brackets in the correct order in the extracts.

1 … growth in tourism in both more and less developed countries. As I said a few minutes ago tourism is now the world's largest industry … (minutes / I / ago / a / few / as / said)

2 … income flowing into poor countries, and I'll _____, both the positive and negative effects … (about / say / I'll / more / a / while / in / that)

3 … effects of this income. What _____ the effect of tourism on health in developing countries. (I / what / about / talk / is / to / now / want)

4 … so _____ the effects of tourism on health and education … (so / about / I've / talked / far)

5 … help protect a number of important sites, and I'll _____ . (in / I'll / back / moment / that / a / to / come)

6 What _____ the question of how the arrival of large numbers of people … (focus / on / like / here / I'd / is / to / what)

7 Having _____ some of the environmental problems, … (about / talked / having)

8 … I'll _____ steps … taken to try to minimise … (on / now / I'll / to / move)

9 Before _____ give some examples of ecotourism in practice, … (going / to / before / on)

10 … I _____ some general principles of ecotourism projects. (I / outline / want / to)

b (◀6.1) **Listen and check your answers. Decide which extracts refer to:**

1 what was said **earlier**. ___I___ ___ ___
2 what will be said **next**. ___ ___ ___ ___
3 what will be said **later**. ___ ___ ___

5.2 **You are going to give a presentation on *The 'nature' vs. 'nurture' debate*. To help you prepare, look again at the notes you made in 1.2b. In pairs, give a short presentation of two or three minutes referring forwards and backwards, using as many phrases from 5.1 as possible.**

6 Writing conclusions in essays

➤ Essay types
Unit 1, 9 p20

6.1 a **The contents of an essay conclusion depends on the type of essay you are writing. In pairs, decide which elements (1–6) you are likely to put into a *describe*, *discuss* and *defend* essay.**

	describe	discuss	defend
1 A brief **reminder** of your aims	✓	✓	✓
2 A **summary** of the main points of your description			
3 A **summary** of the different positions on the topic			
4 An **evaluation** of how the evidence you have presented supports *each* position	✓		
5 A **restatement** of your position			
6 An **evaluation** of how the evidence you have presented supports *your* position			

b **What other elements might go in a conclusion?**

6.2 Read the conclusion to an essay with the title *People are more alike than different. How far do you agree with this statement?* and decide which of the elements in the table in 6.1 are included. Write the words in bold in 6.1 next to the relevant sections of the conclusion.

Conclusion	
In this essay I have examined the ways in which people are similar and the ways in which they are different. On the one hand, all people have certain basic physical needs, such as food, drink, and sleep, and psychological needs, such as respect from others. However, beyond these needs there is huge variety in the way that people behave. Heredity and environmental factors interact in ways that make each individual unique, with their own interests, values, behaviour, and so on. These individual differences outweigh the similarities between us. Overall, then, I would disagree with the statement that "People are more alike than different" and claim, in fact, that "People are more different than alike".	*reminder (of aims)*

6.3 Read the introduction to an essay with the title *To what extent should large international companies make acting in a socially responsible manner more of a priority than increasing their profits?* Then read the notes for the body of the essay which follow and decide what elements you should include in the conclusion. Write a short conclusion to the essay.

Introduction

Large international companies play an increasing role in the everyday lives of people across the world. It is perhaps in developing countries, however, that they have most impact. In countries where governments do not have the resources to provide social support for all of their citizens, international companies may be the only organisations able to maintain and improve quality of life. Some would say that the priority of international companies is to make profits and, therefore, provide income to their owners and shareholders. However, I will argue in this essay that their first duty is in fact to support the communities in the developing countries in which they are based, by providing good working conditions, a safe and clean local environment, and health care and educational facilities for workers and their families.

Argument that profits should come before social responsibility –
· without first making profit, there is no money to help poor (Roberts, 2007)
· company's first duty is to its shareholders (Klein, 2000)
· motives of some companies which have implemented social responsibility programmes have been questioned: do they only do it as a public relations exercise? (Roberts, 2007; example of Conco in Botswana)

Arguments that social responsibility should come before profits –
(i) ethical argument –
· basic human rights of all people should be respected; international companies should recognise this in their dealings with employees (Howarth, 2005)
(ii) economic arguments –
· provision of good working and living conditions for employees can increase levels of productivity, and therefore profits to companies (Howarth, 2005; example from Bangladesh)
· focus on profits can lead to involvement in corruption scandals and environmental accidents; can severely damage reputation of a company (Smith, 2008; example from India)

6.4 a Look at the work you did to prepare for writing the essay in 1.2 with the title '*Do we, as individuals, behave in a certain way because we were "born that way"* [...]'. Now write a conclusion to the essay of about 100 words.

b In pairs, read and evaluate your partner's conclusion.

7 Language for writing: hedging

In academic writing claims are often hedged. *In other words, they are expressed tentatively, as possible rather than certain.*

7.1 Compare examples a and b and answer the following questions.

1   In which one is a claim hedged? Underline the language used to hedge the claim.
2   Why is it better to hedge this claim?

a   A focus on profits can lead to involvement in corruption scandals.
b   Large international companies play an increasing role in the everyday lives of people across the world.

There are a number of types of hedge, including:

1 Modal verbs indicating possibility	e.g. *might, could*
2 Verbs distancing the writer from the claim or showing that the writer is speculating	e.g. *seem, indicate*
3 Adjectives, adverbs and nouns showing the degree of certainty	e.g. *possible, possibly, possibility be likely to*
4 Other expressions qualifying or limiting a claim	e.g. *generally, tend to, in most cases*

➤ *Hedging adverbs*
Unit 5, 6.1 p74

7.2 The following extracts are from the conclusions of journal articles in the field of Applied Linguistics. Underline the hedges and add them to the table.

1   Responses to questions are likely to impose greater demands on subjects' second language skills.
2   Inadequate language proficiency and writing skills may be the main reason for students' problems with plagiarism.
3   The function of 'please' is to some extent to convey the speaker's attitude.
4   The lectures used in this study were mainly descriptive in nature.
5   This study suggests the value of gathering more data on social cultural factors.
6   The lack of motivation among students appeared to be related to their attitudes toward the role of English in science.
7   Information from intercultural communication can be a valuable tool for teacher educators.
8   Perhaps the use of taped oral feedback can provide focused assessment for students.

7.3 In pairs, look at the following claims from academic texts and decide which of them should be hedged. Add a hedge from the table above where appropriate, and make any other necessary changes. There may be more than one possible answer.

1   Cities in the Northern Hemisphere ~~will~~ become hotter over the next century. *are likely to*
2   Air pollution is not a new phenomenon. _____
3   Half of the Earth's species will disappear within the next 75 years. _____
4   Evidence proves that there is a clear human influence on global climate. _____
5   By far the worst concentrations of pollutants are found in urban areas. _____
6   Climate change is the most important danger currently facing humanity. _____
7   Eventually it will no longer be profitable to use oil as the primary fuel for the world. _____
8   Air pollution has got worse in developing countries because of economic growth. _____

7.4 Look again at the conclusion you wrote in 6.4a and add hedges where appropriate.

8 Giving references

At the end of every academic text you write, you will normally be expected to give a list of references.

- *This list should be headed* References.
- *It should include **all** the sources (books, journal articles, newspaper articles, websites, etc.) you have referred to in your text.*
- *It should **not** include any sources you have read but not referred to.*
- *References are normally listed in alphabetical order.*

➤ *References: other sources*

Appendix 3, p168

8.1 **The following table shows a very common style of referencing, used by the APA (American Psychological Association). In pairs, look at the table and answer the questions (1–15).**

Type of source	Example reference
Book with a single author	Jenkins, J. (2003). *World Englishes: A resource book for students.* London: Routledge.
Book with two or more authors	Trudgill, P. & Hannah, J. (1994). *International English.* London: Arnold.
Edited book	Pakir, A. (Ed.) (2001). *Words in a cultural context.* Singapore: UniPress.
Book without a named author	World Bank (2006). *Investment Framework for Clean Energy and Development.* Washington, DC: World Bank.
An article in a journal	Erhardt, D. & Baker, B. L. (1990). The effects of behavioural parent training on families with young hyperactive children. *Journal of Behaviour Therapy and Experimental Psychiatry,* 21, 121–132.
A paper in an edited book	Hung, T. T. N. (2002). Towards a phonology of Hong Kong English. In K. Bolton (Ed.) *Hong Kong English: Autonomy and creativity,* pp.119–40. Hong Kong: Hong Kong University Press.

1 What font style is used for the title of a journal? *Italics* _____
2 What font style is used for the title of an article in a journal? _____
3 What font style is used for a book title? _____
4 What abbreviation is used for *pages*? _____
5 What abbreviation is used for *editor*? _____
6 In a publication with two or more authors, do you use *and* or *&* (ampersand) before the last named author? _____
7 Do initials usually come before or after the author's surname? _____
8 When do initials come before the author's surname? _____
9 In which of the types of source listed is the publisher also the 'author'? _____
10 Which comes first in a reference to an article in a journal: volume number or page numbers? _____
11 Which comes first in a reference to a book: publisher or place of publication? _____
12 In which journal can you find the paper by Erhardt and Baker? _____
13 In which book can you find the paper with the title *Towards a phonology of Hong Kong English*? _____
14 Who published the book edited by Pakir? _____
15 What is the subtitle of Jenkins' book? _____

Grammar and vocabulary

Grammar and vocabulary
- Avoiding repetition: expressions with *so*
- *Wh-* noun clauses
- Using viewpoint adverbs to restrict what is said
- Verb/adjective + preposition combinations

1 Avoiding repetition: expressions with *so*

We can use an expression with so *or* do + so *to avoid repeating an adjective, verb, verb phrase or whole clause.*

1.1 Look at the following sentences. What do the expressions in bold replace?

1 It has been suggested that the expansion of the universe will continue forever. **If so**, it will eventually become too cold to support life.
= *if the expansion of the universe continues forever*

2 Grammar teaching has long been seen as an important aspect of language teaching, and there are several reasons why **this should be so**.

3 Zola's influence on his contemporaries was pronounced, perhaps **more so** in America than in Europe.

4 The term 'aliteracy' refers to the state of being able to read but uninterested in **doing so**.

5 Firms may want to increase their production but are unable to **do so** because of insufficient resources.

6 Dobson (2009) has argued that it is now unimaginable that nuclear weapons would be used in war. **This being so**, possession of such weapons must also be called in question.

(i) · *Other modal verbs are also used before* be so: can, would, will, could. *(Sentence 2)*
· *In so doing is a more formal version of* in doing so. *(Sentence 4)*
· *That being so can be used with a similar meaning to* this being so, *although it is less common in academic writing. (Sentence 6)*

1.2 Use the expressions with *so* in 1.1 to replace repeated parts in the following extracts.

1 Barack Obama won the United States presidential election in 2008, and in ~~winning the presidential election~~ became the first African American to hold the office. _____ *doing so* _____

2 It is often assumed that people in urban areas have different transport needs from those in rural areas, although why people in urban areas have different transport needs from those in rural areas is never fully explained. _____

3 Research has shown (e.g. Hewson, 1998; Charles, 2005) that school is the setting in which teenagers encounter most problems. If school is the setting in which teenagers encounter most problems, teachers have a responsibility to provide adequate support for pupils. _____

4 The research examines whether teachers have used communicative language teaching in the classroom and, if they have used communicative language teaching in the classroom, whether they view it positively or negatively. _____

5 Oxygen and hydrogen do not combine explosively at room temperatures, but combine explosively if the temperature is raised. _____

6 Margaret Thatcher went on to radically transform Britain; perhaps she transformed Britain more than any other prime minister since the Second World War. _____

2 *Wh-* noun clauses

A noun clause is a type of clause that functions like a noun or noun phrase. A noun clause begins with a wh- *word (what, why, where, when, how). For example:*
· The particular content of **what is assigned to men and women** can vary from culture to culture.
· There is no clear way of knowing **what the percentage of nature and nurture mix is**.

2.1 Complete the following sentences using *why*, *where*, *when* or *how*. Use the same word in each pair.

1a Researchers have only recently discovered _____ the birds spend the winter.

b It is impossible to predict _____ meteorites will hit the Earth.

2a In this section we will consider _____ language is used in different ways for different purposes.

b Smith (2011) provides an interesting example of _____ wikis can be used to help younger children improve their reading ability.

3a It is not clear _____ the two studies gave such different results.

b Their theory does not explain _____ boys read less than girls of the same age.

4a Subjects were asked _____ they first noticed symptoms.

b We do not know exactly _____ the temple was constructed, but it was certainly more than a thousand years ago.

2.2 **Match the beginnings (1–6) to the endings (a–f) of the following sentences. Replace the words in bold with *what, why, where, when* or *how*.**

1 Fisher's principle is an explanation of ~~why the sex ratio of most species is approximately 1:1.~~

2 A marketing organisation needs to understand

3 In planning medical care, it is important to be able to predict

4 Pragmatics is a branch of linguistics which studies

5 Landscape history is the study of

6 Recent observations will help cosmologists settle the question of

a **the places that** disease outbreaks may occur.

b ~~the reason~~ ~~the sex ratio of most species is approximately 1:1~~.

c **the ways in which** people have changed the physical appearance of the environment.

d **the time at which** the universe was formed.

e **the ways in which** context contributes to meaning.

f **the kinds of** benefits that its customers are seeking.

3 Using viewpoint adverbs to restrict what is said

Viewpoint adverbs can be used to say what point of view a subject is being considered from. Often these end -ally. For example:

· **Historically**, they have worked outside the home, sometimes as the sole wage earners … (= this was the case over a long period of past time, but not now)

· **Medically**, there is no reason to vaccinate children who were already immune to a disease. (= there is no medical reason, but there may be other reasons to vaccinate them)

· **Physically**, he was never very strong. (= his body was not strong, but he may have been strong in other ways)

Viewpoint adverbs like these are usually in front position, but may occur in mid-position in a sentence (e.g. They have historically worked outside the home.).

3.1 **Rewrite the following sentences using the adverbs in the box and make any (other) changes necessary.**

| conventionally ~~culturally~~ financially globally |
| scientifically symbolically theoretically visually |

1 The city is a mixture of African and European cultural influences.
   Culturally, the city is …

2 The President has wide powers in theory, but most are rarely used. _____

3 Infinity is represented by the symbol ∞ . _____

4 Black is the absence of colour from a scientific point of view. _____

5 Coral reefs all over the world are under threat from climate change. _____

6 The TV station is heavily dependent on the government for monetary support. _____

7 The eclipse of June 1984 was unimpressive in terms of what could be seen. _____

8 The usual way of doing things is to include employment in mining, transport and construction under the heading 'industrial jobs'. _____

> ◔ *Research shows that in the spoken academic English corpus less formal phrases are used in preference to -ally adverbs. For example instead of, 'Culturally speaking' say: As far as culture is concerned, …; From a cultural point of view, …; From the point of view of culture, …; In cultural terms, …; In terms of culture, …*

4 Verb/adjective + preposition combinations

4.1 **Some verbs and adjectives that are common in academic writing are frequently followed by a particular preposition. Complete the following extracts from the texts you read in section 2, pages 85–86 using a suitable preposition. Check your answers in the texts.**

1 … one of the most consistent differences between males and females cross-culturally is that women **participate** _in_ more childcare …

2 … the particular content of what is **assigned** _____ men and women can vary from culture to culture …

3 … men **engage** _____ more violence against other males than females do against other females …

4 There are also cross-cultural similarities in gender roles **related** _____ dating and mating …

5 In these groups, boys are more **concerned** _____ dominance and social status …

6 … girls are more likely to **care** _____ younger children …

7 Gender-role socialization varies **depending** _____ one's cultural background.

8 Traditional Asian American families are patriarchal, with status and power **determined** _____ age, generation, and gender …

9 Gender and birth positions were **associated** _____ certain duties and privileges.

10 … family lineage was passed through the male, while females were **absorbed** _____ the families of their husbands.

Lecture skills C

Preparing for lectures

1 Thinking about the purposes of lectures

1.1 a In pairs, discuss which three of the following purposes of lectures are most important.

1 To encourage students to be enthusiastic about the subject
2 To allow the lecturer to give their evaluation of a topic
3 To tell students where they can find further information about a topic
4 To present new information
5 To help students understand the language of the subject
6 To outline a topic before students study it in more detail
7 To make information memorable
8 To entertain students

b Can you suggest any other purposes of lectures?

Listening

2 Understanding evaluations

2.1 You are going to watch extracts from two lectures where the lecturers give their evaluation of different topics. Listen and answer the following questions.

C.1 Lecture 1: The origins of human diversity

1 Dr Mormina talks about mitochondrial DNA: the part of cells that is inherited only from our mothers. What is her view of the term *mitochondrial Eve*?
2 Dr Mormina talks about the migration of early humans out of Africa. What is her evaluation of the hypotheses on this that have been suggested?
3 Dr Mormina talks about the fossil record: all the fossils so far collected. How does she evaluate the fossil record?

C.2 Lecture 2: An introduction to macroeconomics

4 Dr Vlamis talks about GDP. What does GDP stand for? How is it defined?
5 What disadvantages of GDP does Dr Vlamis point out? How does Dr Vlamis evaluate GDP at the end of this extract?

3 Understanding lists

Study tip *Lecturers often present lists of items. These might be, for example, possible solutions to a problem, factors that produce some effect, or competing hypotheses. It is important to identify the number of items in each list and key information about each item. This information should be recorded in your notes.*

3.1 a ▐C.3▌ Watch Dr Mormina introducing one obvious type of diversity in humans. What is it?

b Dr Mormina goes on to list a number of hypotheses to explain this diversity. Before you watch, in pairs, predict what these hypotheses might be.

c ▐C.4▌ Watch and check your answers. How many hypotheses does she put forward?

d ▐C.4▌ Watch again and make notes on these hypotheses, using symbols or abbreviations where possible. In pairs, compare your notes.

3.2 a ▐C.5▌ Watch another extract from Dr Mormina's lecture, in which she talks about human migration out of Africa. Make notes to answer the following questions.

1 Why did humans migrate out of Africa?

2 How did humans spread out of Africa?

b ▐C.6▌ Watch part of the extract again and compare your notes with those on the slides. Did you make a note of the main points which she lists?

3.3 ▐C.7▌ Watch the next extract of the lecture, in which Dr Mormina evaluates evidence for how humans might have spread out of Africa. Which of these possibilities does she say is most likely?

► Taking notes
Unit B, 6.1 p68

Language focus

► Lecture styles
Unit A, 1.1 p38

► Academic writing style
Unit 7, 8 p106

4 **Noticing differences in the language of lectures and academic writing**

Particularly in conversational and interactive styles, lecturers often use features of informal conversational English that are unlikely to be used in formal academic writing.

4.1 The following table contrasts extracts from lectures by Dr Mormina and Dr Hunt in the left column with extracts from academic writing in the right column. In pairs, underline differences in the language in the lecture extracts. Can you explain why the parts you have underlined would not be used in academic writing?

Lecture extract	Academic writing
1 In the Malay Peninsula <u>we</u>[1] also have populations that have retained their hunter-gatherer lifestyles and they <u>don't</u>[2] <u>look</u>[3] Asian <u>at all</u>[4]. <u>They're</u>[5] short and <u>very, very</u>[6] dark.	In the Malay Peninsula populations also exist that have retained their hunter-gatherer lifestyles, and who do not appear at all Asian. They are short and very dark.
2 ... for most of the time, populations both in Africa and outside Africa have remained more or less constant. Yes, there has been a steady increase in population size, but that has been, well, small, if you like.	... for most of the time, populations both in Africa and outside Africa have remained more or less constant. There has certainly been a steady increase in population size, but that has been quite small.
3 And you'd have thought that something nice and simple like a tennis racket ... if I chuck it up in the air, well, we sort of understand how it behaves.	When a simple object is thrown into the air it spins, and this behaviour should be easy to explain.

1 We try to avoid personal reference (e.g. I, we as subjects) in academic writing as far as possible.

2 We avoid contracted forms in formal writing.

3 'Look' is rather general; 'appear' is a little more precise.

4 This generally only comes at the end of a sentence in conversational English.

5 Contracted form

6 We don't usually repeat words for emphasis in formal writing.

 Study tip *In your lecture notes, you might write down some of the informal language that your lecturer uses. However, remember that you may need to rephrase this if you use your notes to write academic texts.*

5 Noticing prominent words

In any stretch of speech, a speaker makes certain words prominent; that is, they make them stand out from the rest by saying them louder or making the voice rise or fall on them.

> **Study tip** *Most of the important information is carried in the words that are made prominent. If you focus attention on these words, you should be able to follow most of what the lecturer says even if you don't understand the rest.*

5.1 a **C.8** **Listen to the following extract from Dr Mormina's lecture and notice the words in bold in the second sentence that are made prominent.**

> And this is what has fascinated Darwin, who was the first one to think about why is it that, erm, there are so many different biological forms. **So**, the **key message** is that in **order** to **understand human diversity** we **need** to **look** into the **past** – we need to **look** at the **evolutionary mechanisms** that have **generated** it.

b **Compare the types of word that are made prominent with those that are not made prominent. What do you notice?**

> **Study tip** *Non-prominent words are spoken very quickly, are run together and are less clear than the prominent words. However, you can often guess the words from the context.*

5.2 a **Read the next extract, which has the non-prominent words removed. Can you understand what Dr Mormina says?**

> ... how evolution _____ acted _____ human species _____ create _____ vast array _____ biological forms. _____ these _____ exciting times _____ study human evolution.

b **C.9** **Listen to the full extract and fill in the gaps.**

Some prominent words are given particular focus with a step up to a relatively high pitch. This is done to show that information contrasts with something that comes before, what follows, or what might be expected.

5.3 a **C.10** **In the following extract Dr Vlamis talks about how unemployment and inflation have changed in the second half of the 20th century. Listen and notice the step up on** *seventies***. In pairs, predict what he will say next.**

> In the fifties and sixties there was an environment of low inflation rate and low unemployment rate. While in the seventies ...

b **C.11** **Listen to what Dr Vlamis says next and check your answer.**

c (C.12) **Listen to the following extracts from Dr Vlamis's lecture. For each extract, insert an arrow in one of the three places (1, 2 or 3) when you hear a step up. In pairs, explain what is being contrasted.**

Extract 1

So unemployment rate, er, was very close to zero, yeah? Because companies, they wanted to employ and they kept demanding to get more people. Er, that was the case up until you see, up until, er, the seventies where again in the, … er, early seventies onwards we see that the trend changes. The **1** unemployment **2** rate starts **3** increasing. It starts, er, increasing in Britain and in the eighties you see, it got up to about ten percent.

Extract 2

Dr Vlamis has been talking about the policies of the British government during the 1980s.

So the main objective was price stability at whatever cost and you see the cost: huge increase in unemployment in the eighties. **1** Though **2** then it **3** decelerated and, er, now it's about, er, more reasonable levels, er, rather, er, that the picture that we've seen in eighties.

Follow-up

6 Taking notes: annotating

6.1 a **You are going to watch the beginning of the lecture given by Dr Vlamis. Before you watch, read the following handout. Use a dictionary if necessary to help you.**

An introduction to Macroeconomics – Dr Prodromos Vlamis
Term 2, Wednesday 11am
Lecture Hall 6

Macroeconomics: a brief introduction

What is macroeconomics?
- studies the whole economy

Macroeconomists are interested in aggregate phenomena e.g.
- unemployment,
- balance of payment

What policy tools can governments use to stabilise the economy?
- monetary policy
- fiscal policy
- exchange rate

b (C.13) **Watch the extract and add notes to the handout, using symbols or abbreviations where possible.**

7 Reconstructing your notes

When you read your notes after a lecture, it is obviously important that you can make sense of them. In other words, you should be able to reconstruct in general terms what the lecturer said by using your notes.

7.1 **In pairs, look back at the notes you took in this unit. Student A, work with the notes from 3.1d and Student B, with the notes you took in 3.2a. Using the notes, explain to your partner what the lecturer said.**

7 Bringing about change

Reading
- Reading critically
- Finding information and taking notes
- Vocabulary in context 1: inferring the meaning of words; 2: hedges
- Retelling what you have read

Listening and speaking
- Concluding your presentation
- Pronunciation: linking words in speech units

Writing
- Using an academic style

Reading

1 Reading critically

1.1 Read the following extract from an essay with the title *As people live longer and medical costs rise, changes need to be made to the funding of health care. Discuss the options facing governments.* Then read the tutor's comments and in pairs discuss what the tutor meant by the term *critical reader*.

> Lumby (2001) says that we cannot treat health care like other commodities to be bought and sold, and that we need to help people who are not able to afford to pay for health care. Herzlinger (2007) shows that American hospitals, for example, have put up their costs and made it difficult for some people to get health care insurance. One way that health costs could be reduced is by using new technology such as email and text-messaging (World Health Organisation, 2005).

This is too descriptive of what you have read. You need to be a more critical reader. Don't just accept what other writers say.

1.2 In pairs, follow the three stages suggested to help you read critically an extract from one of the sources referred to in the essay.

Stage 1: Before you read
Use information on the front and back cover of a book to find out what you can about the text, the writer and their writing purpose.

1 What kind of text is it (e.g. textbook, report)?
2 What authority (e.g. experience or qualifications) does the writer have to talk about the subject?
3 Who is the book written for?
4 What general position does the writer take in the book?

Who Cares?

The changing health care system
Judy Lumby

The story of modern medicine is one of miraculous new life-saving techniques, sophisticated drugs and health professionals with increasingly specialised skills. Yet patients still feel frightened and vulnerable, and mistakes occur far too frequently. Drawing on a lifetime of work in healthcare, Judy Lumby argues that the system continues to serve those who work in it rather than the people it is intended to care for.

Judy Lumby writes from a patient's perspective. From interviews, anecdotes and observations, she paints a vivid picture of what it is like to be sick in an ailing and changing health care system. *Who Cares?* is compelling reading for anyone involved in the health care system; nurses, doctors, administrators and, of course, patients themselves.

Judy Lumby is Executive Director of the NSW College of Nursing, Emeritus Professor at the University of Technology, Sydney, and Honorary Professor at the University of Sydney. Well-known as a nurse leader, Judy was an architect of and activist for many of the changes she describes in this book.

Stage 2: As you read

As you read, critically evaluate the claims made by the writer (a–f). For each claim, ask yourself the following questions.

1 Is the claim fact or opinion?
2 Are claims supported by evidence where they should be?
3 Where evidence is provided, is this convincing?
4 Where opinions are given, do you agree with them?

Another solution to the rising costs of health care and one gaining momentum is to extend privatisation, and (a) there are sections of the community and the professions who believe this is the answer to the funding crisis. That is, they view health care like any commodity – it should be bought by the individual. However, as I have argued previously in this book, (b) the health of individuals is
5 not like other commodities in that it is so often not about choosing to be ill or not to be ill.

(c) Illness certainly touches everyone in some way in their lifetime, regardless of economic circumstance. But we do know that (d) environments – social, economic and cultural – play a vital part in one's health.[7] How, then, do we justify the discrimination that occurs if we demand that everyone pays up-front for health care? While (e) proponents of the user pays model claim that
10 disadvantaged groups would continue to have free care, (f) there is always a proportion of the population not eligible for financial support but who are nevertheless economically disadvantaged who will find it difficult to pay up-front and will simply not be able to access adequate care.

[7] F. Baum, 'Social capital and health: Implications for health in Rural Australia', paper published in conference proceedings, 5th National Rural Health Conference, 1999

Lumby, J. (2001). *Who cares? The changing health care system.* Crows Nest, NSW: Allen & Unwin.

Stage 3: After you read

Ask yourself questions about the text and the writer.

1 What is the writer's position in the extract?
2 Did you get enough information from your reading to decide whether or not you agree with the writer?
3 Are you convinced by what the writer has said?

1.3 In pairs, follow the same stages for the front and back covers and extract on page 100. The first two claims are underlined, but you will need to find and evaluate other claims later in the extract.

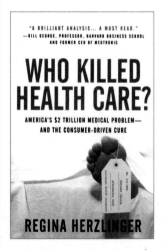

"A BRILLIANT ANALYSIS... A MUST READ."
—BILL GEORGE, PROFESSOR, HARVARD BUSINESS SCHOOL AND FORMER CEO OF MEDTRONIC

WHO KILLED HEALTH CARE?

AMERICA'S $2 TRILLION MEDICAL PROBLEM— AND THE CONSUMER-DRIVEN CURE

REGINA HERZLINGER

Doctors. Parents. Citizens. Employers.
They're all ready for the cure to America's health care crisis:

WHO KILLED HEALTH CARE?

"As it becomes more and more obvious to everyone that our current health care system is unsustainable, this is the book that had to be written."
- Daniel H. Johnson, Jr., MD, former president of the American Medical Association

"Regina Herzlinger's ideas to tackle the crisis of the U.S. health care system introduce the reader to new streamlined choices that have the potential of getting both quality and cost under control."
- Joseph Kennedy, founder, chairman, and president, Citizens Energy Corporation, CEO, Citizens Health Care, former representative (D-Mass)

Regina Herzlinger, DBA, is the Nancy R. McPherson professor of business administration at the Harvard Business School. Dr. Herzlinger has won numerous research awards from U.S. and international health care and accounting organizations and was elected one of the "100 Most Powerful People in Health Care" by *Modern Healthcare.*

Extract from textbook

> The problem begins with the **hospitals** – the bloated behemoths that account for the largest part of our health care system, nearly a trillion dollars' worth, and represent the major reason for its cost increases. (a) <u>Their costs rise at a pace that generally exceeds the growth of their services.</u> They have managed this through shameless manipulation of their nonprofit image and massive political contributions.
>
> (b) <u>Outrageous hospital costs have gravely injured the employers who buy their **employees'** health insurance.</u> Since 2000, health insurance premiums have increased by 73 percent compared to cumulative increases in inflation and wages of about 15 percent.[6]
>
> Some employers, especially small ones, no longer can afford to offer health insurance. As for the other larger employers, in an effort to control costs, they have allowed their human resources (HR) staffs to restrict employees' choice of health insurance plans, frequently offering only one – a managed care insurance plan. The HR types believe that by restricting choice and giving insurance companies a large volume of enrolees, they can achieve meaningful cost control. But they are profoundly wrong in their belief: to the contrary, choice supports competition, competition fuels innovation, and innovation is the only way to make things better and cheaper.
>
> [6] Avera Heart Hospital of South Dakota, "About Us" (www.SouthDakotaHeart.com, accessed January 14, 2007)

Herzlinger, R. (2007). *Who killed health care? America's $2 trillion medical problem – and the consumer-driven cure.* McGraw-Hill.

🎓 **Focus on your subject** *Choose an extract from a text from your subject and read it critically by following the three stages in 1.2.*

---

2 Finding information and taking notes

2.1 a You are preparing for a tutorial where you will give a five-minute talk on *social entrepreneurs*. You decide to take notes from the following book. Before you read the extract, look at the cover and read the beginning of the preface.

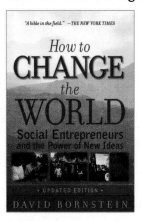

Preface

Is it possible to eradicate poverty? Extend health care to every corner of the world? Ensure that every child in every country receives a good education? These visions may seem beyond reach today, but the stories in this book reveal that we can, in fact, change the world in ways that seem unbelievable. There is a hidden history unfolding today: an emerging landscape of innovators advancing solutions that have the potential to transform life around the globe.

b In pairs, answer the following questions.

1 What do you think the term *social entrepreneur* means?

2 Can you think of anyone (either alive or dead) who might be considered a social entrepreneur?

2.2 Read the following extract and take notes on the four social entrepreneurs for your talk. For example:

Rowland Hill:

Main contribution: Introduced modern postal system
Other details:

While researching this book, I looked at a variety of changes that had occurred in different fields and found a pattern. Frequently, when I traced the change back to its source, I found an obsessive individual working behind the scenes – a person with vision, drive, integrity of purpose, great persuasive powers, and remarkable stamina.

5 The origin of the modern postal system is a classic example.

The system was introduced in England in 1840 by Rowland Hill, a then-unknown British schoolmaster and inventor whose ideas initially met with hostile opposition and ridicule. Hill had noticed that postal revenues in England failed to increase between 1815 and 1835 although the country's economy had grown considerably. Searching for an explanation, he
10 spent five years on his own time studying the cost structure of mail delivery. Through his analysis, Hill demonstrated that the costs for conveyance of mail were actually minor in comparison with handling and administrative costs. He began thinking about ways to simplify the system and came up with the idea of charging a uniform price for all mail in Great Britain (initially a penny for a half ounce) and a prepayment system: an adhesive postage stamp.

15 Hill's proposal met with virulent opposition from the postal bureaucracy. Senior postal officials condemned it as "preposterous" and a "wild and visionary scheme". But his call for a "Penny Post" struck a populist chord and eventually won the endorsement of leading newspapers, which stood to benefit from reduced postal fees. After a protracted political battle, the government authorized Hill to implement his system.

20 Another behind-the-scenes innovator was John Woolman, an eighteenth-century American Quaker whose impact on American society remains largely unrecognized. Among those most active in the campaign to end the slave trade in the United States were the American Society of Friends, or Quakers, who voluntarily emancipated all their slaves between 1758 and 1800. Although individual Quakers had been preaching against the evils of slavery since
25 1680, Quakers did not actually abandon the practice of slaveholding in large numbers until Woolman, a tailor and part-time preacher living in Mount Holly, New Jersey, took it upon himself to travel the country talking them out of it.

In 1743 Woolman set out on a series of walking journeys that, over the decades, took him across New Jersey, Maryland, Rhode Island, and Pennsylvania, where large numbers of
30 Quakers lived. Woolman traveled only on foot ("that I might have a more lively feeling of the condition of the oppressed slaves") and wore only undyed cloth (dyes came from slave plantations in the West Indies). In his soft-spoken but unyielding way, he persuaded Quakers to free their slaves and encouraged them to make slaveholding illegal in their states.

Another remarkably skillful and influential "idea champion" who fits this mold was Jean Monnet,
35 the architect and driving force behind the unification of Europe. Monnet, who is relatively unknown in the United States, was a lifelong proponent of internationalism, a man who spent virtually his entire adult life building one institution after another to allow, or compel, nations to work together to solve common problems. During World War I, as a private citizen without office or title, Monnet initiated joint planning for the distribution of supplies and resources
40 between France and England. During World War II, he organized the combined resources of the Allies. The economist John Maynard Keynes said that Monnet's influence, which led President Franklin Delano Roosevelt to dramatically increase American production of airplanes early in World War II, "probably shortened the duration of the war by a year".

► *Relative clauses*
G&V **1, p108**

► *Abstract nouns + of + -ing / to-infinitive*
G&V **3, p109**

45 After the war Monnet sought to ensure lasting peace in Europe. He conceptualized and hammered out the details of the European Coal and Steel Community and the European Common Market, precursors to the European Union. It's easy to forget that, until the mid-twentieth century, Europe was one of the most dangerous places on earth. Its current stability owes a great deal to Monnet's vision, energy and persuasiveness. There may be few individuals in the twentieth century who played a greater role determining the course of European politics and

50 international affairs.

Even urgent life-saving ideas need champions. In 1966 a leading researcher on blood pressure, Edward Freis, discovered that a drug he was testing offered significant protection for moderate or severe hypertension. Freis immediately halted his study and rushed to publish findings in the Journal of the American Medical Association. For four years, little changed. Then, in 1970,

55 after completing a second phase of research, Freis published another study. This time he got a one-sentence mention on Walter Cronkite's evening news, which caught the attention of Mary Lasker.

Mary Lasker was the driving force behind the creation of the National Institutes of Health and, for five decades, the leading proponent for increased government funding for biomedical

60 research in the United States. After reading Freis's studies, Lasker persuaded officials in the Nixon administration to plan a national campaign to educate the public about blood pressure treatment. She founded an organization, Citizens for Treatment of High Blood Pressure, which began producing an onslaught of messages about "the silent killer". Within a few years, "the nation's attitude toward high blood pressure was transformed".

Bornstein, D (2004). *How to change the world: Social entrepreneurs and the Power of New Ideas*. New York: Oxford University Press.

2.3 **In small groups, discuss the following questions.**

1 What characteristics do the four social entrepreneurs share? Give examples of how the social entrepreneurs show they have these characteristics.

2 Which of the four do you think has made the most important contribution to society?

3 Vocabulary in context 1: inferring the meaning of words

➤ *Inferring the meaning of words*

Unit 1, 5.1 p18

3.1 **Try to infer the meaning of the words in bold in the extracts from the text. Use the questions to help you with question 1. Check your answers in a dictionary.**

1 Through his analysis, Hill demonstrated that the costs for **conveyance** of mail were actually minor in comparison with handling and administrative costs.

· Do you know the meaning of any words in the same family as *conveyance*?

· Handling and administrative costs are mentioned. What other type of cost might be involved?

2 After a **protracted** political battle, the government authorized Hill to implement his system.

3 Monnet, who is relatively unknown in the United States, was a lifelong **proponent** of internationalism …

4 He conceptualized and **hammered out** the details of the European Coal and Steel Community and the European Common Market, **precursors** to the European Union.

➤ Language for writing: hedging

Unit 6, 7 p90

4   Vocabulary in context 2: hedges

4.1   **In pairs, look at the following extracts from the text in 2.2 and add a hedge where appropriate. Make any other necessary changes. The first letters of the hedge are given to help you.**

1   … John Woolman, an eighteenth-century American Quaker whose impact on American society remains unrecognized. (la_____) *remains largely unrecognized.*

2   Jean Monnet, who is unknown in the United States, was a lifelong proponent of internationalism. (re_____) _____

3   Monnet spent his entire adult life building one institution after another to allow, or compel, nations to work together. (vi_____) _____

4   John Maynard Keynes said that Monnet's influence "shortened the duration of the war by a year". (pr_____) _____

5   It's easy to forget that, until the mid-twentieth century, Europe was the most dangerous place on earth. (o_____ o_____) _____

➤ Retelling what you have read

Unit 2, 6 p29

5   Retelling what you have read

5.1   **In pairs, explain to your partner in what way two of the people described in the text were social entrepreneurs. Use the notes you took in 2.2, and try to use some of the new vocabulary you have learnt from the text.**

Listening and speaking

6   Concluding your presentation

6.1   **a   Read the slides from the endings of four presentations on the topic, *Facing the future: the need for change*. Match the titles (1–4) to the slides (A–D).**

1   Air pollution: the need for change   **3**   World poverty: the need for change

2   The future of oil: the need for change   **4**   Our working lifetime: the need for change

A
- sufficient supplies until 2040
- new supplies will be found; sufficient for 100 years
- demand increases rapidly; exceeds supply by 2025
→ need to reduce use and develop new energy sources

B
- increasing proportion of population elderly
- main reasons: longer life & declining birth rates
- huge pressures on health services & care
→ need to change work patterns; longer working lifetime

C
- increasing rapidly as countries industrialise
- damages environment
- impact on human health

→ need for tighter regulation and use of new technologies

D
- too little aid to developing countries
- insufficient spending on health and education
- current trade arrangements disadvantage poorer countries
→ need to change focus of our approach

b   (◄)7.1 Listen and check your answers.

6.2 The following flowchart shows four stages you can use to conclude a presentation.

Stage 1: Announce the ending
Finally, I just want to …   Let me end by …

↓

Stage 2: Summarise the main points
… so let me now summarise the key points   … by going over the main points of the talk again

↓

Stage 3: Thank the audience
So, that's it. Thank you.   Thanks for coming.

↓

Stage 4: Invite comments and questions
If anyone has any questions or comments, we've got a few minutes left.   We've got a few minutes more, and I'll do my best to answer questions if you've got any.

a **In pairs, add the extracts from the presentations (1–8) to the correct stage in the flowchart.**

1   … highlight the most important points in what I've said. …
2   There's some time left, and I'm happy to take any questions or comments you may have.
3   Okay, I'd like to finish by …
4   … by repeating what the major points in my presentation are.
5   We're coming to the end of the talk …
6   Thank you for listening.
7   Many thanks for your attention.
8   We've got a bit of time for questions if there are any.

b **In pairs, try to add other expressions that could be used in each stage.**

6.3 **In pairs, choose one slide each from 6.1 to present to each other. Try to use the language you have seen in 6.2.**

6.4 **In the question–answer stage after a presentation, audience members may:**

   • *ask for further information.*   • *challenge what the presenter said.*
   • *add information of their own.*   • *support what the presenter said.*

Think about presentations you have been to. Which of these have you heard?

6.5 a (◀) 7.2) **Listen to the question–answer stage which took place after each of the presentations in 6.1 and complete the expressions in bold in the following extracts.**

Presentation 1

1   *You* _____ **mentioned that** it might be possible to get oil from oil shale. *Could you*
    say a bit more about where this is found, **please?**

2   **Can I** _____ **that I think** _____ **right** to warn that we're heading for a crisis?

Presentation 2

3   **You** _____ people are living longer because of better health care. **It's** _____
    people have better diets nowadays …

4   **You said** _____ **that** costs rise as a country's population grows older. **But I'm**
    _____ **that** developed countries can't afford to pay for health services and other
    care. **Isn't it** _____ **that** they can afford it, but choose to spend money on other
    things …

Presentation 3

5   **I think** _____ **that** weak regulation has increased air pollution, **but** _____ **that**
    more regulation would be unfair …

6   **I just wanted to** _____ **about** the importance of new technology …

Presentation 4

7   **You've** _____ **that** reducing world poverty has largely been unsuccessful. **I think this**
    _____ in many parts of sub-Saharan Africa.

8   **You** _____ trade agreements. I'm not sure I really understood this. **Can you explain**
    this _____, **please?**

b   **Write the expressions from 6.5a in the correct boxes.**

Ask for information	**Add information**
You mentioned that … Could you say a bit more about … please?	

Challenge what was said	**Support what was said**

Study tip When you listen to question–answer stages at the end of presentations, make a note
of other language used by questioners to ask, add, challenge and support. Try to use this to join
in question–answer stages yourself.

6.6 **Compare what was said in the challenge in these two examples. In what ways is the speaker in
the second example more polite?**

1   "I don't agree that developed countries can't afford to pay for health services and other
    care. It's actually the case that they can afford it, but choose to spend money on other
    things."

2   "You said quite rightly that costs rise as a country's population grows older. But I'm not
    sure I agree that developed countries can't afford to pay for health services and other
    care. Isn't it actually the case that they can afford it, but choose to spend money on other
    things – on defence, for example?"

6.7 In groups of four, take it in turns to present slides and conduct a question and answer stage. Try to use the expressions you have seen in this section.

➤ Dividing speech into units
Unit 4, 9 p60

7 Pronunciation: linking words in speech units

In fluent speech, words within a speech unit are usually linked, without pauses between them. Sounds at the beginnings and ends of words are run smoothly together and to make this possible sometimes sounds are added, left out, or changed.

7.1 a (◀7.3) Listen to the following speech units from the presentations you heard in 6.1 and notice what happens when words are linked together at the point marked *. Answer the questions (1–8).

// should go * into improving education //	1 What sound is added here *?
// a major * impact //	2 What sound is added here *?
// and other care for the * elderly //	3 What sound is added here *?
// around * twenty twenty-five //	4 What happens to the /d/ sound at the end of *around*?
// the last * thirty years //	5 What happens to the /t/ sound at the end of *last*?
// we need to increase * substantially //	6 What happens to the /s/ sounds at the end of *increase* and the beginning of *substantially*?
// let * me now summarise //	7 What happens to the /t/ sound at the end of *let*?
// what are the main * points //	8 What happens to the /n/ sound at the end of *main*?

b In pairs, practise these pronunciation features by saying these speech units to each other. Try to make the same additions and changes you heard.

7.2 a What additions and changes do you expect in the following speech units?

1 // I've tried to show //
2 // for example //
3 // let me end //
4 // to reduce significantly //
5 // will be unable to meet demand //
6 // I'll do my best to answer questions //
7 // just can't afford to pay for these any more //
8 // there will be seven parts //

b (◀7.4) Listen and check your answers.

c In pairs, say the speech units to each other with the additions and changes you heard.

Writing

8 Using an academic style

When writing essays and other academic texts, it is important to use an appropriate style. This will be different from the style of the language you hear and use in spoken academic contexts such as lectures, seminars and tutorials.

8.1 Look at the following extract from a student's essay on attitudes to science and how these might be changed. The tutor commented on the underlined sections of the essay. Match the sections (1–21) to the tutor's comments (a–m). Some comments refer to more than one section.

Today's young people will become tomorrow's scientists, and so their attitudes to science are **1** <u>pretty</u> important. Unfortunately, **2** <u>at this moment in time</u>, many young people are rejecting a career in science, preferring to become **3** <u>businessmen</u> instead. **4** <u>I think</u> one reason for this is that scientists are paid relatively poorly. **5** <u>As you saw</u> earlier, people working in science in the United Kingdom **6** <u>don't</u> earn as much as those in occupations **7** <u>like</u> medicine or law. **8** <u>Besides</u>, at the moment **9** <u>it can be difficult to find a job in science and this</u> can **10** <u>put off</u> young people from **11** <u>thinking about</u> a career in science.

12 <u>Quite a lot of</u> studies have been conducted that try to identify other factors that influence attitudes to scientists and their work (e.g. Campbell, 1998; Adams, 2003). **13** <u>What are some of these factors?</u> **14** <u>Well,</u> one important factor is **15** <u>how scientists are represented</u> in the media. **16** <u>They're</u> often shown as being socially isolated or even **17** <u>mad!</u> Another factor is the quality of science teaching in school. If a science teacher is interesting and enthusiastic, **18** <u>he</u> can have a **19** <u>big</u> impact on whether a student goes on to study science at college or university. Unfortunately, in my experience **20** <u>not many</u> science teachers are inspirational, although **21** <u>the reader</u> may have had a different experience.

a Avoid colloquial words and phrases (i.e. ones used in informal conversation rather than formal writing). _____1_____ _____ _____ _____

b Avoid long expressions where there are shorter ones with the same meaning. _____

c Use a one-word verb rather than a multi-word verb where possible. _____ _____

d Unless you are referring specifically to men or to women, use gender-neutral language. _____ _____

e Avoid referring to the reader as 'you' or 'the reader'. _____ _____

f Avoid contracted forms (e.g. use 'is not' rather than 'isn't'). _____ _____

g Don't use 'like' instead of 'such as' when giving examples. _____

h Don't use 'besides' to add another, stronger reason. _____

i Avoid using questions to organise your writing. _____

j Avoid using 'I' (think/believe etc.) when you express your opinion. _____

k Use nominalisations where possible to express yourself more efficiently. _____ _____

l Don't use exclamation marks to show your surprise. _____

m Use more appropriate negative forms ('few' rather than 'not many', 'little' rather than 'not much', 'no' rather than 'not any'). _____

8.2 In pairs, correct or improve the sections the tutor has commented on.

8.3 Look back at a piece of academic writing you have done recently and, using what you have learnt in this section, find ways to improve the style in your writing.

8.4 Look back at the slide titles in 6.1. Write a short essay of around 750 words on one of the topics using the following structure. Remember to provide evidence for claims you make, and pay particular attention to using an academic style in your writing.

Introduction: Describe the main problem(s) and briefly outline two or more possible solutions that have been suggested.
Body: Present these possible solutions in more detail and evaluate them.
Conclusion: Give your own position.

Grammar and vocabulary

Grammar and vocabulary
- Adding information about nouns: relative clauses
- *It*-clauses: expressing personal opinions impersonally
- Abstract nouns + of + -ing / to-infinitive

1 Adding information about nouns: relative clauses

A relative clause identifies or gives more information about a noun. It begins with a relative pronoun (who, whose, what, which, where, when, whom, that).

Types of relative clause

A defining *relative clause* identifies which or which type of person or thing we mean. The relative pronoun can refer either to the subject (1) of the relative clause or the object (2).	1 I looked at a variety of changes **that had occurred in different fields.** 2 The system **which Hill introduced** is still widely used.
A non-defining *relative clause* simply adds information about the noun. We usually put a comma before and after a non-defining relative clause (3), unless it is at the end of a sentence (4).	3 Monnet, **who is relatively unknown in the United States,** was a lifelong proponent of internationalism. 4 The system was introduced by Rowland Hill, **whose ideas initially met with hostile opposition and ridicule.**

> (i) · We can't leave out the relative pronoun or use that in a non-defining relative clause.
> · We can omit the relative pronoun in a defining relative clause if the relative pronoun is the object. However, in academic writing the relative pronoun is usually included.
> · In academic writing, who is more usual than that to add information about people.
> · Don't confuse whose and who's (= who is).

1.1 Use the information in the table to help you match the following examples (1–6) to the descriptions of relative pronouns.

Relative pronouns are used to add information about:
- **things** (*that, which* and no relative pronoun).
  e.g. ___3___
- **people** (*that, who, whom* (formal) and no relative pronoun). e.g. _____
- **time** (*when*). e.g. _____
- **location, situation** or **point in a process** (*where*).
  e.g. _____
- **'belonging to'** and **'associated with' relationships** (*whose*). e.g. _____
- **how something happens** (*whereby*). e.g. _____

1 He was a man who spent virtually his entire adult life building one institution after another.
2 Hill's postal system was an innovation whose influence is still seen today.
3 His call for a "Penny Post" won the endorsement of leading newspapers, which stood to benefit from reduced postal fees.
4 His walks took him across New Jersey, Maryland, Rhode Island, and Pennsylvania, where large numbers of Quakers lived.
5 Hill improved the process whereby mail was delivered around the country.
6 He lived in a time when Europe was one of the most dangerous places on earth.

1.2 a Add the information in brackets as a relative clause (defining or non-defining) to the sentences in an appropriate place. There may be more than one possible answer.

1 Doctors thought the disease had been wiped out in the 1950s. (it was widespread at the start of the last century)
   Doctors thought the disease, which was widespread at the start of the last century, had been wiped out in the 1950s.
2 Ben Johnson was an English poet and playwright. (he lived from 1572 to 1637)
3 An organic compound is any member of a large class of chemical compounds. (their molecules contain carbon)
4 The patient was 25 years old. (his case is described here)
5 Anaerobic digestion is a simple process. (in anaerobic digestion, organic matter is broken down by microorganisms)
6 The company is in the second stage of business development. (in this stage activities and customer base are expanded)

b Redraft the following extracts by adding information from the notes.

1 Another influential social entrepreneur is the Bangladeshi banker Muhammad Yunus. He was previously a professor of economics at Chittagong University.
   · *Born 1940*
   · *Developed idea of 'microcredit' while at Chittagong Uni.*

2 Victoria Hale founded the Institute for One World Health (IOWH). The IOWH has set up a scheme with major pharmaceutical companies.
  · *aim of IOWH: make medicines available to poor communities*
  · *IOWH scheme: certain drugs developed by pharma. companies can be sold cheaply*

3 Maria Montessori is best known for introducing a method of education. She developed her ideas during the early part of her career.
  · *method uses self-directed learning activities*
  · *at start of career worked with children with learning disabilities – ideas developed then*

2 *It*-clauses: expressing personal opinions impersonally

2.1 In academic writing it is often good style to express ideas in a more impersonal way than in informal contexts. In pairs, discuss which example in each of the following pairs is more appropriate for academic writing and why.

1 a It is necessary to recognise that the pressure for change exists.
  b We have to recognise that the pressure for change exists.

2 a I think that the students' high level of motivation is interesting.
  b It is interesting that the students were all highly motivated.

3 a It is worth noting here that there are multiple causes.
  b I want to note here that there are multiple causes.

4 a We should remember that in 1973 crude oil cost only $2 a barrel.
  b It should be remembered that in 1973 crude oil cost only $2 a barrel.

2.2 What are the three main grammatical forms of *it*-clauses to express opinions? (You can remind yourself by looking back at Unit 3, p 52.) Underline the places in the following extracts where the writer introduces an opinion. Then rephrase the extract using impersonal *it*-clauses.

1 <u>In my opinion</u>, computers may soon take over from the teacher as the main information provider in the classroom. If this happens, <u>I think</u> that the profession of teaching will become seriously devalued.
  It is possible that computers … it is likely that the profession …

2 I don't think it is surprising that so few people turned out to vote in the general election. We need to remember that this was the third general election in as many years.

3 I wish to point out here that oil production is in decline. Consequently, in my view a further rise in petrol prices is inevitable

4 We should recognise that there are few benefits in keeping animals for food. Animals cause damage to the environment, and meat is less healthy than vegetables. Consequently, it seems to me that governments need to discourage people from eating meat, and in turn I believe this will probably reduce the number of animals kept for food.

3 Abstract nouns + *of* + *-ing* / *to*-infinitive

Some abstract nouns that are common in academic writing can be followed by a to-infinitive (e.g. effort*), some by of + -ing (e.g.* idea*), and some by either a to-infinitive or of + -ing with a similar meaning (e.g.* way*).*

· In an **effort to control** (NOT ~~effort of controlling~~) costs, they have allowed their human resources (HR) staff to restrict employees' choice.

· He began thinking about **ways to simplify / ways of simplifying** the system and came up with the **idea of charging** (NOT ~~idea to charge~~) a uniform price for all mail.

3.1 In pairs, complete the table with the abstract nouns in the box. Use a dictionary if necessary.

ability	attempt	capacity	cost	effect
~~effort~~	failure	~~idea~~	means	method
opportunity	possibility	power	problem	
process	right	risk	tendency	~~way~~

+ *to*-infinitive	+ *of* + *-ing*	either *to*-infinitive or *of* + *-ing*
effort	*idea*	*way*

3.2 Correct the following examples from students' writing.

1 This was due to their failure ~~of competing~~ with US companies in Asian markets. *to compete*

2 Children from poor families have a higher risk to become criminals.

3 As more migrants came, there was a tendency of living near people from the same country of origin.

4 There are undoubtedly negative effects to surfing on the Internet.

5 Donors now have the possibility to give online.

 Study tip *When you find new words, make a note of the grammar of what follows them. For example, when you write down an abstract noun, note whether it is followed by of + -ing, to-infinitive, or some other form.*

8 Work and equality

Reading

1 Understanding figures and tables

Although much of the information you read in your academic studies will be in the form of continuous text, some of it will be in other forms, such as tables, maps, formulae, and so on. It is important to develop skills in understanding these other sources of information.

1.1 **Your group has been asked to prepare a presentation on the topic *Employment and inequality in the UK*. You have researched the topic and found four relevant sources online. For each source (A–D) answer the questions (1–4). In pairs, compare your answers.**

1 Is there any information above the figure/table (e.g. the title)? Is there any information below the figure/table (e.g. the source, other notes)?
2 Are there different colours in the figure? What do they indicate?
3 What information is given on the X and Y axes (of a graph) or in the row and column headings (of a table)?
4 What observations can you make that are of relevance to the topic of your presentation?

Men aged 60 to 64 are more likely to be in low income than men in any other age group between 25 and 80

[Line graph: Proportion of the age group in households below 60% of median income after deducting housing costs (Y-axis, 0%–40%) vs Age group (X-axis, 16–19 to 80+). Lines for Men and Women.]

Source: *Households Below Average Income, DWP; UK; the data is average for 2006/07 to 2008/09; updated 2010*

A

Age group	Proportion not working	
	Men	**Women**
18 to 24	39%	42%
25 to 34	15%	29%
35 to 49	13%	24%
50 to retirement	28%	30%

Source: www.poverty.co.uk

B

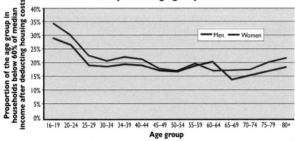

Scotland 19%
North East 25%
North West 24%
Yorkshire and the Humber 23%
East Midlands 23%
West Midlands 25%
Wales
East 20%
London 28%
South East 19%
South West 20%

Proportion of the population in households below 60% of median income after deducting housing costs.

Source: *Households Below Average Income, DWP; UK; Average for 2006/7 to 2008/09; Updated Aug 2010*

C

Four-fifths of the total increase in incomes over the last decade has gone to those with above-average incomes and two-fifths has gone to those in the richest tenth

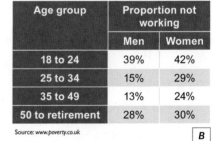

2nd poorest tenth
3rd
4th
5th
6th
7th
8th
Second richest
Richest tenth

Source: *Households Below Average Income, DWP; the data is the difference in real incomes between 1998/99 and 2008/09; Great Britain; updated Aug 2010*

D

► *Presenting charts*
Unit 2, 9 p31

1.2 In pairs, give a short presentation of no more than two minutes using the information from Sources A–D.

- Student A, use Sources A and B to talk about age and gender issues.
- Student B, use Sources C and D to talk about the distribution of income across regions and society.
- Individually, make notes to prepare for your presentation.
- Present the information to your partner.

> 🎓 Focus on your subject *What are the main types of figure used in your subject? Look in a number of textbooks or journal articles to find out if you don't already know.*

2 Scanning for information

2.1 You are going to read a text with the title *Gender Bias and the Glass Ceiling*. Before you read, look at the following scenario. In small groups, discuss the questions.

> Janice, a 35-year-old African American at a business consulting firm, is concerned because her career is not progressing as rapidly as she had hoped. Janice works hard and has received excellent performance ratings every year, but she has noticed that there are very few women in upper management positions in her company. Janice wonders whether she will ever be promoted.

Kail, R. V. and Cavanaugh, J. C. (2010) *Human development: A life span view* (5th edn.).Belmont, CA: Wadsworth, Cengage Advantage Books.

1 What reasons can you suggest for Janice's slow progress?
2 What advice would you give to Janice?

2.2 Look at the following statements made in the text. Scan the text to find out whether the writer says they apply mainly to women (W) or to men (M).
1 They are unusual in high status jobs. ___W___
2 They comprise about a quarter of all CEOs. _____
3 Fewer serve in the highest ranks of major corporations. _____
4 They face gender discrimination in the workplace. _____
5 They have stricter job performance standards applied to them. _____
6 They are largely blind to the existence of the glass ceiling. _____
7 They are more readily promoted to upper-tier grades. _____
8 They are more democratic and interpersonally oriented. _____
9 They earn less in the same occupation. _____
10 They should negotiate salary more effectively. _____

► *Passive voice*
G&V 1, p120

Gender Bias and the Glass Ceiling

Even though the majority of women work outside the home, women in high status jobs are unusual (Mitchell, 2000); in 2006 only about 23% of all CEOs – and only 10 of the Fortune 500 companies – were PT headed by women. Not until 1981 was a woman, Sandra Day O'Connor, appointed to the U.S. Supreme Court; it took another 12 years before a second woman, Ruth Bader Ginsburg, was appointed. As Janice
5   noticed, few women serve in the highest ranks of major corporations, and women are substantially PS outnumbered at the senior faculty level of most universities and colleges.

Why are there so few women in such positions? The most important reason is gender discrimination: denying a job to someone solely on the basis of whether the person is a man or a woman. Lovoy (2001) points out that gender discrimination is pervasive in the workplace. Despite some progress over the past
10 two decades, sex discrimination is still common: women are being kept out of high status jobs by the men at the top (Barnes, 2005; Reid, Miller, & Kerr, 2004). *Re conti*

Research in the United States and Britain also confirms that women are forced to work harder than men (Gorman & Krnec, 2007). Neither differences in job characteristics nor family obligations account for this difference; the results clearly point to stricter job performance standards being applied to women.

15 Women themselves refer to a glass ceiling: the level to which they may rise in an organization but beyond which they may not go. The glass ceiling is a major barrier for women (Maume, 2004), and the greatest barrier facing them is at the boundary between lower-tier and upper-tier grades. Men are largely blind to the existence of the glass ceiling (Heppner, 2007). Women like Janice tend to move to the top of the lower tier and remain there, whereas men are more readily promoted to the upper tier even when other factors
20 (e.g. personal attributes, qualifications, job performance) are controlled (Lovoy, 2001).

The glass ceiling is pervasive across workplace settings (Heppner, 2007), including private corporations (Lyness & Thompson, 1997), government agencies (Reid et al., 2004), and nonprofit oganizations (Shaiko, 1996). The glass ceiling has also been used to account for why African Americans and Asian Americans do not advance as much in their careers as do European American men (Hwang, 2007; Johnson, 2000; Phelps
25 & Constantine, 2001). It also provides a framework for understanding limitations to women's careers in many countries around the world (Mugadza, 2005; Zafarullah, 2000).

What can be done to begin eliminating the glass ceiling? Mitchell (2000) suggests that companies must begin to value the competencies women develop, such as being more democratic and interpersonally oriented than men, and to assist men in feeling more comfortable with their female colleagues. Mentoring
30 is also an important aspect. Lovoy (2001) adds that companies must be more proactive in promoting diversity, provide better and more detailed feedback about performance and where employees stand regarding promotion, and establish ombuds offices (company offices where employees can complain about working conditions or their supervisor without retribution) that help women deal with difficulties on the job.

35 In addition to discrimination in hiring and promotion, women are also subject to pay discrimination. According to the Bureau of Labor Statistics (2007a), in only 13 of the hundreds of occupations they track did women earn at least 95% of men in the same occupations. On average, women are paid about 81% of what men are paid on an annual basis.

Several solutions to this problem have been promoted. One of these is pay equity: equalizing pay across
40 occupations that are determined to be equivalent in importance but differ in the gender distribution of the people doing the jobs. Determining which male-dominated occupations should be considered equivalent to which female-dominated occupations for pay purposes is difficult and controversial. In their comprehensive look at pay inequity, Dey and Hill (2007) suggested several actions to address the problem: encouraging women to negotiate salary more effectively, rethinking the use of hours worked as the primary measure
45 of productivity, creating more work options for working mothers, and ending gender discrimination in the workplace.

Kail, R. V. and Cavanaugh, J. C. (2010). *Human development:
A life span view* (5th edn.). Belmont, CA: Wadsworth, Cengage Advantage Books.

➤ –ing nouns
G&V 3, p121

2.3 **The text focuses mainly on the situation in the United States. In small groups, discuss how this compares with the situation in your country. What evidence do you have (e.g. your own experience, experience of people you know, information from the media) to support your views?**

3 Taking notes

3.1 a **You are preparing for a tutorial on** *Discrimination in the workplace*. **You have been asked to give a short talk on the question** *Why are there fewer women than men in higher-status jobs?* **Read the text again in more detail and make notes in the following table.**

The problem: Fewer women than men in higher-status jobs (at least in US context)
Reasons:

	Gender discrimination	Glass ceiling	Pay discrimination
What is it? (Give definition)			
Info/examples			
Possible solutions			

b **In pairs, compare your notes and if necessary add more detail to them.**

c **Use the notes to explain either the** *glass ceiling* **or** *pay discrimination*. **Define the term, saying why it is a problem and what solutions have been suggested.**

4 Understanding the significance of references

References are used in academic texts to provide evidence or support for the claims made by the writer.

4.1 **In pairs, discuss what kind of evidence or support might be found in the following references taken from the text. For example, Mitchell (2000) (lines 1–2):**

> Mitchell (2000) provides evidence that there are few women in high-status jobs. For example, companies might have been surveyed to find out whether high-ranking jobs are filled by men or women. It doesn't actually say where the figures come from.

1 Mitchell, 2000 (lines 1–2)
2 Barnes, 2005 (lines 9–11)
3 Gorman & Krnec, 2007 (lines 12–13)
4 Maume, 2004 (line 16)
5 Lovoy, 2001 (lines 19–20)

6 Heppner, 2007 (line 21)
7 Lyness & Thompson, 1997 (lines 21–22)
8 Reid et al., 2004 (line 22)
9 Shaiko, 1996 (line 22)
10 Hwang et al., 2007 (lines 23–24)

5 Vocabulary in context: avoiding repetition

5.1 **It can be good style to avoid repeating words and phrases. Which words in the text have a similar meaning to the words in bold? The first letter is given to help you. Look back at the text to check your answers.**

1 ... and only 10 of the Fortune 500 **companies** ... (line 2)
   c*orporations*____ (line 5)

2 ... **gender** discrimination is **pervasive** in the workplace ... (line 9)
   s_____ (line 10) ; c_____ (line 10)

3 Neither differences in **job characteristics** nor family obligations ... (line 13)
   o_____ (line 36) ; a_____ (line 20)

4 ... and **establish** ombuds offices ... (line 32)
   c_____ (line 45)

5 ... deal with difficulties **on the job.** (lines 33–34)
   _____ _____ w_____ (lines 45–46)

6 Several solutions to this problem have been **promoted.** (line 38)
   s_____ (line 43)

 Study tip *When you have produced a first draft of a piece of writing, check it carefully for unnecessary repetition of words and phrases. Try to replace some of the repetitions you find with words or phrases with the same meaning.*

Listening and speaking

6 Taking part in tutorials and joining in discussions

6.1 **◄8.1** **Listen to three students talking about their experience of university tutorials in different subjects. As you listen, make notes in the following table.**

	Anna (Linguistics)	Greg (Chemistry)	Matt (Business Studies)
1 What happens during their tutorials?			
2 What are they expected to do before and during tutorials?			
3 What problems do they face in tutorials?			

6.2 All three students mention the difficulties of joining in with a discussion in a tutorial. Match the following expressions (1–12) to the four ways to start a contribution to the discussion (a–d).

a Indicate that you want to make a point

b Give your own view

c Agree with the last speaker and add a further point

d Disagree politely with the last speaker and add a point

1 Iris makes a good point, and another thing is ...   _c_

2 Could I just say that ...?   _____

3 That may be the case, but don't you think ...?   _____

4 If I could add ...?   _____

5 In my view ...   _____

6 The way I see it is that ...   _____

7 I think that's interesting, and something else to consider is ...   _____

8 I see what you mean, but maybe ...   _____

9 That's right, and also ...   _____

10 I think ...   _____

11 That's partly true, but you've also got to think about ...   _____

12 Can I add something here?   _____

6.3 **a** **You are going to take part in a discussion on the advantages and disadvantages of having a national minimum wage. In pairs, decide which of the following statements can be used as arguments for (F), and which can be used as arguments against (A) having a national minimum wage.**

Note: The national minimum wage is the lowest amount of money that an employer is legally allowed to pay someone who works for them. In some countries, workers have the right to a national minimum wage.

1 It provides an incentive for people without jobs to look for work.   _F_

2 The total wage bill of companies will be higher, which means that they have less to invest in research, development and worker training.   _____

3 The cost of a company's products may be pushed up by the national minimum wage. This means they may lose orders to countries with lower wage rates.   _____

4 A national minimum wage reduces levels of poverty; people are paid a wage that they can live on.   _____

5 If people are paid a wage they can live on, they need government support less. This can save money for the government.   _____

6 A national minimum wage means that it is more expensive for companies to employ people. The consequence of this is that they will cut jobs and/or reduce hours of work, and unemployment will rise.   _____

7 It prevents employers exploiting workers by paying them too little.   _____

8 Companies are more likely to employ older, more experienced workers. This means that it will be more difficult for younger people to find work.   _____

9 A national minimum wage does not take into account regional differences. It is often more expensive to live in a big city than a rural area.   _____

10 There is a fairer distribution of wealth across society. It also reduces differences in pay levels between women and men, as women tend to be lower paid than men.   _____

11 If people are paid more, they pay more taxes. This goes to the government, who can invest it in social benefits.   _____

12 Workers who are already paid above the minimum wage will ask for increased pay in order to maintain pay differentials.   _____

b **In small groups, discuss the advantages and disadvantages of having a national minimum wage. Use some of the arguments you saw in 6.3a and try and use the expressions from 6.2.**

6.4 **Use what you have learned about the national minimum wage to write a short essay of around 750 words with the title *Discuss the advantages and disadvantages of a national minimum wage in a country you are familiar with.***

7 Pronunciation: stress in compound nouns 1

> ⓘ *A compound noun is a fixed expression which is made up of more than one word and which has the function of a noun. Some are written as two words (e.g.* wind farm*), some with a hyphen (e.g.* wind-chill*), and some as one word (e.g.* windmill*).*

7.1 **a** 🔊 **8.2** **Listen to these compound nouns used in the discussion of the national minimum wage and underline the part with main stress.**

minimum wage   wage bill

b **Complete the following rules about stress in compound nouns by writing** *first* **and** *second* **in the gaps.**

·   *Noun + noun* compounds usually have main stress in the _____ part (e.g. *wage bill*).
·   *Adjective + noun* compounds usually have main stress in the _____ part (e.g. *minimum wage*).

7.2 🔊 **8.3** **Using the rules in 7.1b, underline the part with main stress in these compound nouns. Listen and check your answers.**

bullet point	global warming	middle management
early retirement	health centre	mixed economy
earthquake	income tax	periodic table
gender bias	jet lag	social security

7.3 🔊 **8.4** **Listen to the definitions (1–12) and match them to the compound nouns in 7.2.**

1   *health centre*   5   _____   9   _____
2   _____   6   _____   10   _____
3   _____   7   _____   11   _____
4   _____   8   _____   12   _____

Study tip *It is important to place main stress in the correct place in compound nouns to help people understand you. When you are preparing a presentation, identify compound nouns you may use, make sure you know where main stress comes, and practise saying them aloud.*

Writing

8 Looking at the structure and content of reports

8.1 **a** 🔊 **8.5** **Students studying on different courses may be asked to write different types of texts. Listen to three university students, Frederike, Sabesan and Anitha, talking about their experiences. What text types did each student have to write?**

b **Do you know what text types you will have to write during your studies?**

8.2 **In many subjects, students and academics need to write up their research into a structured report. Reports often include some or all of the following sections. In pairs, decide on the order which you think they are most likely to come in.**

Abstract _____	Literature survey _____
Acknowledgements _____	Methods _____
Appendices _____	References _____
Conclusion _____	Results _____
Discussion _____	Title page _____1___
Introduction _____	

Notes: An *abstract* is a summary of the entire research report; *acknowledgements* thank people who have helped in writing the report; *appendices* contain additional information not central to the report; a *literature survey* is a review of sources relevant to the research.

> 🎓 **Focus on your subject** *Are you familiar with how reports are written in your subject? If so, do reports in that subject usually have all these sections? Do they usually have any other sections?*

8.3 **a** Look at the following extracts from a Business Administration report with the title *The influence of organisational change on employee motivation: A study of university secretaries.* For each extract (1–11) decide which section of the report from 8.2 you think it is likely to come from.

1 A questionnaire was distributed to all 372 secretaries in the university. *Methods*

2 A number of studies have shown that organisational change can have a negative impact on the motivation of employees (e.g. Ledman, 2002; Griffin, 2007). _____

3 The study investigated the effect of recent organisational changes on the motivation of secretaries at the University of Northport. _____

4 On the basis of the findings, it is recommended that decisions on major organisational change should take more account of the views of the employees they most affect. _____

5 The results of this study support Denon's (1999) claim that organisational change is seen as negative by most people affected by it. _____

6 Circle A, B, C, D or E for options i–iv.

A = Greatly increases my motivation to work
B = Slightly increases my motivation to work
C = Has no effect on my motivation to work
D = Slightly reduces my motivation to work
E = Greatly reduces my motivation to work

i Working in an open-plan office	A	B	C	D	E
ii Having flexible office hours	A	B	C	D	E
iii Taking greater responsibility for tasks	A	B	C	D	E
iv Having annual work appraisal	A	B	C	D	E

_____

7 This study aims to investigate the factors which affect motivation at work.

_____

8 My supervisor, Dr Marta Lopes, has provided excellent guidance and support throughout this project. _____

9 Gray, P S, Williamson, J N, Kark, D A & Dalphin, J R (2007). *The research imagination: An introduction to quantitative and qualitative methods.* Cambridge: Cambridge University Press. _____

10 73.4% said that having flexible office hours increased their motivation to work.

_____

11 Jay Grimmet, Department of Business Administration, University of Southland

_____

b In pairs, compare and discuss your answers.

9 Language for writing 1: describing events in a time sequence

In many types of written academic text you will need to describe a sequence of events in the order that they occurred. For example, in a report you might write a description of a procedure, or in an essay you might write an account of an historical event.

9.1 **a Read the following extract from the *Methods* section of a report in the field of English language teaching, ignoring the spaces for now. In pairs, decide if the aim of the research is to help students improve their listening, speaking or reading ability.**

> **1** ___*During*___ the session, four short texts were handed out to students, and the same steps followed for each text. **2** _____ students worked in small groups, trying to guess the meanings of any unknown words in the text. This group stage **3** _____ a demonstration to the students of how I inferred meanings. In this demonstration I spoke aloud my thought processes **4** _____ working through the same task. **5** _____ , students again worked in groups to discuss the clues that I had used. This **6** _____ a whole-class discussion of the strategies that I had used. The whole process was recorded using a video camera with external microphone, which I had set up in the classroom **7** _____ the beginning of the session. This recording was **8** _____ transcribed using the conventions which I had established **9** _____ in the pilot study. **10** _____ the session, I wrote down my impressions of the investigation, giving special attention to the discussion.

➤ *Past perfect*
G&V 2, p121

b Complete the extract using the time phrases in the box.

after this	~~during~~	earlier	first of all	while
Immediately after	later	prior to	was followed by (x2)	

c In pairs, answer the following questions.

1 Which of the time phrases you have written indicate *at a later time*?
2 Which ones indicate *at a previous time*?
3 Which one indicates *at the same time*?
4 What events are reported out of chronological order? What tense is used to report these events?

9.2 **a Look at the following notes made by a research student who was studying the effect of background music on how vocabulary is recalled. In pairs, put the steps in the order you think that they occurred.**

a Procedure repeated (same participants; next day); but played heavy metal music quietly in background. _____

b I read ten lists of words aloud to participants (ten words in each list); played classical music quietly in background. _____

c I selected words with similar level of difficulty for the two tests. __1__

d I collected in papers. _____

e Participants wrote down all the words they could remember after each list read; any order; given 90 seconds. _____

f I gave participants blank sheets of paper to write answers; they wrote name on top. _____

g I analysed the results statistically. _____

b Write a short paragraph for a report describing the research procedure, adding appropriate information where necessary. Try to use some of the time phrases from 9.1b and start with the following sentence.

Thirty participants aged either 15 or 16 were tested during a class meeting. ...

10 Language for writing 2: cause and effect

10.1 In reports, you may need to use expressions which signal a cause–effect relationship. What are the causes and what are the effects in the example sentences in the table? For example:

<u>The Caribbean sugar boom</u> brought about <u>a steady decline</u> in world sugar prices.

cause   *effect*

Structure	Examples
verbs (+ prepositions) bring about; cause; give rise to; produce; result in; is caused / produced / brought about by; result from	The Caribbean sugar boom **brought about** a steady decline in world sugar prices. Food poisoning can **result from** eating food contaminated with bacteria or toxins.
nouns (+ prepositions) consequence (of); result (of)	The Scramble for Africa was the **result of** conflicting European claims to African territory.
conjunctions because; so that; thereby	Adjacent areas often merge into each other **so that** the boundaries are blurred.
prepositional expressions because of; due to; on account of	He had to retire early **on account of** deafness.
sentence connectors as a consequence; as a result; consequently; therefore	The region is largely rural and **therefore** does not have a dense transport network.
***-ing* form** e.g. *producing*	With modern machinery farmers can look after larger fields, **producing** more food with less effort. (= *as a result*, they can produce more food ...)

10.2 a Match the following causes (1–5) to the effects (a–e).

1 An economic crisis hit the country.
2 In 2010, there was an ash cloud from a volcano in Iceland.
3 There was huge foreign direct investment into the country last year.
4 There was a ban on cigarette advertising.
5 Agricultural prices were depressed after the First World War.

a There were major disruptions in air transport.
b The economy of the country grew by 15% last year.
c The number of smokers rapidly decreased.
d Farmers intensified their demands for government assistance.
e There was a change in government.

b Combine the sentences using a variety of cause–effect expressions from 10.1. For example:

An economic crisis hit the country, **bringing about** a change in government.
The change in government **was brought about by** the economic crisis that hit the country.

Grammar and vocabulary

1 Passive voice

*The passive voice is commonly used in academic
writing in order to focus on the action or process (what
was done, found, believed, etc.) rather than the agent
(who performed the action). For example:*
In 2006 only about 23% of all CEOs **were headed** by
women. *(the agent – women – is mentioned in a 'by...'
phrase)*
Women **are** substantially **outnumbered** at the senior
faculty level of most universities and colleges. *(no
agent mentioned)*

1.1 **Compare the following extracts from the text in 2.2 on
pages 111–112, which use the passive voice, with the
equivalent sentence in the active voice. Why do you
think the passive voice was chosen in the text?**

1 Women are substantially outnumbered at the
senior faculty level of most universities and
colleges.
(Active voice: Men substantially outnumber women
at the senior faculty level of most universities and
colleges.)

2 Women are being kept out of high status jobs by
the men at the top.
(Active voice: Men at the top are keeping women
out of high status jobs.)

3 What can be done to begin eliminating the glass
ceiling?
(Active voice: What can people do to begin
eliminating the glass ceiling?)

4 The glass ceiling has also been used to account
for why African Americans and Asian Americans
do not advance as much in their careers as do
European American men (Hwang, 2007; Johnson,
2000; Phelps & Constantine, 2001).
(Active voice: Hwang (2007), Johnson (2000), and
Phelps and Constantine (2001) have used the
glass ceiling to account for why African Americans
and Asian Americans do not advance as much in
their careers as do European American men.)

> ◎ *Research shows that it is very common to omit the
> agent in academic writing. In the written academic corpus
> 86% of passive verbs had no agent. The agent is often
> left out because it is not important or because it can be
> understood from the context.*

> ⓘ *In academic writing the agent is sometimes indicated
> in an in-text 'non-integral' reference. For example, in the
> following sentence, the agent is Aldcroft, who made the
> claim.*
> It has been claimed that "from an economic point of view
> Britain's educational provision during the postwar period
> has been little short of disastrous" (Aldcroft, 1990: 239).

1.2 **Complete the following sentences using the verbs in
the box. Decide whether each verb should be used in
the passive or active voice. A number of tenses are
possible in each case.**

> base   belong   depend   design   ~~estimate~~
>
> happen   link   rise   subject   undergo

1 The global incidence of malaria _____ *is estimated*
to be nearly 120 million cases each year.

2 Interviewers _____ extensive
training prior to the research.

3 35 years later, the population of the city
_____ to 490,000.

4 This analysis _____ on the
works of Lenin and Mao.

5 The present study _____ to
compare quantitatively the relative effectiveness of
these two methods.

6 They argue that global economic development
_____ on a strong American
economy.

7 Vitamin D deficiency _____ to
higher risk of heart disease.

8 The caracal is an animal found in Africa and
western Asia which _____ to
the cat family.

9 The water temperature rise in the lake
_____ at the same time as
increased seismic activity in the area.

10 Tiny cracks appeared in the concrete when it
_____ to high temperatures.

2 Past perfect

We can use the past perfect to talk about a past event:
a *that took place before another past event.*

___ ___

b *that took place before or up to a particular time in the past.* ___ ___

c *reported after a past tense reporting verb.*

___ ___

2.1 Match the following sentences (1–6) to the uses of the past perfect (a–c).

1 Throughout the 1990s unemployment rates among those in their 20s were substantially higher than those in their 30s. However, by 2003 this difference **had** largely **disappeared**.

2 Animals were removed from the apparatus after they **had found** all of the sunflower seeds or after ten minutes, whichever came first.

3 Two weeks after the questionnaires were sent out, over 75% **had been returned**.

4 Richards and Kassin (2001) claimed that Holding Theory **had made** a major contribution to the treatment of children with autism.

5 The survey asked current smokers if they **had seen** a dentist in the previous six months.

6 At that time they did not have sufficient proof to say they **had discovered** a new element.

3 *-ing* nouns

Some -ing *forms can be used as nouns. These nouns often refer to the action or an instance of doing something. For example:*

- **Mentoring** is also an important aspect. (*verb = mentor*)
- In addition to discrimination in **hiring** and promotion, … (*verb = hire*)

Some verbs have only an -ing *noun form (e.g.* hire *(v)* ⟶ hiring *(n)), whereas other verbs have two nouns with a similar meaning, one of which is an* –ing *noun. For example:*

```
          promotion (n)              assessment (n)
promote (v)                assess (v)
          promoting (n)             assessing (n)
```

Where two forms of noun are possible, we generally avoid using the –ing *noun when there is no following noun. Compare:*

- It is a method for **assessment**. (NOT ~~It is a method for assessing.~~)
- It is a method for **assessing risk**. *or* It is a method for **the assessment of risk**.

3.1 Complete the table, using a dictionary where necessary to help you. Some verbs only have one noun form.

verb	-ing noun	other derived noun forms
assess	assessing	*assessment*
analyse	analysing	
apply	applying	
build	building	
conclude	concluding	
create	creating	
establish	establishing	
fund	funding	
identify	identifying	
invest	investing	
learn	learning	
obtain	obtaining	
plan	planning	
remove	removing	
respond	responding	
research	researching	
structure	structuring	
teach	teaching	
transcribe	transcribing	
undertake	undertaking	

3.2 Complete the following sentences using a noun form of the verbs in brackets, and adding any other words necessary. Give alternatives where possible.

1 In this section I will discuss *applying / the application of* visual aids in ___*teaching*___. (apply; teach)

2 The model provides both a framework for _____ intonation and its _____. (transcribe; analyse)

3 He played a fundamental role in _____ the discipline of biomechanics. (establish)

4 When the managerial changes were introduced, we noted the _____ of employees. (respond)

5 The World Wide Web has grown rapidly since its _____ in 1991. (create)

6 The programme aims to improve the environment for _____. (learn)

7 The first stage of the project was _____ strengths and weaknesses in the company. (identify)

8 We developed a technique for _____ feedback from students. (obtain)

9 _____ trees from the mountains has led to severe erosion. (remove)

Lecture skills D

Preparing for lectures

1 Building basic information

Some course programmes give only a list of lecture titles, but others may give a brief description of their content, too. If so, you can use this to prepare for lectures.

1.1 a **Read the following description of a lecture and in pairs predict what the lecture might be about.**

> **Why we read Shakespeare**
> Dr Charles Moseley will be investigating why Shakespeare matters to us now, particularly in terms of his impact on the English language. He will also look at why fictions, and reading and studying them, matter to the moral and political health of a society.

b **What information would you like to have before the lecture starts to help you understand it?**

c (▮D.1) **Watch the first part of the lecture. What more do you now know about what it will be about?**

Listening

2 Understanding the relationship between parts of the lecture

Lecturers will expect you to understand the relationship between one part of the lecture and what has been said before. The lecturer might use linking words or phrases (usually a sentence connector or conjunction) to make this relationship clear, or expect you to infer the relationship.

2.1 **Underline the linking word in the following extract from a lecture given by Dr Moseley. What is the relationship between the second sentence and the first?**

> Shakespeare had no advantage from any connection with any noble house. Rather, he made his way simply by his extraordinary facility with words and what they could do.

2.2 a (▮D.2) **Watch extracts from the lectures by Dr Mormina and Dr Hunt. The first part of each extract is given below. For each extract, write down the linking word or phrase that introduces the second part, if there is one. If there is no linking word or phrase, write '–'.**

1 So what's happening here is that when the ball goes around in a circle the force is at right angles to the velocity. _____Which means that_____

2 So then we start thinking, 'Well, what fun experiments can I do?' Well, what I can do is I can go to the bike shop and I can buy something called a *stunt peg*, and I've got one here, I've got a stunt peg with a piece of string attached to it. _____

3 Lift on a plane is just a simple thing really – people love to make it sound complicated – but if air flows over a wing, the wing contrives to deflect the air downwards and by Newton's third law of motion every action has an equal opposite reaction: if the air is being pushed downwards, the wing must be being pushed upwards. And we know from lift that the faster you go, the more lift you get. _____

4 If I have backspin on a ball, then the ball comes back towards me. _____

5 Basically, in these high latitudes, people tended to prefer people with light skin colour and therefore that all led to the predominance of light skin colour in high latitudes.

_____

6 So if you put together all of us, our genetic diversity is much smaller than that of African populations and that indicates that African populations are older. _____

b Check your answers in the audioscript on pages 162–163.

c Which of the following labels best describes the relationship between the first and second parts of the extracts? Match the extracts (1–6) to the labels (a–f).

    a Additional point _____   **d** Example _____
    b Consequence __1__   **e** Explanation _____
    c Contrast _____   **f** Reason _____

3 Understanding descriptions of processes

Study tip *Lecturers often describe processes; that is, series of events or actions with a particular result. If it is important for you to understand the process, you should try to note the steps in the process and some information about each step.*

3.1 a (D.3) **Watch an extract from Dr Mormina's lecture, where she describes the process of climate change about 12,000 years ago and how humans adapted to it. Complete the following notes.**

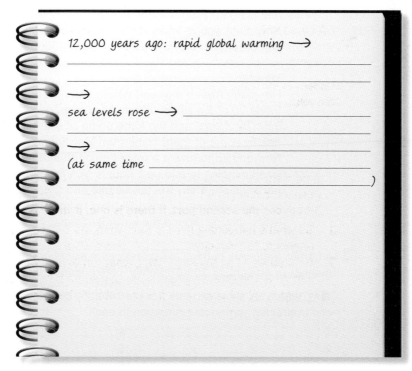

12,000 years ago: rapid global warming →
_____
_____
→
sea levels rose → _____
_____
→ _____
(at same time _____
_____)

b In pairs, compare your notes.

c (D.3) **Here are some words and phrases commonly used to introduce steps in a process or to describe the relationship between them. Watch again and tick (✓) the ones you hear Dr Mormina use.**

1	after that	___	**7**	in order to	___
2	afterwards	___	**8**	next	___
3	and that produced	___	**9**	so	___
4	as a consequence	___	**10**	then	___
5	as a result	___	**11**	therefore	___
6	first	___	**12**	with that	___

d **In pairs, think of some additional words and phrases which are commonly used in describing processes.**

Language focus

4 Understanding vague language

Particularly in conversational and interactive lectures, you will hear informal, vague language of the type you find in everyday conversation. In academic writing we tend to be more formal and precise, and such language is rarely found.

Study tip *You can sometimes use clues in the context to understand vague language in lectures. For example, pay attention to the lecturer's gestures, objects used in demonstrations, or information on slides.*

4.1 **In pairs, look at the vague expressions in bold in the following extracts from Dr Hunt's lecture and explain what each one means.**

Extract 1

That's just that's obvious. In fact if it didn't start to spin you'd think there was something wrong it looks wrong you'd think the brakes are on **1 or something**. So we know it's intuitive that that ball will start to spin. Okay. Now what? That ball is heading up towards the top now spinning. Is this top spin or back spin? Now most people know a little bit about tennis or squash or or or er um er golf or football **2 or whatever**, to know about spin

Extract 2

I've made myself a wheel. What I can now do is to think of a wheel as being made up of **3 a zillion** different particles each one of those particles acted upon by a force and the force some of the forces come from other particles nearby some of them come from gravity some come from all over the place. Newton had to invent a way of doing this mathematically and what he said was I'm going to add up F equals M A for all the particles but because the particles are **4 tiny weenie weenie** and there's **5 a billion zillion** of them I can't just add them up by hand I'll have to add them up mathematically ... Now the moon moving around the earth is circular motion **6 pretty much.**

4.2 *Informal, imprecise numerical expressions – words or phrases that mean a small or large number or amount, or approximately – are common in lectures.*

(D.4) **Watch six short extracts from lectures by Dr Hunt and Dr Mormina and make a note of one imprecise numerical expression in each.**

1	_____	**4**	_____
2	_____	**5**	_____
3	_____	**6**	_____

Follow up

5 Listening for a lecture summary

 Study tip *At the end of a section, or at the end of the lecture, the lecturer will often give a brief summary of what they have covered and the most important information they have provided. This is a useful opportunity to edit the notes you have made so far by checking them and, if necessary, adding to or changing them.*

5.1 (D.5) **Look at the following notes on the history of human populations which a student made earlier in Dr Mormina's lecture. Watch her summary section and add to the notes.**

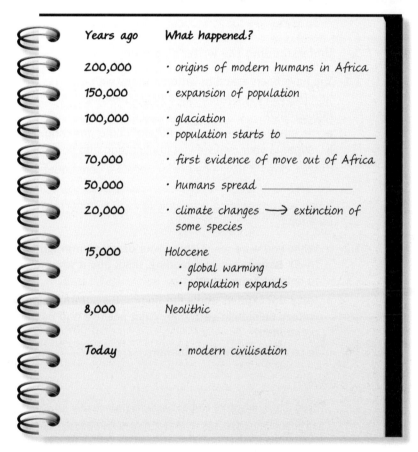

Years ago	What happened?
200,000	· origins of modern humans in Africa
150,000	· expansion of population
100,000	· glaciation · population starts to _____
70,000	· first evidence of move out of Africa
50,000	· humans spread _____
20,000	· climate changes ⟶ extinction of some species
15,000	Holocene · global warming · population expands
8,000	Neolithic
Today	· modern civilisation

6 Comparing notes

6.1 a **Some students find it helpful to compare notes with other students after a lecture. In pairs, think of two advantages and two disadvantages of doing this.**

b (D.6) **Watch Frederike talking about her experience of working cooperatively with her fellow students after lectures, and answer the following questions.**

1 How did the students share their material?

2 What surprised Frederike about this experience?

c **In pairs, discuss ways in which you have shared material or helped other students.**

9 Controversies

Reading

1 Understanding the writer's opinion

1.1 You have been asked to write an essay with the title *Discuss the advantages and disadvantages of immigration*.

a In small groups, make a note of some pros and cons of immigration.

b What is your own view of immigration into your country?

Overall, does it have positive or negative consequences?

When you are reading academic texts, it is important to understand the writer's general opinion on a topic.

1.2 **a** While you were researching your essay on immigration you found the following extracts (A–F). Before you start reading, think about what information you hope to find in the extracts to help with the essay.

b Read the extracts and write brief notes summarising what you understand about the writer's opinion in each one. What positive and negative consequences of immigration are mentioned?

c In pairs, compare your answers.

Extract A

> Where illegal migrants and/or their children qualify for social benefits or education, social programs and educational systems may be stressed as transfers occur from indigenous residents to migrants. Ethnic tensions may rise as cultures clash. Those migrants who do not speak the country's primary language often have difficulty assimilating, and some of these problems may spill over into the educational system through higher costs of bi-lingual education and in other ways.

Greenwood, M. J. (2007). Population: Migration, in Lomborg, B. (Ed.) *Solutions for the World's Biggest Problems: Costs and benefits*. Cambridge: Cambridge University Press.

Extract B

> One consequence of today's patterns of intense global migration is the creation of multicultural societies composed of groups representing very different cultural histories, values, and practices. In many respects nations and economies that embrace and encourage multiculturalism can reap tremendous economic and cultural benefits from the energy, creativity, and productivity that diversity generates.

Lull, J. (2006). The push and pull of global culture. In Curran, J. and Morley, D. (Eds.) *Media and cultural theory*. Oxford: Routledge.

Extract C

> As the earth's population has continued to grow, a new kind of fear has emerged in the developed countries: an environmental one. The added population of new migrants increases the demographic pressures on all of a country's environmental resources. It reduces the amount of natural, undeveloped land remaining, leaving it farther away from many people and more crowded with visitors, as well as threatening plant and animal species which rely upon these habitats. And immigration adds more "automobile-using and toilet-flushing residents,"[72] contributing to air and water pollution.

Erler, E. J., West, T. G. and Marini, J. (2007). *The Founders on Citizenship and Immigration: Principles and challenges in America*. Maryland, U.S.:Rowman and Littlefield Publishers.

Extract D

> In the long run, dependence on cheap labor is not profitable – it delays modernization of plants, facilities and farms. As a rule, American labor is better educated and more productive and higher wages are justified by greater productivity. Not many years ago, grain was harvested by great armies of agricultural workers armed with scythes. Now, the crops are harvested by giant machines which are more efficient and more cost effective.

Meilander, P. C. (2001). *Toward a theory of immigration*. New York: Palgrave Macmillan

Extract E

> Indeed, demographic pressures within the developed world will make it difficult (at least costly) to continue ignoring the political and economic potential of international migration. The developed world's population is both shrinking (in number) and ageing. Across most of Europe, national birth rates are below their replacement rates. Russia and Japan face the same dire situation, while America and Canada are hovering on the brink. Soon there will be too few workers in these countries to pay for their elaborate welfare and social security needs (which they otherwise fight so hard to protect). Without an injection of young immigrant workers, the welfare of the developed world risks being retired along with its population.

Moses, J. W. (2006). *International Migration: Globalization's last frontier*. London: Zed Books

Extract F

> Immigration, therefore, has two distinct consequences and these consequences propel the immigration debate. The nation, as a whole, gains from immigration. In other words, immigration increases the size of the economic pie available to natives. Immigration also redistributes income – from native workers who compete with immigrants to those who hire and use immigrant services. Immigration changes the way the economic pie is split between workers and firms.

Borjas, G. J. (1999). *Heaven's Door: Immigration policy and the American economy*. Princeton, NJ: Princeton University Press

> 🎓 **Focus on your subject** *Each academic subject has particular issues of debate and controversy. Being able to recognise writers' opinions can help you understand and evaluate the arguments on either side. When you are reading about these issues, try to work out whether the writer takes a particular position and what evidence they provide to justify this position.*

2 Identifying main ideas and supporting information

2.1 You are going to read a text with the title *Isolates or socialites? The social ties of internet users*. What controversial issue do you expect the text to be about?

2.2 Read the text. For each paragraph tick the sentence (a–c) which summarises the main idea.

Paragraph 1
a The internet gives us access to enormous amounts of information, and also allows us to buy things without going into shops.
b The internet makes it possible both to keep in touch with people who live far away and also to avoid personal contact.
c Railways, the telephone, and the internet are some of the most important developments in how people communicate.

Paragraph 2
a Through the internet we can keep in contact with people using words, photos, video clips, and other images.
b Email has had an important effect on social relationships mainly because it is cheap and because we can reply to emails at some time after we have received them.
c Some argue that the internet has made it easier to make contact with friends and relations, so that relationships between people become closer.

Paragraph 3
a Face-to-face communication develops trust between people and encourages them to help each other.
b Face-to-face communication is more important than electronic communication for a healthy society, but some argue that the internet can encourage face-to-face communication.
c We can use the internet to arrange to meet friends, or to encourage people to come to social activities organised for a particular community.

Paragraph 4
a Some argue that electronic communication replaces face-to-face communication, and this can be a bad thing for people.
b The same criticisms of the internet for its negative impact on social relations were previously made about watching television.
c Because using a computer is a solitary activity, this can make people lonely and depressed.

➤ Adverbials
G&V 3, p137

1 The advent of the internet has been one of the biggest developments in the history of communications technology. Like the railways and the telephone before it, the internet has helped to make the world a smaller place, making it easier to undertake both business and pleasure with individuals and organisations located far away. At the same time it has enabled individuals to acquire from the comfort of their office or front room access to both a hive of information and a wide range of commercial services, activities that previously would have necessitated a trip to the high street. Seemingly the internet has both made it easier to maintain contact with our fellow human beings, especially those who do not live locally, and, at the same time, reduced the need to engage in social contact with others in order to conduct the everyday business of commercial or social life.

2 These apparently divergent features of the internet have resulted in a lively debate about whether its advent has strengthened or weakened the social bonds and ties between individuals. One school of thought argues that it has had a beneficial impact. It points out that the internet makes it much easier to get into contact with individuals who have similar interests to oneself, irrespective of where they live, thereby making it possible to create 'virtual communities'. Contact with friends and relatives who live some distance away can more easily be maintained too – not

Non-finite relative clauses

G&V 2, p136

just using words but also exploiting the ability to send photos, video clips and scanned images via the internet too. These apparent consequences derive principally from the opportunity afforded by e-mail to communicate asynchronously and to do so at no greater cost with someone halfway round the world than with a neighbour living next door (Hauben and Hauben, 1997; Wellman and Gulia, 1999; Wellman et al., 2001; Horrigan, 2002). 20

3 These arguments, though, do not address the possible impact of the internet on face-to-face communication. It is often argued that face-to-face communication helps develop bonds of trust and reciprocity between individuals in a manner that no other form of communication can achieve (Putnam, 2000; though for a dissenting view see Uslaner, 2002). Such bonds, fostered by and 25 embedded in social networks, provide a stock of 'social capital' that helps make societies healthier, more caring and more efficient. Thus, whether or not the internet makes it easier for people to organise face-to-face meetings rather than just maintain electronic contact with those living far away is a vital question. Certainly, those who are optimistic about the impact of the internet think it does. After all, it can be used to make an appointment to meet a friend in the local pub or to 30 advertise and encourage people to attend a communal social activity. Moreover, friends initially made on-line may subsequently be met face to face. In short, the ability to engage in 'on-line' social activity could help to stimulate greater 'off-line' social activity too (Robinson et al., 2000; Shah et al., 2001; Hampton and Wellman, 2002) – with consequential beneficial impacts on the stock of social capital. 35

4 On the other hand 'on-line' activity could serve to displace 'off-line' activity. Those engaged in a virtual network may spend less time participating in their local social networks. Even if they are not particularly predisposed to withdraw from face-to-face contact, time spent on the internet is time not spent doing something else, and one of the activities that might be displaced is socialising with friends and family (Nie and Erbring, 2000; Nie, 2001). Similar arguments have been, indeed, 40 previously made about the growth in the second half of the 20th century of television watching (Steiner, 1963; Putnam, 2000); but whereas watching television can, in fact, be turned into a communal activity, using a computer is usually a solitary activity. Indeed, it has been argued that the solitary nature of internet use may result in people becoming lonely and depressed, thereby undermining their ability to form or sustain friendships (Kraut et al., 1998). 45

Park, A. et al (Eds.) (2007). *British Social Attitudes: Perspectives on a changing society*. 23rd report. National Centre for Social Research/Sage.

2.3 a **The writer reports that there is a debate about whether the internet has strengthened or weakened the social bonds and ties between individuals. Take notes from the text on the arguments on both sides of this issue. Include notes on any supporting evidence. Then in pairs, compare your notes. Make any changes to your notes you think necessary.**

   b **In pairs, discuss your views on this issue.**

3 Recognising general nouns

General nouns are often used to refer to previous or following parts of a text. It is important to recognise these general nouns in order to understand the relationships between parts of the text. For example, in the following extract the general noun arguments *is used to refer to and label the points made in the previous three sentences.*

On the other hand 'on-line' activity could serve to displace 'off-line' activity. Those engaged in a virtual network may spend less time participating in their local social networks. Even if they are not particularly predisposed to withdraw from face-to-face contact, time spent on the internet is time not spent doing something else, and one of the activities that might be displaced is socialising with friends and family (Nie and Erbring, 2000; Nie, 2001). Similar **arguments** have been, indeed, previously made ...

3.1 **Find the general nouns in bold in the text in 2.2. What do they refer to?**

1 ... **activities** that previously would have necessitated a trip to the high street. (lines 6–7)

2 These apparently divergent **features** of the internet ... (line 11)

3 These apparent **consequences** derive principally from ... (line 18)

4 These **arguments**, though, do not address the possible impact of the internet on face-to-face communication. (lines 22–23)

➤ Hedges

Unit 5, 6.1 p74,
Unit 6, 7 p90

4 Understanding hedges

4.1 **a** **The following extracts from the text in 2.2 are missing the original hedges. In pairs, add the hedges in the box to the extracts and make any other changes necessary. Look back at the text to check your answers.**

could	helped to	may	might	~~one of~~	usually

1 The advent of the internet has been ∧ the biggest development ∧ in the history of communications technology.
(one of above the first ∧; s above the second ∧)

2 The internet has made the world a smaller place,

3 The ability to engage in 'on-line' social activity helps to stimulate greater 'off-line' social activity too

4 Those engaged in a virtual network spend less time participating in their local social networks.

5 One of the activities that is displaced by spending time on the internet is socialising with friends and family

6 Whereas watching television can, in fact, be turned into a communal activity, using computer is a solitary activity.

b **Can you suggest different hedges that could be used instead?**

c **Which other ideas in the sentences in 4.1a could be hedged?**

➤ Using academic style

Unit 7, 8 pp106–107

5 Vocabulary building 1: formal and informal verbs

5.1 **Complete the following sentences using formal verbs from the text in 2.2 with the same meaning as the words in brackets.**

1 The internet has made it easier to _undertake_ business. (do)

2 Individuals can _____ information from the comfort of their office. (get)

3 It is now possible to _____ 'virtual communities'. (make)

4 Friends and relatives can _____ contact via the internet. (keep)

5 The consequences of the internet _____ principally from the opportunity _____ by email to communicate asynchronously and cheaply. (come; given)

6 The internet may undermine people's ability to _____ or _____ friendships. (make; keep)

6 Vocabulary building 2: opposites

Many academic texts include pairs of words with an opposite meaning. Often these are used in presenting contrasts or arguments on two sides of an issue.

6.1 **What words are used in the text in 2.2 as the opposites of the following words? Look back at the text to check your answers.**

1 far away (line 8)   *locally*
2 strengthened (line 12)   _____
3 divergent (line 14)   _____
4 face-to-face communication (line 28)   _____
5 on-line (line 36)   _____
6 engaged in (line 38)   _____
7 subsequently (line 41)   _____
8 solitary (line 43)   _____

Listening and speaking

7 Tutorials: asking for and giving more information

7.1 **(◄)9.1) A student is finishing her presentation on the advantages of genetically modified (GM) crops over conventional plant varieties. She invites others in the tutorial group to ask questions. Listen and complete the following extracts with phrases for asking for and giving information.**

Raquel: … Does anybody want to ask any questions at all?

Nik: Yes, Raquel, *you used the abbreviation* FOE. *What does that stand for*?

Raquel: Oh, right, that means Friends of the Earth …

Elena: You only talked about the advantages of GM crops. So _____ *that* there are no disadvantages?

Raquel: Well, no, not at all. _____ at the moment there's no actual evidence of health risks, …

Richard: Raquel, *you* _____ 'selective breeding' of plants. _____ *exactly*?

Raquel: Well, _____ *is that* researchers grow plants that have particular characteristics …

Tim: _____ GM foods have better nutritional value. _____?

Raquel: *To be honest,* _____ . *I'll need to* _____ .

Tutor: Okay, thanks Raquel.

7.2 a **Add the underlined phrases in 7.1 to the following table.**

Asking for information	Introducing more information
· Could you give an example of that? · Have you got any other examples of … ? · What did you mean by …? · What did you mean when you said … ? · You used the term/word … – what's that? · I didn't quite understand (what you said about) …	· What I meant was (that) … · The main reason is … · It's to do with …
	Saying that you don't know
	· I'm sorry, I don't know. · I'll have to find out and let you know. · I need to go away and look at that a bit more.

b **Can you suggest any other possibilities?**

7.3 a **Prepare notes for a short talk no more than two minutes long. This should be on a topic from your academic field, or on a special subject that interests you.**

b **In small groups, give your talk. Afterwards, invite questions and be prepared to give more information or say that you don't know. In the question-answer stage try to use language from the table in 7.2.**

🎓 **Focus on your subject** *In your academic studies you may be asked to give longer presentations in tutorials or seminars. Research a controversial issue from your own subject and prepare a presentation of about ten minutes. Be ready to explain terms which students from other subject areas may not be familiar with.*

---

8 Pronunciation: intonation in *wh*-clefts

Wh-*cleft sentences often begin with* what. *The wh-clause (in bold below) is usually old information, and attention is focused on the new information at the end (in italics). The wh-clause usually ends with a fall-rising tone, ↘↗ and the new information ends with a falling tone ↘ . For example:*

Elena: So are you saying that there are no disadvantages?
Raquel: Well, no, not at all. **What I'm SAYing** ↘↗ is that *at the moment there's no actual EVidence* ↘ *of health risks …*

Richard: You talked about 'selective breeding' of plants. What does that mean exactly?
Raquel: Well, **what it MEANS** ↘↗ is that *researchers grow plants that have particular characterIStics.* ↘

8.1 ◄))9.2 **Listen to the examples above. In pairs, take it in turns to read them aloud, and try to copy the intonation in the *wh*-cleft sentences.**

8.2 a ◄))9.3 **Rewrite the answers in the dialogues using a *wh*-cleft. Listen and check your answers.**

1 A: How do you feel about the government's healthy eating campaign?
B: I think they need to target children more.

_____

2 A: What did your survey tell you about motivation levels among students?
B: I found that older students were better motivated than younger ones.

_____

3 A: You said that businesses need to spend more on IT. Can you explain that a bit more, please?
B: I was talking about how difficult some websites are to use.

_____

4 A: You said that the mobile phone was the most important invention of the 20th century. Why do you think that?
B: I actually said that it was the most important communications device invented.

_____

5 A: You mentioned the new vaccination programme. Where can we get more information about that?
B: I suggest that you have a look at the WHO website.

_____

b **In pairs, take it in turns to ask and answer the questions. Try to use the pronunciation for *wh*-clefts you heard in 8.1.**

Study tip *Wh-clefts are often used during presentations to say how they are organised. Listen for these in lectures and presentations, and try to use them in your own presentations.*

8.3 (4)9.4) **In pairs, take it in turns to read the following organising sentences aloud. Listen and check each other's pronunciation.**

What I'll be TALKing about ↘↗ is *the GM conTROVersy.* ↘
What I've done SO far ↘↗ is *outline the advantages of GM FOODS.* ↘
What I want to do NEXT ↘↗ is *discuss some of the potential PROBlems.* ↘

Writing

9 Describing information in figures and tables

Numerical evidence is often presented in essays and reports in the form of a figure or table. When describing information in figures or tables we often follow the four stages listed below.

9.1 **Complete the description of each stage using the words in the box.**

aspect	column	detail	limitations	significance	statement

Stage 1: Introduce the topic

Describe the general topic the figure or table relates to, or give other background information.

Stage 2: Explain what the figure or table shows

Briefly expand on the title of the figure or table. Sometimes more **1** _____ is given, such as what is shown by each axis on a graph, or each **2** _____ in a table.

Stage 3: Highlight information of particular interest or relevance

This stage may be repeated a number of times, each focusing on a new **3** _____ of the information. Often a general **4** _____ is followed by supporting detail.

Stage 4: Comment on the information

This may be, for example, on the **5** _____ of the information to the essay or report more generally, or on the **6** _____ of the information.

9.2 **You have been asked to discuss the controversial statement "Women work harder than men". In pairs or groups suggest what types of evidence you would look for in order to research and evaluate this controversial point of view (e.g. working hours).**

9.3 a **Complete the following extract from a report, which describes information in Table 4.1 on page 134, by putting the sentences (a–g) in the correct order.**

a The main differences between men and women are in the time spent in paid and domestic work. _____

b Table 4.1, for example, shows the time spent on activities by people in Great Britain in 2005 by gender. _____

c However, because more women have entered the workforce since this survey was conducted in 2005, it seems likely that these differences will now be less marked. _____

d In some countries, national surveys have gathered information on how much time people spend on certain activities during the day, and have also compared time spent on these activities by men and women. __1__

e Free and unspecified time amounts to about a fifth of each day, and work, both paid and domestic, and study together take about a quarter. _____

f As can be seen, for the group as a whole the main activity is sleep, which takes over a third of each day. _____

g Men spend substantially more time in paid work and study, while women spend over 50 percent more time on domestic work than men. _____

Table 4.1 Time spent on main activity by gender, 2005

Activity	Men	Women	All
	Average minutes per person per day		
Sleep	527	546	537
Meals, personal care	125	127	126
Free time, unspecified time use	342	311	326
Paid work, study	225	146	184
Domestic work	129	228	180
Travel	92	82	87

Office for National Statistics (2006). *The Time Use Survey, 2005.* London: Office for National Statistics

b Match the sentences (a–g) to the four stages for describing figures in a report.

1 Introduce _____   **3** Highlight ___a___ ____ ____ ____
2 Explain _____   **4** Comment _____

➤ 'Figure 2 displays'
G&V 1, p136

10 Language for writing 1: referring to figures and tables

ⓘ *We can use an* as-*clause to refer to the information in tables and figures (e.g.* As can be seen … *or* As shown in Table 4.1 …*). Notice that we do not use* it *in this kind of* as-*clause (NOT* As ~~it~~ can be seen … *or* As ~~it~~ is shown in Table 4.1 …*).*

10.1 In pairs, look at the following extracts from reports of research on language learning. Identify four grammatical forms that are used to refer to figures and tables.

1 The stages of acquisition of sounds are shown in Figure 1.
2 As shown in Table 1, the most frequent tense used was the present perfect.
3 Each workshop was spread over one or two days (see Table 4).
4 The worksheet that I produced is presented in Figure 3.
5 Figure 1 shows in diagrammatic form the training practices that have been described.
6 In order to preserve the meaning of the original utterance, it is necessary to manipulate the three variables of person, place, and time (see Table 2).
7 Figure 1 gives the opening page on the internet as viewed by the student.
8 The result may be the copying of teaching techniques, as illustrated in Figure 2.

11 Language for writing 2: referring backwards and forwards

11.1 A number of words and phrases are commonly used in academic writing to point backwards or forwards in a text (e.g. *As shown in table 1*). Underline the examples in the following sentences.

1 The composition of the diet was <u>as follows</u>: 50% sugar, 20% casein, 20% corn starch, and 10% corn oil.
2 As mentioned earlier, alcohol contributes significantly to motor vehicle crashes.
3 There are many exceptions to the above rules.
4 Employment data, as noted above, is not a particularly accurate indicator of output.
5 Cell identity and purity were determined, as previously described.
6 Halliday (2006) criticises those against the war for the following reasons. First, there is …
7 These criticisms were rejected for the reasons discussed below.

11.2 In pairs, look at the following extracts from students' writing. Underline the language the students used to point backwards or forwards and correct their mistakes in each sentence.

1 The population can be divided into four age groups as <u>~~following~~</u> *follows*: 15 to 24 year olds, 25 to 34 year olds, 35 to 44 year olds, and those 45 and over.
2 As it was mentioned earlier, red meat is an important source of protein.
3 In addition to above factors, customers have other reasons to complain.
4 As being noted above, the early childhood years are vital for full development of cognitive, emotional and social skills.

5 As I described before, radio became an important means of communication from the middle of the twentieth century.

6 The reasons are following. First, work pressures have become so great that parents have less time to spend with their children. Second, ...

7 I increased the number of participants in the study for the below discussed reasons.

Corpus research shows that the most common past participle that goes in the structure As .... *in table/figure/section/chapter ... is shown. What do you think are the next most common? The first letters are given to help you.*

1 sh<u>own</u>	3 de_____	5 in_____	7 def_____	9 gi_____
2 di_____	4 il_____	6 se_____	8 dep_____	10 ou_____

---

12 Writing practice

12.1 a **You have been asked to write an essay on gender differences in behaviour. You want to include a section on sleep habits and have found the following information. In pairs, identify the main information and any supporting information you wish to highlight.**

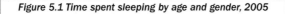

Figure 5.1 Time spent sleeping by age and gender, 2005

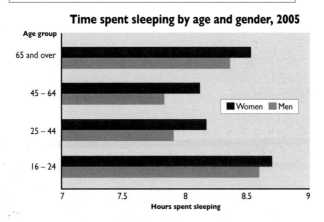

Table 5.20 Time spent on leisure activities by age and gender, 2005

Leisure activity		Age group				All
		16-24	25-44	45-64	65+	
		Average minutes per person per day				
Social Life	Men	132	81	57	58	77
	Women	135	79	80	79	87
Entertainment & culture	Men	4	4	6	4	5
	Women	11	6	3	4	5
Sport & outdoor activities	Men	32	10	9	12	13
	Women	4	7	9	4	7
Hobbies & games	Men	54	27	37	42	37
	Women	25	13	26	34	23
Reading	Men	10	11	22	57	23
	Women	9	13	24	61	26
TV & Video/DVDs, radio, music	Men	149	137	178	241	170
	Women	126	113	142	214	145
All leisure	Men	382	269	309	414	325
	Women	311	231	284	396	293

Office for National Statistics (2006). *The Time Use Survey, 2005*. London: Office for National Statistics

b **Write two paragraphs, one describing Figure 5.1 and the other describing Table 5.20. Follow the four stages in 9.2.**

Grammar and vocabulary

Grammar and vocabulary
- Verbs followed by a noun phrase or *that*-clause
- Non-finite relative clauses
- Adverbials used to comment

1 Verbs followed by a noun phrase or *that*-clause

A number of verbs can be used to say what is in a table or figure. Some of these verbs can be followed by a noun phrase or by a that-clause; other verbs can only be followed by a noun phrase. For example:

- Table 1 **shows** the budget for the project.
- Table 1 **shows** that most users were satisfied with the website.
- Figure 1 **summarises** the characteristics of market competition for the product. *(NOT* summarises that*)*

1.1 In pairs, complete the table with the verbs in the box. Check your answers in a dictionary.

compare   contrast   demonstrate   display
give   illustrate   indicate   list   present
provide   reveal   show   suggest   summarise

+ noun phrase or *that*-clause	+ noun phrase only
show	summarise

 Study tip *As you read texts in your subject that include tables and figures, make a note of any other verbs that are used to refer to them.*

1.2 In pairs, decide whether the following sentences are correct (✓) or incorrect (✗). If they are incorrect, suggest an improvement. There may be more than one possible answer.

1 Figure 1 displays that the cinema attendance in Australia between 1990 and 2010. ✗
2 The table provides that there was a substantial increase in receipts last year. ___
3 Table 4 compares that the readership for ten open access journals with ten non-open access journals during 2008. ___
4 Figure 3 indicates that there were large differences between the answers in the two groups. ___
5 Table 1 gives that the 52,000 births recorded in 2010 represent a 4.2 per cent increase over the preceding year. ___

6 Figure 3 demonstrates quite clearly that boys spend less time reading on average than girls. ___
7 The figures suggest that some of the increase in internet advertising expenditure occurred at the expense of direct mail. ✗
8 Figure 1 presents that the majority of the investment in the sector (46%) came from Germany. ___

2 Non-finite relative clauses

2.1 Complete the following explanation of non-finite relative clauses by adding the examples (a–h) in the appropriate place (1–8).

We can often add information to a noun phrase using a clause beginning with a non-finite verb form. These sometimes correspond to a relative clause. For example, we can use:

- *an -ing (present participle) clause. For example:*
  1 __e__ *which corresponds to* **2** __b__
- *an -ed (past participle) clause. For example:*
  3 _____ *which corresponds to* **4** _____
- *a being + -ed (past participle) clause. For example:*
  5 _____ *which corresponds to* **6** _____

-ing clauses correspond to relative clauses with an active verb.

-ed and being + -ed clauses correspond to relative clauses with a passive verb.

We can't use a non-finite relative clause when the subject of the verb and the noun we are adding information to are different. For example:

7 _____ *but NOT* **8** _____

a   the equipment being used was faulty
b   ~~a neighbour who lives next door~~
c   organisations located far away
d   the subject studying
e   ~~a neighbour living next door~~
f   the subject that they were studying
g   organisations which are located far away
h   the equipment that was being used was faulty

2.2 Match the pairs of sentences (1–8 and a–h). For each pair, combine the sentences using a non-finite relative clause. If a non-finite relative clause is not possible, use a relative clause with a finite verb.

1 The proposal was part of a new marketing strategy. __g__
The proposal was part of a new marketing strategy designed to increase sales in India.

2 Simmons (2008) talks about the increased opportunities for employment. _____

3 The government will give more funding to research. _____

4 The police began by arresting demonstrators. _____

5 Ultrasound energy is a form of therapy. _____

6 An investigation was held to look into the patients' claims. _____

7 The Education Department is to introduce a new curriculum. _____

8 'Verbatim' is a Latin term. _____

a They hope it will have immediate economic benefits.

b They are being created by the development of green technologies.

c They were handing out political leaflets.

d It aims to improve science teaching in schools.

e It is being studied as a possible cancer treatment.

f It is used to mean 'word for word'.

g ~~It was designed to increase sales in India.~~

h They were receiving inadequate care in the hospital.

3 Adverbials used to comment

One way in which writers of academic texts comment on what they are saying is by using adverbials (adverbs or phrases that function like an adverb).
For example:
· Using a computer is usually seen as a solitary activity. **In fact**, it turned into a communal activity.
· **Seemingly** the internet has made it easier to maintain contact with our fellow human beings.

3.1 **a** Underline the adverbials used to comment in sentences 1–10.

1 Inflation rose during the 1970s. <u>No doubt</u> increases in oil prices played a part.

2 As might be expected, the brain size of animals increases with body size.

3 Although many people claim to have found remedies for the common cold, there is actually very little research published on the subject.

4 Both Cars (2006) and Wills (2010) studied the impact of social networking sites on friendship groups, but interestingly their findings were different.

5 Although most researchers have measured children's body weight monthly, this high frequency is in fact unnecessary.

6 Unemployment rate arguably provides the best indicator of employment opportunities.

7 Of the two, roller bearings are probably better as they are easier to fit.

8 Surprisingly, left-handers showed a higher preference for careers in medicine.

9 Certainly, the features of Standard English are hard to define.

10 The number of respondents who were in favour of tax increases was predictably small.

b Complete the following explanation of adverbials which are used to comment with the adverbials you underlined in 3.1a.

We can use sentence adverbials to:

a *express certainty (e.g.* __no doubt__ *and _____)*

b *express a level of doubt (e.g. _____ and _____)*

c *say what we think is really the case (e.g. _____ and _____)*

d *say that something is expected (e.g. _____ and _____)*

e *give our reaction to what we are talking about (e.g. _____ and _____)*

3.2 Add an adverbial from 3.1 to each of these extracts in an appropriate place.

1 *As might be expected, the* The amount of exercise people took varied with age.

2 When students (100 in total) were asked what they intended to do after completing their first degree, not one of them said they wanted to go on to do postgraduate studies.

3 The abstract is the most important part of an article in an academic journal because it is the only part of an article that many people read.

4 There are many limitations of the research, but I would like to point out two.

5 Although creativity seems to be a simple phenomenon, it is very complex.

10 Health

Reading
· Reading for evidence
· Thinking about what you already know
· Preparing for essay writing
· Vocabulary in context: inferring meaning
· Understanding connections in texts: *this/these*
· Developing hedging skills

Listening and speaking
· Summarising what has been said
· Evaluating visual aids
· Pronunciation: stress in compound nouns 2

Writing
· Contrasting information
· Taking a stance: expressing disagreement

Reading

1 Reading for evidence

1.1 **a** In pairs, identify four main findings in the following table, which gives information about life expectancy at birth.

Life expectancy at birth (years)						
	Male			Female		
WHO REGION	1990	2000	2008	1990	2000	2008
African Region	49	49	51	53	52	54
Region of the Americas	68	71	73	75	77	79
South-East Asia Region	58	61	63	59	63	66
European Region	68	68	71	75	77	79
East Mediterranean Region	59	62	63	62	65	66
Western Pacific Region	68	70	72	71	74	77
INCOME GROUP						
Low income	52	53	56	55	56	59
Low middle income	61	63	65	63	66	69
Upper middle income	65	65	67	72	73	75
High income	72	75	77	79	81	83
GLOBAL	62	64	66	66	68	70

World Health Organization (2010). *World Health Statistics 2010*. WHO.

b Suggest four factors that might influence the differences in life expectancy you can observe in the table. Report these to the class.

1.2 You have been asked to write an essay with the title *Despite the increase in life expectancy over the last 200 years, not all groups of people have the same chances of good health. What factors affect health?*

a Using your ideas from 1.1 and what you already know, add general factors that affect health and examples of these to the following table. (You will look for evidence in the following activity.)

General factors that affect health	Examples of factors	Evidence
· Genetic / biological factors	· Gender	

b **Read the following extracts and add notes to the table which are relevant to the essay.**

Extract 1

The WHO estimates 2.8 million annual deaths from indoor air pollution, making it one of the largest single mortality factors in the world – 5.5 percent of all deaths. This is an extremely large figure and backs the World Bank's decision to name indoor air pollution as one of the world's four most crucial environmental problems.

Lomborg, B. (2001). *The skeptical environmentalist: measuring the real state of the world*. Cambridge: Cambridge University Press.

Extract 2

It has consistently been reported from developed countries that although male death rates are higher than women's at all ages, women report more symptoms, disability days, use of medications and contacts with the medical profession. *gender*

Macintyre, S. (1993). Gender differences in the perceptions of common cold symptoms. *Social Science and Medicine*, 36, 15–20.

Extract 3

Nutrition is important for children's development and long-term health. Eating fruit during adolescence, for example, in place of high-fat, sugar and salt products, can protect against health problems such as obesity, diabetes, and heart problems. Moreover, eating fruit when young can be habit forming, promoting healthy eating behaviours for later life.

OECD (2009). *Health at a glance: OECD indicators*. OECD.

Extract 4

Several studies provide strong evidence of socio-economic differences in smoking and mortality (Mackenbach *et al.*, 2008). People in lower social groups have a greater prevalence and intensity of smoking, a higher all-cause mortality rate and lower rates of cancer survival (Woods *et al.*, 2006). The influence of smoking as a determinant of overall health inequalities is such that, in a non-smoking population, mortality differences between social groups would be halved (Jha *et al.*, 2006).

OECD (2009). *Health at a glance: OECD indicators*. OECD.

Extract 5

This study found no clear evidence to support the hypothesis that damp housing has a detrimental effect on the physical health of adults; nevertheless, there was evidence that those living in damp houses have more emotional distress. The principal finding, however, was of significant associations between living in a damp and, more specifically, "mouldy" house and ill health among children. Not only respiratory problems but other symptoms suggestive of infections and stress were more common in children in damp dwellings.

Martin, C. J. Platt, S. D. and Hunt, S. M. (1987). Housing conditions and ill health. *British Medical Journal*, 294, 1125–1127.

Extract 6

Tobacco is the second major cause of death in the world after cardiovascular disease, and is directly responsible for about one in ten adult deaths worldwide, equating to about 6 million deaths each year (Shafey *et al.*, 2009).

OECD (2009). *Health at a glance: OECD indicators*. OECD.

Extract 7

In the late 1970s, the Sultanate of Oman had only a handful of health professionals. People had to travel up to four days just to reach a hospital, where hundreds of patients would already be waiting in line to see one of the few (expatriate) doctors. All this changed in less than a generation. Oman invested consistently in a national health service and sustained that investment over time. There is now a dense network of 180 local, district and regional health facilities staffed by over 5000 health workers providing almost universal access to health care for Oman's 2.2 million citizens. Life expectancy at birth, which was less than 60 years towards the end of the 1970s, now surpasses 74 years.

WHO (2008). The World Health Report 2008. *Primary Health Care: Now more than ever*. World Health Organization.

Extract 8

There is a growing body of evidence demonstrating that it is relative inequalities in income and material resources, coupled with the resulting social exclusion and marginalization, which is linked to poor health (Blane et al 1996, Wilkinson 1996). In the developed world it is not the richest countries which have the best health but the most egalitarian. Whilst the exact mechanisms linking social inequality to ill health are uncertain, it is likely that both physiological pathways (e.g. the effect of chronic stress on the immunological process) and social pathways (e.g. support networks) are relevant. Healthy, egalitarian societies are more socially cohesive and have a stronger community life.

Naidoo, J. and Wills, J. (2000). *Health Promotion: Foundations for practice* (2nd edn.). Bailliere Tindall/Elsevier.

Extract 9

In the United States, African Americans develop high blood pressure more often, and at an earlier age, than whites and Mexican Americans do. Among African Americans, more women than men have the condition.

Race or Ethnic Group	Men (%)	Women (%)
African Americans	42.2	44.1
Mexican Americans	24.8	28.6
Whites	31.2	28.3
All	31.8	30.3

Centers for Disease Control and Prevention: www.cdc.gov/bloodpressure/facts.htm.

c In pairs, compare your notes. Identify any gaps in the information in the table in 1.2a. What additional information would you now look for before you start writing the first part of the essay?

2 Thinking about what you already know

2.1 You are going to read an extract from a textbook on the subject of how different cultures perceive health and the consequent treatment of ill health.

The extract refers to 'western scientific medicine'. Before you read, discuss the following questions in pairs and report back your answers to the class.
1 What do you understand by the term 'western scientific medicine'?
2 What alternatives to western scientific medicine do you know?
3 Do you have any experience of these alternatives?

▶ *Supporting claims and referencing*
Unit 2, 13 p35; Unit 3, 10 pp48–50; Appendix 3 p168

3 Preparing for essay writing

 Study tip *Remember that in your academic writing you should include a reference to the source of any ideas that are not your own.*

3.1 The following statements are from the first draft of a student's essay, *Approaches to health care*. For each statement, decide whether the student needs to include a reference to the textbook source below. Tick (✓) if the idea is mentioned in the extract and cross (✗) if it is not.

1 Western scientific medicine is not only used in modern western societies.   ✓
2 Some health care workers from other societies train in the west.   _____
3 Many health care workers are trained to believe that health means no illness or disease.   _____
4 The media tries to encourage western scientific medicine.   _____
5 People often take for granted that a particular view of health is true without ever questioning whether it is true or not.   _____
6 The British National Health Service provides both western scientific medicine and alternative therapies.   _____
7 Some traditional Chinese medical treatments have been shown to be as effective as western scientific medicine.   _____
8 There is a parallel between economics and health in western societies.   _____

The western scientific medical model of health

A In modern western societies, and in many other societies as well, the dominant professional view of health adopted by most health care workers during their training and practice is labelled western scientific medicine. Western scientific medicine operates with a narrow view of health, which is often used to refer to no disease or no illness. In this sense, health is a negative term, defined more by what it is not than what it is.

▶ *Connecting with this/these*
G&V 3, p149

B This view of health is extremely influential, as it underpins much of the training and ethos of a wide variety of   5
health workers. These definitions become more powerful because they are used in a variety of contexts, not just in professional circles. For example, the media often present this view of health, disease and illness in dramas set in hospitals or in documentaries about health issues. By these means, professional definitions become known and accepted in society at large.

▶ *Referring to quantities*
G&V 1, p148

Cultural views of health

C We are able to think about health using the language of scientific medicine because that is part of our cultural heritage.   10
We do so as a matter of course, and think it is self-evident or common sense. However, other societies and cultures have their own common-sense ways of talking about health which are very different. The Ashanti view disease as the outcome of malign human or supernatural agencies, and diagnosis is a matter of determining who has been offended. Treatment includes ceremonies to propitiate these spirits as an integral part of the process. Ways of thinking about health and disease reflect the basic preoccupations of society, and dominant views of society and the world.   15
Anthropologists refer to this phenomenon as the cultural specificity of notions of health and disease.

D In any multicultural society such as the UK, a variety of cultural views coexist at any one time. For example, traditional Chinese medicine is based on the dichotomy of Yin and Yang, female and male, hot and cold, which is applied to symptoms, diet and treatments, such as acupuncture and Chinese herbal medicine. Alternative practitioners offer therapies based on these cultural views of health and disease alongside (or increasingly within) the National Health   20
Service, which is based on scientific medicine.

▶ *Evaluative adjectives and adverbs*
G&V 2, p148

E The influence of culture on views of health is most apparent when other societies are being studied. However, Crawford (1984) applies the same analysis to western society, with provocative results. Crawford argues that capitalism is the bedrock of western society. Capitalism is an economic system centred on maximum production and consumption of goods through the free market. These economic goals have their parallel in views about health. Health is concerned with both release (consumption) and discipline (production) (Fig. 1.4). Hence the coexistence of apparently opposite beliefs in relation to health.

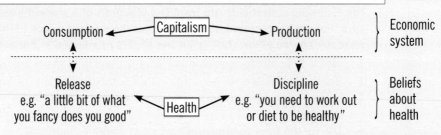

Figure 1.4 Cultural views about health in capitalist society. Adapted from Crawford (1984)

Naidoo, J. and Wills, J. (2000) *Health Promotion: Foundations for practice* (2nd edn.). Bailliere Tindall/ Elsevier.

3.2 a In pairs, you are going to report back on the main ideas in the extract. Read the text in detail and make relevant notes.

- Student A, prepare to explain differences between western scientific medicine and other views of health (paragraphs A–D).
- Student B, prepare to explain Crawford's view of health in a capitalist society (paragraph E and Figure 1.4).

b Using your notes, report back to your partner.

4 Vocabulary in context: inferring the meaning of words

4.1 Try to infer the meaning of the words in bold in the following extracts from the text in 3.1. Use the questions to help you. Use a dictionary to check your answers.

1 The Ashanti view disease as the outcome of **malign** human or **supernatural** agencies, ...
   - What other words could go in this space?
   - Do you know the meaning of other words with the prefix *super-*? *Supernatural* is contrasted with *human*, so what might it mean?
2 Treatment includes ceremonies to **propitiate** these spirits ...
   - Are these spirits good or bad? What might a ceremony aim to do to these spirits?
3 ... the **dichotomy** of Yin and Yang, female and male, hot and cold ...
   - Do you know what the prefix *di-* means? Do you know any other words with this prefix?
   - Do the pairs of terms that follow give you a clue to the meaning?
4 Crawford argues that capitalism is the **bedrock** of western society.
   - What two words make up *bedrock*? Does this give you a clue to its meaning?

5 Understanding connections in texts: *this/these*

Expressions using this/these + noun are often used in academic writing to refer back to something that has been mentioned earlier in the text.

5.1 Find the phrases in bold with *this* or *these* in the text in 3.1 and explain what they refer to.

1 In **this sense**, health is a negative term, ... (lines 3–4) *'this sense' refers to the definition of health given in the previous sentence i.e. no disease or illness.*
2 **This view of health** is extremely influential, ... (line 5)
3 **These definitions** become more powerful ... (line 6)
4 By **these means**, professional definitions become known ... (line 8)
5 Treatment includes ceremonies to propitiate **these spirits** ... (line 14)
6 Anthropologists refer to **this phenomenon** ... (line 16)
7 Alternative practitioners offer therapies based on **these cultural views of health and disease** ... (lines 19–20)
8 **These economic goals** have their parallel ... (line 25)

> → *This/these*
> **G&V** 3, p149

6 Developing hedging skills

6.1 In pairs, insert the hedges in the box in an appropriate place in the following sentences. Look back at text 3.1 to check your answers.

apparently	most	much of	often

1 Western scientific medicine is adopted by health care workers in their training and practice. (lines 1–2)
2 This view of health underpins the training and ethos of a wide variety of health workers. (lines 5–6)
3 The media presents this view of health in dramas and documentaries. (lines 7–8)
4 Health is concerned with both release and discipline, and so opposite beliefs in relation to health coexist. (line 25–26)

b Can you suggest different hedges that could be used in these places?

c Are there other ideas in any of these sentences that could be hedged?

Listening and speaking

7 Summarising what has been said

Often we summarise what someone else has said before making a related point ourselves. For example:

Introducing the summary

The summary

Introducing a related point

> "Can I just make a point here? As Jackie said earlier on, governments need to play a part in educating people about health and life style. And I think in particular, they need to focus on young people – telling them about diet, for example ..."

7.1 ◀)10.1 Listen to eight extracts from presentations and group discussions about health education. For each extract, decide what is being summarised.

a What was said during a small group discussion _____ _____
b An entire presentation __1__ _____
c What a previous presenter said _____ _____
d What the speaker has said so far during a presentation _____ _____

7.2 Match the phrases from the extracts (1–8) to the contexts (a–d) in 7.1. Listen again and check your answers.

1 One of the things that Mei mentioned was that ... __c__
2 Our general view was that ... _____
3 Okay, let me just recap so far. _____
4 Up to now I've tried to ... _____
5 Overall, we thought that ... _____
6 Let me round off by summarising my main points. _____
7 I want to pick up one of the topics that Zak touched on briefly. _____
8 I'll finish by giving a brief summary of my talk. _____

7.3 Here are some useful phrases for introducing a related point. Can you add any more?

· And I think ...
· Yes, and also ...
· A similar point is ...

 Study tip *Being able to summarise what has been said before, either by you or by another speaker, is an important skill. For example, in a presentation you may want to give a summary at the end of each main section to help the audience follow what you are saying.*

7.4 (◄►10.2) **Listen to three extracts from tutorials on** *Health and lifestyle*. **In pairs, after each extract summarise what the speaker said and make a related point based on the notes.**

1

Smoking is still one of the main causes ...

Olga

Parents shouldn't set a bad example to their children – if we don't want children to smoke, their parents shouldn't either.

2

If you don't exercise you have a higher risk ...

Maria

Can be difficult for people to fit exercise into their daily lives – busy with jobs, study, travel, child care, etc.

3

It's important for companies ...

Ben

Companies often want to create good work-life balance for employees. But may not know what's best. Up to employees to tell managers how best to help (e.g. flexible working, child-care facilities).

8   Evaluating visual aids

Many speakers in presentations, seminars and tutorials present words and images visually using PowerPoint, handouts, a whiteboard or blackboard, projector transparencies, or a flip chart.

8.1   a   **In groups, think of three advantages and three disadvantages of using each of these visual aids in your presentations. One member of the group should take notes during the discussion.**

b   **Report back to the class. Use the expressions you saw in 7.2 and 7.3 to summarise your group's discussion and to add to what other groups have reported.**

9   Pronunciation: stress in compound nouns 2

➤ Stress in compound nouns 1

Unit 8, 7 p116

9.1   a   (◄►10.3) **Listen to the following sentences and underline the part which has the syllable with main stress in the compound noun** *mental health*.

1   There's a link between exercise and *mental health*.

2   There's a link between physical and *mental health*.

b   **Why do you think there is a difference in the stress pattern?**

9.2   a   **In pairs, take it in turns to say the following** *adjective + noun* **compound nouns. Put the main stress on the syllable in bold in the second part (the noun).**

1	human deve**lop**ment	**6**	economic deve**lop**ment
2	industrial **waste**	**7**	municipal **waste**
3	natural **sci**ence	**8**	social **sci**ence
4	direct **ob**ject	**9**	indirect **ob**ject
5	micro-eco**nom**ics	**10**	macro-eco**nom**ics

b   (◄►10.4) **Listen and check your pronunciation.**

9.3 a When *adjective* + *noun* compound nouns are used in context, main stress may move to the first part in order to show a contrast. In pairs, underline the syllable with the main stress in the compound nouns in italics in the following sentences.

1 The UN has come up with an index of *human development*.
2 *Human development* is the ultimate aim of *economic development*.
3 One of the key problems to be overcome is *industrial waste*.
4 The landfill tax has probably led to *industrial waste* entering *municipal waste*.
5 The *social sciences* include subjects studying the social life of human groups.
6 Some methods from the *natural sciences* are applied in the *social sciences*.
7 What's the *direct object* in this sentence?
8 In English, the *indirect object* usually precedes the *direct object*.
9 He was a specialist in *micro-economics*.
10 The course begins with *micro-economics* and goes on to *macro-economics*.

b ◀)10.5 Listen and check your answers.

c In pairs, take it in turns to say the sentences.

Writing

10 Contrasting information

In both academic speech and writing, we often need to contrast two or more items. For example, we might contrast:
a advantages with disadvantages.
b one definition with another.
c certain research findings with different research findings.

10.1 Read these extracts from written academic texts. Which of the three types of contrast (a–c) do they contain?

Extract 1

> 1 Health has two common meanings in everyday use, one negative and one positive. 2 The negative definition of health is the absence of disease or illness. 3 This is the meaning of health within the western scientific medical model. 4 The positive definition of health is a state of well-being, interpreted by the World Health Organization in its constitution as 'a state of complete physical, mental and social well-being, not merely the absence of disease or infirmity' (WHO 1946).

Naidoo, J. and Wills, J. (2000). *Health Promotion: Foundations for practice* (2nd edn.). Bailliere Tindall/Elsevier.

Extract 2

> 1 Over the years, coaches and athletes have reported beneficial effects of caffeine for endurance exercise such as cycling or cross-country skiing. 2 So far, however, research has produced inconsistent results. 3 Several small studies have shown that the caffeine in two or three cups of brewed coffee (220 to 330 milligrams), taken within a few hours of endurance exercise, postponed exhaustion in well-conditioned athletes. 4 But other studies have found little or no benefit from caffeine.

University of California at Berkeley (1995). *The New Wellness Encyclopedia*. University of California at Berkeley.

Extract 3

> 1 Consumption refers to the goods, services, energy and resources that are used up by people, institutions and societies. 2 It is a phenomenon with both positive and negative dimensions. 3 On the one hand, rising levels of consumption around the world mean that people are living under better conditions than in times past. 4 Consumption is linked to economic development – as living standards rise, people are able to afford more food, clothing, personal items, leisure time, holidays, cars and so forth. 5 On the other hand, consumption can have negative impacts as well. 6 Consumption patterns can damage the environmental resource base and exacerbate patterns of inequality.

OECD (2009). *Health at a glance: OECD indicators*. OECD.

10.2 Contrast texts often follow the three stages shown in this table. Match the sentences in extracts 1–3 in 10.1 to the stages (a–c). Write the sentence numbers in the table.

Stage	Extract 1	Extract 2	Extract 3
a Introduce topic/contrast	*1*		
b First contrasting item			
c Second contrasting item			

10.3 In pairs, underline phrases in extracts 1–3 which might be useful for writing contrast texts. Write the phrases in the appropriate column in the table.

Introduce topic/contrast	First contrasting item	Second contrasting item
... two common meanings in everyday use, one negative and one positive.	*The negative definition of ... is ...*	*The positive definition of ... is ...*

10.4 Add the following phrases for contrast texts to the table in 10.3.

In contrast ...   According to (author + date) ...   Other researchers ...   However, ...
A number of writers have claimed that ...   There are divergent views on the subject.

10.5 Write short contrast paragraphs based on the following notes. The main topic of each paragraph is in bold. Follow the stages in 10.2 and use appropriate language from this section.

1 poverty – *definition problematic*
a monetary approach; poverty = having an income of less than a certain level per day vs.
b multidimensional approach; poverty = includes a number of factors e.g. income, health, literacy, access to safe water

2 biofuels *(= fuel made from living things e.g. plants)*
+ produce less CO₂ than fossil fuels; cheaper than petrol (when cost of petrol high)
– natural forests cleared to grow crops for biofuel (so loss of habitat); farmers may grow crops for biofuel rather than food (make more money from it)

3 online learning *– research shows: increased access to education (esp. more mature students) (Murray, 2008); students contribute more in online learning environments than in face-to-face classroom situations (Ryman, 2006) vs. high dropout rates in online learning (Thomas, 2010); students discouraged by isolation of online learning (so poor motivation) (Karlson, 2006).*

11 Taking a stance: expressing disagreement

11.1 Read the following contrast text and in pairs discuss whose views are being contrasted. Underline the different views that you find.

1 For Illich (1975), health is a personal task which people must be free to pursue autonomously. 2 Doctors and health workers contribute to ill health by taking over people's responsibility for their health. 3 In addition, the practice of medicine leads to iatrogenic ill health caused by doctors and health workers. 4 Health workers come to be seen as disabling elements in the lives of ordinary people. 5a Whilst it is possible to agree with Illich that doctors and health workers wield enormous power in people's lives, which is not always exercised in accordance with their patients' wishes or beliefs, 5b it does not follow that we would all be better off without any health care system at all. 6 Medicine has made some remarkable contributions to people's health (for example the widespread use of antibiotics discovered in the 1950s).

Naidoo, J. and Wills, J. (2000). *Health Promotion: Foundations for practice* (2nd edn.). Bailliere Tindall/Elsevier.

In academic writing, disagreement with, for example, what another writer says or with a course of action, often follows the four stages shown in this table.

Stage	Sentence(s)	Useful language for each stage
a Describe the other position		A number of writers have … It has been suggested that … *Author (date)* claims that … According to *author (date)* …
b Acknowledge the truth of some part of this position		Although … / Even though … This is true to some extent … It is no doubt the case that … It can certainly be argued that …
c Disagree with this position		However, … On the other hand … Nevertheless, … In fact, …/ In reality, … Having said that, …
d Support your position with evidence		For example, …

11.2 a Match the sentences (1–6) in the text in **11.1** to the stages (a–d). Write the sentence numbers in the table.

b Add any useful language from this text to the third column.

11.3 a Read the first stage (Describe the other position) of the following extracts from contrast texts (1–3). In pairs, discuss what the content of the other stages might be.

Extract 1

A number of writers (e.g. Duff, 1989; Harbord, 1992) have encouraged the constructive use of the students' mother tongue in the English as a foreign language classroom.

Extract 2

A considerable amount of advertising on television is aimed at children, promoting toys, games, food, drink, and so on, and concerns have been expressed about its impact. For example, since 1991 Sweden has banned all television advertising aimed at children under the age of 12.

Extract 3

It has been suggested that parents should be held responsible when their children play truant from school. Zoltman (1998), for example, argues that the possibility of prosecution encourages parents to take a more active role in the lives of their children and this will eventually reduce levels of juvenile crime.

b Write sentences for the other stages of each extract using your ideas and the language in **11.2**.

c In pairs, compare your texts and make any improvements you think are necessary.

12 Writing practice

12.1 Look again at the essay title in **1.2**: *Despite the increase in life expectancy over the last 200 years, not all groups of people have the same chances of good health. What factors affect health?* Do you think it is a *describe*, *discuss* or *defend* type essay? Write an essay with this title of about 1,000 words. Use the information in this unit and, if necessary, research other relevant information.

Grammar and vocabulary

Grammar and vocabulary
· Referring to quantities
· Evaluative adjectives and adverbs
· Phrases connecting sentences: *this/these*
· Non-finite relative clauses

1 Referring to quantities

A number of quantifying expressions are commonly used in academic writing to refer to a quantity of something without saying the exact number or amount (e.g. a wide variety of health workers).

1.1 Look at the table and decide whether the quantifying expressions are usually followed by a plural noun or an uncountable noun.

Expression	Followed by
1 a(n) (…) variety of … (e.g. a great variety of environments; a large variety of tasks)	*plural noun*
2 a great/good deal of … (e.g. a great deal of money; a good deal of time)	*uncountable noun*
3 a (…) number of … (e.g. a substantial number of patients; a small number of computers)	
4 a(n) (…) amount of … (e.g. a considerable amount of work; a limited amount of material)	
5 various … (= many different) (e.g. various kinds of bird; various aspects)	
6 several … (= more than two or three, but not many) (e.g. several occasions; several years)	
7 numerous … (= many) (e.g. numerous examples; numerous studies)	
8 a substantial number of (= a large amount) (e.g. a substantial number of birds)	

1.2 Write two statements about each of the words in the box using the quantifying expressions in 1.1. For example:

A substantial number of migrating birds are killed by hunters around the Mediterranean.
A great deal of research has been conducted on how birds fly.

> animals   birds   films   knowledge
> languages   occupations   technology

2 Evaluative adjectives and adverbs

One way in which writers express their views in academic texts is through their choice of evaluative adjectives and adverbs.

2.1 a Match the beginnings of the sentences (1–6), ending in evaluative adjectives, to the endings (a–f).

1 They made the exciting +   _b_
2 Her work offers a fascinating + _____
3 The results of their work had a significant + _____
4 Hatton (2003) raises the interesting + _____
5 Flowerdew (2007) makes a useful + _____
6 The article provides a valuable + _____

a question of how genes are controlled between the two nuclei.
b ~~discovery of a geothermal hot spot at the bottom of 3 km thick ice.~~
c impact on the practice of cost engineering.
d contribution to evolutionary research on entrepreneurship.
e insight into life in Victorian England.
f distinction between scholarly and practitioner-oriented work.

b Complete the following sentences using an evaluative adjective and noun of your own. There may be more than one possible answer.

1 In the conclusion she makes _____ _____ on how to improve team working.
2 Jackson's findings have _____ _____ for agricultural water management in the tropics.
3 In general, the results showed a _____ _____ between metropolitan and non-metropolitan areas.
4 Sinclair played a _____ _____ in establishing the field of applied linguistics.
5 This research was an _____ _____ in changing childcare practices.

A number of evaluative adverbs can be used at the beginning of a sentence to express the writer's view of what follows.

> ❷ *Research shows that the most frequent sentence-initial evaluative adverb in the written academic corpus is* interestingly. *What do you think are the next most common? The first letters are given to help you.*
>
> 1 *Interestingly*   2 N_____ sur_____
> 3 Sig_____   4 Sur_____
> 5 Imp_____   6 Cur_____
> 7 Rem_____   8 Pre_____
> 9 Od_____ (enough) 10 Str_____ (enough)

2.2 The following sentences describe the findings from research into the career plans of university students studying Business Studies. Express your view of these findings by adding an evaluative adverb from the Corpus research box on page 148.

1 _____, less than half of the students wanted to get a job immediately after completing their university degree.

2 _____, nearly 90% said they wanted to retire before they were 60 years old.

3 _____, 60% of male students said that they wanted to run their own business while the corresponding figure for female students was 42%.

4 _____, only one student said that they wanted to become a university teacher.

5 _____, all of the students said that their Business Studies degree would improve their career prospects.

> 🎓 **Focus on your subject** *As you read texts in your subject area, identify evaluative adverbs that are often used. Make a note of these and try to use them when you give evaluations in your own writing.*

3   Phrases connecting sentences: *this/these*

A number of common phrases that have the structure preposition + this/these + noun *are used in academic writing at the start of a sentence to connect the sentence to what has come before. For example:*

> Western scientific medicine operates with a narrow view of health, which is often used to refer to no disease or no illness. **In this sense**, health is a negative term, defined more by what it is not than what it is.

> … the media often present this view of health, disease and illness in dramas set in hospitals or in documentaries about health issues. **By these means**, professional definitions become known and accepted in society at large.

3.1 Complete the following phrases using a preposition in the box.

At   By   For   From   In   On

1 _____ this reason/purpose, …
2 _____ this regard/respect/way, …
3 _____ this method/criterion/process, …
4 _____ this point/stage/juncture, …
5 _____ this basis/issue/point, …
6 _____ this perspective / viewpoint / point of view, …

3.2 Match the beginnings (1–6) to the endings (a–f) of the following extracts. Connect them using a connecting phrase from 3.1. The first letter of the noun is given to help you.

1 Hanson's (1998) study looked at high school students, while Franks (2005) investigated students in their first year at university. __*b*__

2 Some writers believe that a text has a single, correct meaning within it that is independent of the reader. _____

3 The transport costs of natural gas are high, so most of it is consumed in the countries where it is produced. _____

4 Tramcon began to export to North America in 2004. _____

5 Lacy (2009) claims that capitalism is expanding the gap between rich and poor. However, _____

6 Each informant was asked to operate a mobile phone, a personal data assistant (PDA), and digital still camera (DSC). _____

a _____ this s_____, it had a workforce of only about 50.

b __*For*__ this *reason*, it is difficult to compare their results.

c _____ this p_____, a reader's job is to try to find the "correct" meaning in the text.

d _____ this m_____, we were able to compare the use of these hand-held devices.

e _____ this r_____, it is similar to electricity and, to a lesser extent, to coal.

f _____ this p_____, there is considerable disagreement among economists.

4   Non-finite relative clauses

4.1 Look again at the text on pages 141–142 and answer the following questions.

1 How many non-finite relative clauses can you find in the text? Underline the past participle at the beginning of each clause.

2 How many full relative clauses with a relative pronoun (e.g. *which*, *who*) can you find?

3 Which of these full relative clauses could be reduced to a non-finite relative clause?

Lecture skills E

Preparing for lectures

1 Overcoming problems in listening to lectures

1.1 a ▐E.1 Watch Larissa, Frederike and Zaneta talking about the problems they faced in listening to lectures in English.

 Larissa
 Frederike
 Zaneta

Tick (✓) the problems that each student mentions.

Problems in listening to lectures in English	Larissa	Frederike	Zaneta	You
1 Understanding fast speech				
2 Understanding colloquial language				
3 Understanding specialist terminology				
4 Understanding the large amount of content				
5 Concentrating for a long time				
6 Understanding lecture organisation				

b Have you experienced any of the problems above? Tick the two biggest problems for you, and in pairs discuss your answers.

1.2 In pairs, suggest a possible solution for each of the problems in 1.1a.

Listening

2 Understanding specialised terms

Most lecturers use lectures to introduce and explain specialised terms that are important in their subject area or important for understanding the topic presented.

2.1 a ▐E.2 Watch three extracts from Dr Mormina's lecture where she is defining some specialised terms, and make notes on the following terms.

1   modern humans _____

2   a parsimonious explanation _____

3   interbreeding _____

b In pairs, compare your notes.

Language focus

2.2 Dr Mormina explains the following specialised terms twice during her lecture. For each term, watch the first extract and make notes on the meaning. Then watch the second extract and check your notes.

1 (E.3) interglacial _____

2 (E.4) glacial maximum _____

3 (E.5) mitochondrial DNA _____

 Study tip When an unfamiliar term is introduced and explained in a lecture, try to write it down in your notes. (If it is particularly important, it may appear on a slide or the board.) If you don't understand the explanation given by the lecturer, listen for the term used later in the lecture and try to pick up more clues to its meaning.

3 Understanding reasons

3.1 (E.6) Watch six extracts from Dr Vlamis's lecture, *Introduction to Macroeconomics*. Underline one of the following expressions in each pair that he uses to signal that he is giving a reason.

1 which is why / because
2 because of / on account of
3 for that reason / this is one explanation why
4 it has to do with / as a result of
5 the cause of this / that's why
6 that explains why / that means

3.2 (E.6) It is often important to record reasons in your notes. Watch the extracts again and complete the following notes with the reasons Dr Vlamis gives. In pairs, compare your notes.

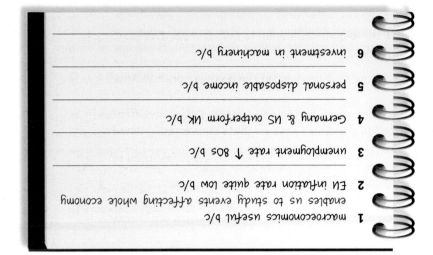

1 macroeconomics useful b/c
enables us to study events affecting whole economy
2 EU inflation rate quite low b/c
3 unemployment rate ↑ 80s b/c
4 Germany & US outperform UK b/c
5 personal disposable income b/c
6 investment in machinery b/c

4 Understanding signals of incomplete information

Lectures are often intended only to give you an outline of a topic. It may be that the lecturer will give further details in a later lecture, or you may be expected to fill the gaps in what the lecturer has said from follow-up reading. Sometimes the lecturer will signal that they are giving incomplete information.

4.1 a Read the following extract from the beginning of Dr Vlamis's lecture and underline language that signals he is giving incomplete information about a topic.

I'm gonna just give you a brief introduction of *What is macroeconomics?* and the main questions that macroeconomists are interested [in].

b What does the language you have underlined tell you about what Dr Vlamis will *not* be speaking about in his lecture?

4.2 ▣ E.7 **Listen and complete the following extracts from the lectures by Dr Mormina and Dr Vlamis, where the lecturers signal they are giving incomplete information about a topic.**

1 ... I'm going to be talking _____ about natural selection and adaptation to different environments ...

2 ... there are only small pockets where people have retained the hunter-gatherer lifestyle. So I _____ but one of the things that have interested me most over the years ...

3 ... The governments they _____ have two policy tools in their hands. ...

4 ... if you want to disinflate you have to be ready to accept the higher cost in terms of higher unemployment. Um so _____ why unemployment rate increased in the in the in the eighties. ...

5 Understanding forward and backward reference

To help you recognise connections between parts of a lecture, lecturers often refer forwards to what they will say later, or backwards to what they have already said.

5.1 a ▣ E.8 **Watch four extracts from Dr Vlamis's lecture. Part of each extract is given below. Write down the phrase that follows. Does it refer forwards or backwards?**

1 ... without getting into much detail about specific sectors or specific products.
So as I said _____ (backwards)

2 ... Why was there this huge, erm, increase in inflation rate in this country?
And _____

3 ... Okay. So it has certain limitations. We'll _____

4 ... So increases in real gross domestic or gross national product I will _____

b **Watch the extracts again and make brief notes on what the phrase you have written in 5.1a refers to. For example:**

1 *So as I said ... some key issues in Macroeconomics: Inflation*

c **In pairs, compare your notes.**

5.2 **In pairs, think of words and phrases which you might use to refer forwards and backwards in academic writing. Discuss whether you would use the phrases Dr Vlamis used in his lecture.**

6 Listening and annotating slides

6.1 a **You are going to watch another extract from Dr Vlamis's lecture. Before you do, check that you know the meaning of the following words. Use a dictionary where necessary to help you.**

decelerate   domestic   histogram   remuneration

b ▣ E.9 **Watch the extract and annotate the following slides. Use symbols and abbreviations that you find helpful.**

Unit B, 6 p68

► symbols and abbreviations

More key issues in macroeconomics

• Economic growth
  – increases in real GNP

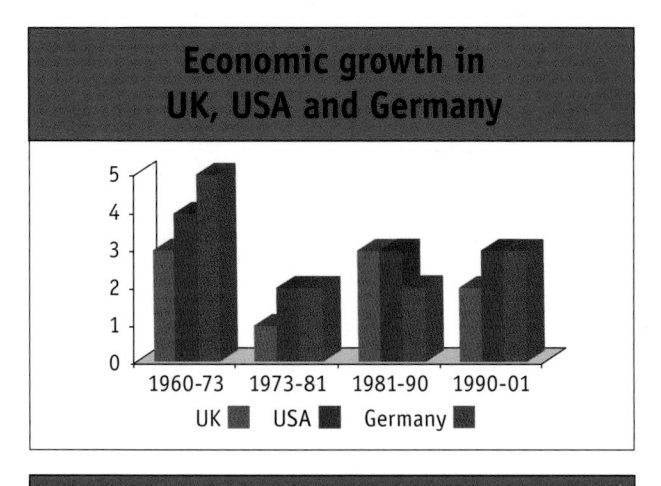

Economic growth in UK, USA and Germany

1960-73   1973-81   1981-90   1990-01

UK ■   USA ■   Germany ■

GDP and GNP

- Gross domestic product (GDP)
- Gross national product (GNP)
- GNP =
- GDP measures the value of what is produced in this country
- GNI / GNP

c In pairs, compare your notes.

7 Writing up your notes

Sometimes you will write up the notes which you took in lectures as parts of assignments (e.g. essays).

7.1 a (▮ E.10) Watch an extract from Dr Vlamis's lecture, where he compares unemployment in the UK, USA and Germany from the 1960s. Take notes on the extract, and then in pairs compare your notes.

b Write up your notes in a short paragraph and then in pairs compare your paragraphs.

8 Overcoming problems

As you gain experience of listening to lectures in English, it is likely that you will understand more and more. However, if you continue to face problems, here is some advice on what action you might take.

- *Do more preparatory reading.*
- *Record lectures and listen again later.*
- *Talk to your lecturers about your difficulties.*

8.1 a In pairs, evaluate each of these pieces of advice and answer the following questions.

1 Is the advice useful?
2 What problems might arise in putting it into practice?
3 Do you have any other advice on listening to lectures?

b Report back your ideas to the class.

The transcripts of lectures and interviews are from authentic recordings and there may be some slips of the tongue or grammatical errors which are normal for both native and non-native speakers. These are shown as [*]

Academic orientation

◄0.1

Zaneta: Thinking about interaction between the student and a lecturer, teacher in England I think there's a big difference between the relationship which I experienced in Poland and here. Er, because in Poland –in my country –it's more formal so you have to call ['] "Mr" or "Mrs" or "Professor" you're not allowed to just call the person by its[*] first name because it's considered rude. But I think it's not also nice because it builds a barrier between you and the lecturer and what I find here –which I'm really happy about and I've been always saying that– that you can call your lecturer, or your professor doesn't matter whether he's got Master or PhD, you can actually call him simply by his or her first name. What, what I think also, erm, makes you feel more comfortable if you've got any problem, to go to a person and talk to them.

Unit 1

◄1.1

Fei He: Mhm. When I studied in Chinese university I think students are passive. That is a huge problem. And students seldom find papers by them, by themselves they just learn what the teacher taught. So the only ac- academic sources is the textbooks. Students just work on their textbooks and then take the examinations. That is all fine, you can pass the examination get your degree. But this thing is different in British university[*]. You have to find the useful resources by yourself. You have to know, you have got to know where you can find the resources. There are many resources used in British universities not only for the textbook monographs online journal papers. Er, the three resources are very, very important.

Talk 1

◄1.2 – 1.4

I want to begin by talking about the different voting systems that democracies have to choose from, and here I'll focus on the three main ones. First, there's proportional representation. This is when the number of seats a political party wins matches the number of votes the party gets. Second, there's alternative voting. What's meant by this is that voters rank candidates in order of preference – first, second, third, and so on. Essentially, the candidate who gets more than half the votes is elected. Third, there's the so-called first-past-the-post system. In other words, a candidate just has to win more votes than any of their rivals in a particular area, not a majority of the votes. Let me go on to talk about each of these in more detail, and I'll discuss the advantages and disadvantages of each ...

Talk 2

◄2.1

What I'd like to do is outline the ways in which governments raise money. Basically, they do this from taxing the people and businesses in the country. In this session I'm going to highlight three major types of taxation, although there are plenty of others that I'll come on to later. The first one is income tax. That's to say, the government takes a share of any income earned by individuals through their work or investments, and of any profits made by companies. The second is sales tax. What happens here is that a percentage is added to the price of any goods or services bought – you, the customer, pays this and it goes back to the government. Thirdly, there's property tax. In this case, owners of buildings – houses, offices, and so on – pay tax to the government, with the amount they pay depending on the value of the property.

Unit 2

◄2.1

Can you have a look at Figure 2 on the second page of your handout? That's the horizontal bar chart. Has everybody got it? Right. OK, what this chart shows is the causes of death in the United States. The figures are for the annual death rate on average for the last decade. The causes of death are listed on the left, and the death rate represented by the length of the bar. So, for example, the death rate from homicide – that's the fifth figure down – was 9.9 per 100,000. Although there's a lot here of interest, I'd like to pick out three pieces of information. The first is that by far the major cause of death is disease. The figure is 652 per 100,000. The second is that, apart from car accidents, which kill large numbers of people, death from accidents – in falls, drowning, airline crashes, and so on – are relatively small in number. And the third – and of particular relevance to this talk - is that natural hazards kill a relatively tiny number of people. Even if we add together deaths caused by floods, lightning, earthquakes, and so on, they kill far fewer people than those who die in fires. So, the main thing I want to highlight here is that while the risks of natural hazards can sometimes seem very serious, in a country like the United States, the dangers are relatively small for the population in general. However, hazards like flooding and earthquakes can be a serious risk in particular areas, and potentially could be dangerous for large numbers of people. And it's these hazards I want to focus on in the rest of the talk.

◄2.3

1 Cardinal numbers
a 0; 101; 466
b 1200; 1201; 12,245
c 111,456; 1,222,567
d 100; 1000; 10,000
e 100,000; 1,000,000

2 Ordinal numbers
a 1st; 2nd; 3rd
b 14th; 21st; 32nd
c 100th; 1000th

3 Dates
a 1234; 1954; 1987
b 2008; 2012; 2020
c 21st May 1956; 2/9/1989

4 Decimals and fractions
a 0.1; 0.02; 0.009
b 3.4; 56.78; 39.197
c ½; 1/3; ¾

◄2.4

1 So, for example, the death rate from homicide – that's the fifth figure down – was 9.9 per 100,000.
2 The second is that, apart from car accidents, which kill large numbers of people, death from accidents – in falls, drowning, airline crashes, and so on – are relatively small in number.
3 And the third – and of particular relevance to this talk - is that natural hazards kill a relatively tiny number of people.

Lecture Skills A

▣ A.1

Extract 1

Dr Moseley: By Shakespeare' - again in quotation marks - we can signify William, son of John, born probably in 1564 in Stratford where he died in 1616. A man who was variously referred to as, 'an upstart crow', our 'Roscius,' 'sweet Mr Shakespeare' and who was known as a writer, a poet, a successful plays and a very shrewd buyer of real estate. He is quite an interesting chap to talk about and to speculate about.

Extract 2

Dr Mormina: The fossil record is difficult to interpret. So when you see a skull and it … the skull is so old and it's got has got lots of cracks you really, you're really hard pressed to say this, this is human. And that's why the fossil record has lots of ambiguities. The interpretation of the fossil record is full of ambiguities and these ambiguities gave rise to a number of hypotheses with regard to the origin of modern humans.

Extract 3

Dr Hunt: … the force is at right angles to the velocity, which means that it doesn't change how fast I'm going, it changes the direction I'm going. So the ball doesn't get any slower but the direction of its travel is continuously changing. It is accelerating because the direction changes and that's very important as we'll see later when we start thinking about, er, spin and angular momentum. Now what I wanna do now is really start getting into the, the thick of spinning things. Now I want to start talking about what happens, er, as you change the geometry of spinning things and for this I'm gonna need a a volunteer who'd be willing to come. You wanna volunteer for me OK? Very good I've got a willing volunteer. Now I have here a spinning platform you see so what I'm gonna try and, er, emulate is ice skater ballet dancer type thing. Erm, and what you wanna do is, I want you to stand on there. Your name is?

Volunteer: Steve.

Dr Hunt: Steve. So stand on there Steve OK.

A.2

Dr Mormina: So I'm going to be talking to you, erm, about some of the evolutionary mechanisms that are responsible for generating, er, the astonishing biological diversity of human populations. Er, I'm going to be talking about them on mostly from a biological perspective but I will also make some reference to cultural evolution. Erm, in particular I want to focus on three of these mechanisms, er, migration adaptation and culture but I have to say that I'm going to focus mostly on migration.

A.3

Dr Mormina: Right. Erm, this is the outline of, of this talk I'm going to spend a little bit of time giving you the science behind so you won't escape there is a bit of scientific talk. Erm, I'm going to give you a general background on these biological mechanism generating diversity, er, mutation natural selection and gene flow migrations. And the rest of the talk is going to be about how these mechanisms have contributed to structure the biological diversity that we see today in human populations. So I'm, I'm going to be talking about the role of geography in migrations in human prehistory. Erm, I'm going to be talking a little bit about natural selection and adaptation to different environments and the role of, of culture in, in all this process.

A.4

Dr Mormina: OK so let's start with this first part. I like using this picture because to me it represents the diversity of, of our human species. Er, as you can see we come in different sizes and different shapes and different colours. And, why is that?

A.5 See transcript on page 40.

A.6

Dr Mormina: I said gene flow also, er, plays a role in generating diversity. And if you think, erm, have represented here two populations: population A and population B these are two different populations. Erm, one could think individuals in these populations have different characteristics look different, erm, what happens if we allow gene flow if we allow, er, these two populations to intermix. They're going to the frequency of certain traits are going to change. So we're not going to have populations that are either yellow or green only. But they are going to have, erm, various at various frequencies individuals from, from the other population. But it could also happen that migrations or gene flow occurs in one direction and this is what we geneticists call a genetic bottleneck. So we have this population as you can see it's very polymorphic has many, many different forms and a subset of that population has migrated to a different area to a different location. Therefore carrying some of these forms into the new the new the new region. And therefore the, erm, characteristics, the diversity in this new region is going to be affected, is going to be changed.

A.7

… So I spoke about mutations because at the heart of, at the centre of it all, there's the process of mutation. Mutation is what generates diversity.

… However at about ten thousand years the agricultural populations communities that were developing or that were domesticating, er, species were only in these pockets.

… and therefore they evolved independently, er, finding different ways different solutions to the different environments so migrations human dispersals have played a role in generating this, erm, array of biological diversity.

… But then the weather changes again and at around twelve thousand years we enter into the Holocene. And the Holocene is the period the epoch we're living in now.

… It is around this time that some species like, er, begin, begin to dwindle begin to, erm, be reduced in numbers.

… But we can also use indirect evidence which is the distribution of genetic diversity today and from that we infer back we look back and try to understand how this, erm, diversity might have, erm, been generated.

A.8

Dr Mormina: And therefore the, erm, characteristics, the diversity in this new region is going to be affected, is going to be changed. However … it's not always possible, erm, to have this exchanging of genes between populations and that is also going to affect the fate of, of the genetic diversity in the populations. So imagine that we have here, erm, two individuals and they can mate freely and the offspring of these two individuals is going to be, erm, neither dark neither light it's going to be something different because of the laws of inheritance. But what happens if we introduce a barrier. Er, in this case a bunch of hungry cats. If we introduce a barrier those two individuals those two individuals are not longer going to be able to freely mate. And they're going to have to mate with individuals from their own group. This is called interbreeding and the result of interbreeding is a reduction of genetic diversity. So basically they're all going to look more or less the same although there are always going to be some, erm, brave individuals that are going to be able to cross the barrier so. But genetic barriers, erm, tend to reduce the diversity within populations and in the case of humans these barriers are not, erm, hungry cats but are geographic barriers for example mountains or rivers, er, climatical, er, barriers or cultural barriers if you think of the caste system in India for example it's a tremendous, er, cultural barrier.

Unit 3

3.1

1 Rachel: It would be good to start by reminding people of what the company produces.

Sebastian: Maybe we could download one of their adverts from Youtube and show them that? Would you be able to do that, Carlos?

Carlos: Sure. Great idea.

2 Rachel: We need to give the audience some time at the end to ask questions. How are we going to do that?

Sebastian: Well, I think it's best if just one person deals with the questions. Perhaps you could do that, Kate, as you're the last speaker in the presentations.

3 Rachel: We've really got to grab their attention. I think we jump straight in and talk about the company's problems.

Sebastian: I see what you mean, but what about the history of the company? Wouldn't it be more sensible to do that before talking about the problems it's facing today? Shall I do that?

4 Rachel: So we need to end with a set of recommendations, don't we?

Sebastian: Yes, er, how do you feel about putting those as a series of bullet points – just on one slide so they're quite memorable. Who wants to do that?

5 Sebastian: ... I think it's best if just one person deals with the questions. Maybe Christian could do it?

Rachel: That's a possibility. Or we could all sit at the front and take the questions that are to do with our part of the presentation.

6 Rachel: I'm not sure of the best way of presenting all these tables. They wouldn't look good projected on screen.

Sebastian: How about if we put them on a handout? We could give that out at the beginning. You're good at that kind of thing Francoise. Can you sort that out?

◀)) 3.2

1 There've been huge technological improvements since they were introduced.
2 Overall, the economic effects have been very positive.
3 In theory children are safer when they've got a phone with them.
4 There's been quite a lot of research in psychology on their effects on people.
5 Isn't there supposed to be some health risk from the magnetic field around mobile phone masts?
6 I think mobiles have been a catastrophe for some people. They can't get away from work any more.
7 Haven't mobiles got some kind of magnet inside them?
8 It'd be catastrophic for businesses if the mobile phone network stopped working. We're too dependent on them.
9 They've had a big impact on the economy of some countries.
10 There's a theoretical chance of them causing brain damage.
11 I'm sure there's no evidence of psychological damage from using mobiles.
12 The technology's improving all the time.

Unit 4

◀)) 4.1

Tutor: Can we go to group three now? Who's going to summarise?

Student: Me.

Tutor: OK, Steve, do you want to tell us what you discussed?

Student: Right. Well, we thought that this picture was showing that people in different cultures greet each other differently. So in some cultures people shake hands, for example while others avoid contact and might just bow. There's also the question of gender here which prompted us to talk about the different behaviour of men and women, er, you know, childcare, household tasks ... One member of the group suggested that in some cultures men and women greet each other in different ways. So Zubaidah, er, mentioned that for most groups in Indonesia it wouldn't be

appropriate for men and women to touch when they greet each other. Erm, turning now to the third question, we came up with a number of other aspects that could be investigated. One possibility would be to look at how young people treat their elders. Kerry said something similar for group one. So, for example, do they show respect in particular ways? We also talked about attitudes to punctuality. This was something that group two talked about as well. We thought it would be interesting to see whether people from different cultures thought it was OK to turn up late for lectures.

◀)) 4.3

OK Steve, do you want to tell us what you discussed?

◀)) 4.4

1 So in some cultures people shake hands for example, ...
2 ... while others avoid contact and might just bow.
3 There's also the question of gender here which prompted us to talk about the different behaviour of men and women.
4 One possibility would be to look at how young people treat their elders.
5 This was something that group two talked about as well.

Lecture skills B

■ B.1

Anitha: Usually before a lecture I'd read through the notes of all the previous lectures to refresh my mind of what's going on because a lecturer does tend to go straight into it and doesn't spend a lot of time reviewing the material leading up to it. So I do that, erm, I try to do that before each lecture. And also after a lecture I'd read through the notes immediately so that if there's anything, erm, the lecturer's said that was really useful in understanding I'll, I'll jot it down and make sure I've got everything he says then and there before I forget it. Erm, apart from that like reading texts we don't really have a lot of textbooks and things for maths but, erm, at the start of the course they'll give us a list of, erm, reading material. So sometimes I would go and read ahead. But usually it's just, er, a lot of effort enough to sort of keep up and reading ahead sometimes I try to in the beginning but if I sort of get swamped by all the example sheets that you've got to do. So generally at the very minimum I'd read through the notes before the lecture and yeah take it from there.

Anna: What I found most interesting about lectures I think was that the whole process isn't standardised. I think at any usual university any university it's, erm, it's quite, it isn't standardised because you have some lecturers who will introduce everything when they start they'll go through what they're going to cover in the lecture

and other lecturers who just go straight into it. Other lecturers will give you a handout before you start before you even arrive at the building and will let you know what's on next week. So you very much had to, erm, really, er, be flexible in the way you, erm, came to the lecture. Erm, I found that it was difficult to fit in preparation before the lecture because often they're back to back. So they're y'know you have one at eleven, finishes at twelve, another one starting at five past twelve and, erm, and that would mean that you would have to just listen carefully, make notes and then ideally go back home and write up your notes afterwards so you have that bank of reference.

■ B.2

Dr Hunt: What I'm going to be talking about is, er, the topic of spinning things and you might think that that is a fairly silly thing to talk about. But what I'm hoping to show you is just perhaps a large number of things that you've never seen before and perhaps things you've seen before but you've never quite understood. And I'm gonna start with a little demonstration to do with um, er, bouncing balls and what physicists would, er, call the particle theory of light.

■ B.3 **See transcript on page 67.**

■ B.4

Dr Hunt: ... So what's that got to do with boomerangs? Well it helps generally speaking in science and in mathematics if we try and not look at a boomerang-shaped object cos it's not very symmetrical. I'd rather look at a um, er, two boomerangs stuck together to make this sort of cross-shaped object. Erm, a cross-shaped object like this, has the virtue of symmetry we do in, in science and maths we'd much rather work with circles and squares and spheres rather than with, erm, trapeziums and, er, ellipses and, and funny-shaped objects we, we like symmetry. So this object here is actually a boomerang, er, it's got nice rotational symmetry about it. When you throw a boomerang it has a direction of travel – it also has some spin. Now the spin means that not all points on the boomerang are moving at the same speed. The middle is moving at a certain speed but as any part of the boomerang moves across the top it's going faster than the middle. Just like when you're on a train and you're walking towards the front of the train you're going faster than a train, and when you're on a train and you walk towards the back of the train you're going slower than the train. So this boomerang is spinning, this bit is going faster now it's going slower through the air. So that means we've got more lift generated by the little bit of wing that's moving across the top of the boomerang because it's moving faster and less lift when it's moving slower.

B.5

Dr Hunt: Let's suppose I have two mirrors. So my beam of light is gonna come in here bounce off this mirror go up onto *that* mirror back and out. And if the mirrors went on forever, then this light beam would keep on reflecting backwards and forwards that would then be a, er, a bit like a, er, an optic fibre. A, er, a light pipe, a wave guide of some sort. Well, I'm gonna try and reproduce this experiment, er, here with this, er, table representing the top, er, mirror if you like and this table here representing the bottom mirror. And I'm going to throw a ball, a bouncy ball – I've got one here – an ordinary bouncy ball and I'm gonna throw that under the table and it's gonna go out the other side like this. Now to make my job a bit, er, more difficult I've got a pile of glasses here which I'm gonna stack up. And there's a neat little gap through here which I think I can aim for. Right here goes. And the ball is still in my hand. So there's something funny going on here. Maybe this table is the wrong way round? Erm. Mn. Er, maybe the glasses don't have anything to do with it. I'll move the glasses away. ...

B.6

Dr Hunt: And the first thing we have to notice is that there are three collisions you can hear the three collisions 'ba-da-dum'. Well I can do it under this table here more slowly. You can hear the three collisions. In fact I can use a nice big ball here. You can hear those three collisions, OK? What happens on each one of those collisions? First collision. Now can you see what happens? What do you notice about that ball? See what happens? It starts to spin.

B.7 See transcript on page 67.

B.8

Dr Moseley: We make our view of Shakespeare the man according to the parameters and the concerns of the age that we live in and our own culturally attuned sense of priorities which reflexively are demonstrably affected by what he was and what he did. But no matter let's deal with Shakespeare the man first. Now we must start by recognising him as a man of the later Renaissance in the very peculiar form that it took in England and we do him a great disservice if we ever forget that.

B.9

Dr Mormina: But why Africa? Why did we evolve in Africa? Here it's probably useful to look a little bit of what the environment was[*] around that time. About 200,000 years around here we went through a period of cold. So we were in what palaeoclimatologists call the interglacial so, warm periods, and at around 200,000 years we, the, climate, changed and got colder so we went into a glacial. So how did the, erm, how did organisms respond to colder climatic conditions? Well it depends. They respond differently, er, depending

on where they live. So 'cold' in the tropics means drought. Means that the water gets trapped in the ice course therefore, erm, the climate in the tropics gets extremely dry. And that means that loads of species are going to struggle. And that means that the species feeding on those species are also going to struggle. So if there are less resources, you have to develop, erm, some system of making savings and this is what happens to our body. This is a Neanderthal and this is a modern human as you can see a modern human is a lot more gracile than a Neanderthal. So basically we're the economy version of Neanderthals. We evolved a cheaper biology because there were less resources.

B.10

Dr Mormina: Another example of how, erm, natural selection acts to generate diversity is in the body shape. And these two individuals come from lower latitudes from Africa and from higher latitudes from Alaska and as you can see the body shapes are very, very different and that has to do with the fact that in the tropics where it's very hot and very humid you need to reduce the inner body surface in order to avoid the loss of, erm, ... in order to favour the loss of heat. So this individual here is adapted to an environment where you were you need to lose heat. Whereas this individual here is shorter and more robust, is adapted to colder environments where the body needs to prevent the loss of heat. So here you have bigger inner surface that keeps the body warm.

B.11

Dr Mormina: And finally, with this I want to finish the role of culture. So culture has also played a role in generating diversity and one of the most classical examples of how culture has driven human evolution is the case of the lactase persistence. The lactase persistence is our ability to digest milk beyond the age of weaning. Most species most mammal species, er, drink milk only when they're young and once they've, er, been beyond the age of weaning they are not able to digest milk any more. However, we are the only species that has the ability to digest milk in adult-adulthood although there are some exceptions like myself who can't stand milk. So why is that? That is because there is a gene called the LCT gene and a mutation in that gene allows people to drink milk and not get sick. And that mutation interestingly enough is about ten thousand years old. That mutation, that change in that gene happened 10,000 years ago and that coincided with the beginnings of agriculture. So when communities started to domesticate plants and animals - particularly cattle - they were probably in close contact with cattle and dairy products and therefore if a mutation appears in the genetic pool of those populations that allows them to consume dairy products that mutation is going to be very, very favourable and natural selection is going

to say, 'Oh OK good let's spread this mutation because it's advantageous.' And this is what happened.

B.12

Dr Vlamis: So macroeconomics and microeconomics they do use the same style of thinking about economic issues. The difference is that macroeconomists they're looking at the wider picture while microeconomists they are just looking at specific sectors, er, specific products, specific individual decisions. And why do we need macroeconomics? Macroeconomics is useful because it enables us to study events that affect the economy as a whole. Without getting into much detail about specific sectors or specific products. So as I said some key issues in macroeconomics. Inflation. What is the inflation[*]? Inflation is the rate of change of the general price level, OK? And how can we measure inflation? There are different indices that we can use. The Bank of England or government other government sponsored authorities, er, they produce these statistics. The wholesale price index or the consumer price index are used as proxies for inflation rate. Let me just, er, give you a kind of an idea of what was the inflation rate in this country in United Kingdom[*], er, from the fifties onwards. So this figure, er, measures on the vertical axis we have the percentage inflation rate per annum. The annual inflation rate. Er, and on the, er, horizontal axis we have, er, different decades. So what can we make of it? You see that just after the Second World War yeah? In the early fifties inflation rate you, you see the trend. OK there was a kind of fluctuation but the trend was around three, four percent OK annual. So quite low inflation rate in Britain. Then there was a huge increase in the early seventies you see in 1973 there was a huge increase in inflation rate and it got up to twenty-two percent as you can see. Then it decelerated in the mid seventies and again there was another, er, increase in, er, late um, er, seventies in nineteen seventy-nine. And then you see since then it decelerated and now inflation rate is around two point five percent. Why there was this huge, er, increase in inflation rate in this country?[*] And as we will see in a minute it wasn't just in this country it was across the industrial, er, the industrialised, er, world. Er, what was the cause of this huge, er, increase in inflation rate? Um the cause if we relate what we were talking about a few minutes later it was the increase in the two oil shocks that took place in 1973 and 1979 because of the increase in the price, er, of oil, er, by the OPEC –, er, economies, the oil-producing economies – that created this, er, effect on inflation. Why? Because oil is an important raw material in the production process, so when the price of oil increases, that considered, economists used to call that 'supply shock' because that increases the cost of production – not just for oil but for throughout the production process – the cost of production increases. So that gives you a picture of what was the inflation rate [*], how inflation evolved since the fifties and the next slide gives you a kind of comparative picture between, er, the three key, er, world economies. Er, the US, the UK and, er, Germany.

Unit 5

◀)5.1

Antonia: Hello, Dr Jones. I was wondering if I could ask you about the comments on my essay. I thought it was important to include information that I had found in my research. You know, to show that I had understood everything and–

Dr Jones: Yes, of course it's important to back up what you've found, and to support your own ideas, but you have to be careful how you do it, otherwise this is called plagiarism.

Antonia: Mmn, I've already read about plagiarism in the manual we were given at the start of term, but I'm still not really sure what it involves. I mean, what it is exactly.

Dr Jones: Well, put very simply, it's copying other people's work. Maybe I can explain it best if I give you some examples, or types of plagiarism. One way of committing plagiarism might be when you copy material directly from a textbook or a journal but don't give a source. This way you're not admitting, or rather acknowledging, that the idea is someone else's.

Antonia: Erm, what do you mean?

Dr Jones: Well, if I just show you the original textbook that you used to write your essay, we can see that the words in your essay are the same, or only slightly different from the original, but you haven't included the reference in your text ... here. For example *this* paragraph ... , and then your essay ...

Antonia: Mmn, I see. Yes, OK.

Dr Jones: Other examples of where you might copy are when people just cut and paste material from a website, or when they copy another student's work. This may be, for example, an essay, or even another student's data from a lab experiment.

Antonia: Mmn, OK. So basically you can't copy any information directly from someone else.

Dr Jones: Well, you can copy small quotes but you have to make sure you reference them. For example, if we look at your essay, you've used a large amount of information which you found in Steele, but you need to either give a reference or try and paraphrase it. I mean, you know, put it into your own words more.

Antonia: Right. That makes things a bit clearer. But I don't really understand why it affects my grade so much. Why is plagiarism such an important part of my essay mark?

Dr Jones: Well, if you're saying that words or ideas are yours when they belong to someone else, then this is a kind of stealing. And it's important to avoid that.

Antonia: Yes, of course.

Dr Jones: The other thing is that we have to try to assess what students have learnt. If a student copies, then we might give them credit for something that's not their own work.

Antonia: OK, right. Yes, it's clearer now. So have you got any advice on how I should avoid plagiarism?

Dr Jones: Mm, well, I think there are probably three main things that you can do. First, you should always acknowledge the source of your information by putting in a reference. The exception is where this information is common knowledge.

Antonia: OK, er, let me write this down ... reference ... except common knowledge ... OK.

Dr Jones: Then, as far as possible, try to paraphrase what you read; in other words, try to put it in your own words. You should still give a reference to the source, though.

Antonia: OK ... own words ...

Dr Jones: And third, where you use the exact words of another writer always put this in quotation marks and add a reference. I realise that all of this can be difficult, but it's very important in your academic studies. We can look at how to reference and put in sources in your texts later if you like?

Antonia: Thanks, Dr Jones, that would be good. I'll certainly do my best. Can I also ask you a question about this other comment you made later, about paragraph order ...

◀)5.2

Tom: ... so, we've decided that we're going to cover five topics: the side-effects of antibiotics, how antibiotics work, the impact of antibiotics on public health, resistance to antibiotics, and the discovery of antibiotics. We haven't got much time left and we need to agree an order for presenting these.

Susana: It's sensible to put how antibiotics work first. That way we can explain what they are and what they're for, so that people know what we're talking about.

David: Well, that's possible, but it seems more logical to talk about their discovery before saying how they work. We can start with the discovery of penicillin, and then end with problems of resistance. That can be the conclusion. So we talk first about the past, and then about the future.

Ann: Yeah, er, I agree.

James: Me, too.

Tom: OK, most people are in agreement that we start with their discovery and then end by looking at overcoming problems of resistance. What about the order of the other three topics?

Ann: Well, we can't really introduce side-effects before we've talked about how antibiotics work. So we need to do side-effects later.

Susana: Yes, that's sensible.

David: Agreed.

Tom: Right, the consensus seems to be that we talk about how antibiotics work and then go on to side-effects. What about the impact of antibiotics

on public health?

James: Can I make a suggestion? Maybe we should put that second, after their discovery. That's likely to grab people's attention before going on to the more technical side of how they work.

Ann: That might be right, but I think the presentation would flow better if we had impacts after how antibiotics work and their side-effects. We'd be going from the specific to the more general effects of antibiotics.

Susana: That's right.

David: Yes, that sounds very sensible.

Tom: Right, that's it then. Our agreed order is ...

◀)5.3

Giving reasons for a preferred order

1 It's sensible to put how antibiotics work first.
2 Well, that's possible, but it seems more logical to talk about their discovery before saying how they work. We can start with how ...
3 Well, we can't really introduce side-effects before we've talked about how antibiotics work. So we need to do side-effects later.
4 ... I think the presentation would flow better if we had impacts ...

Reaching a consensus

5 We haven't got much time left and we need to agree an order for presenting these.
6 OK, most people are in agreement that we start with ...
7 Right, the consensus seems to be that we talk about how antibiotics work ...
8 Right, that's it then. Our agreed order is ...

◀)5.4

So we talk first about the past, and then about the future.

We'd be going from the specific to the more general effects of antibiotics.

◀)5.5

1 We'd expected the material to expand, but in fact it contracted.
2 Some of the results were expected, but others were totally unexpected.
3 Rather than being temporary, as we'd anticipated, the effects were permanent.
4 We collected a lot of quantitative data, but more interesting was the qualitative data.
5 Having outlined the situation in the regions, I'll now look at the national position.
6 I first counted the concrete nouns in the text, and then the abstract nouns.
7 While some of our results support previous findings, others contradict them.
8 I've outlined the results of our physical health survey, and now Stephan will look at mental health.

Unit 6

◄)) 6.1

Over the last thirty years or so, there's been a massive growth in tourism in both more and less developed countries. As I said a few minutes ago, tourism is now the world's largest industry with over 10 per cent of global GDP – that's gross domestic product – directly related to tourism activities. Although this growth has had a pretty big impact in developed countries, it's in developing countries that the effects have been most significant. Obviously, there have been major economic effects with massive amounts of income flowing into poor countries, and I'll say more about that in a while, both the positive and negative effects of this income. What I want to talk about now is the effect of tourism on health in developing countries. …

… so far I've talked about the effects of tourism on health and education, but another important issue is the impact of tourism on the local culture. Of course, cultural heritage sites have attracted tourists for many years, and mass tourism can lead to substantial damage. Organisations like UNESCO – that is, the United Nations Educational, Scientific and Cultural Organization – help protect a number of important sites, and I'll come back to that in a moment. What I'd like to focus on here is the question of how the arrival of large numbers of people from different cultures affects the attitudes, beliefs, and ways of thinking of the host community and spreads new ideas about work, money, and human relationships.

… and the tourism industry needs to take a more responsible attitude. Having talked about some of the environmental problems, I'll now move on to steps that have been taken to try to minimise negative environmental and cultural impacts. A form of tourism known as ecotourism – that is to say, tourism that preserves the environment and improves the well being of local people – is growing rapidly in some developing countries. Before going on to give some examples of ecotourism in practice, I want to outline some general principles of ecotourism projects. First of all …

Lecture skills C

C.1

Dr Mormina:

1   So I have two sisters. Our mitochondrial DNA joins up in that of my mother. My mother has two siblings. Their mitochondrial DNA joins up in their mother so in- as we work backwards the number of ancestors gets smaller and smaller and smaller until we reach the point where we find the common ancestor of all living modern humans. And this common ancestor has been dubbed 'the mitochondrial Eve', which is an unfortunate term because it doesn't mean that there was just one

person as in the Bible story, but is one DNA type that gave rise to all modern humans.

2   So, populations – humans – spread out of Africa but when did they spread and how did they spread? And here well there have been several, hypotheses. Some people have suggested that humans spread out of Africa through a northern route – through northern Africa – through a southern route – Ethiopia – round there. Some people have proposed that humans spread only once out of Africa. Some people have suggested that they spread in different waves. Some people have proposed some combination of the above and the discussion, the debate continues.

3   Before this, time before ninety thousand years, er, the fossil record suggests that humans were only living in Africa. So what was happening at that time elsewhere? Well, Europe for example was populated by Neanderthals. Whereas in Asia we had homo-erectus and more recently we know we also had the hobbits 'homo floresiensis' but no modern humans, and when I say 'modern humans' I mean people looking like you and me. No modern humans were present outside Africa at around two hundred thousand years. However the fossil record is difficult to interpret. So when you see a skull and the skull is so old and it's got has got lots of cracks you really you really hard pressed to say this is human.

C.2

Dr Vlamis:

GDP stands for 'gross domestic product'. Gross domestic product. Gross domestic product is the measure of economic, *the* measure, not one of the measures, *the* measure – the most efficient let's say – measure of economic activity that we have. Okay? And it measures the output and services, not just output, and services brought you produced by factors of production located in the domestic,er, economy. Gross domestic product, er, is a specific measure of output in the market economy and is not a measure of welfare or happiness. Okay? So it has certain limitations. What are the limitations? Well this, er, measure, er, can measure certain things and certain things cannot be measured by GDP OK. So whatever is quantitative GDP can pick up. Whatever is qualitative it can not be measured by GDP. For example, er, leisure. OK leisure. When you go out with your friends and you have drinks you do have a certain satisfaction out of doing that. GDP cannot pick up that. Cannot measure something that is not quantitative. OK. Or it doesn't, it cannot measure anything that does not pass through the market mechanism. If companies tax evade, OK, that is output that cannot be measured by, er, the gross domestic, er, product, erm, and doesn't measure everything that contributes to human, er, welfare when you socialise with people and you spend time drinking beers or going out or going, er, to see,

sightseeing[*] or whatever. This has a certain value for you OK, er, it it brings a certain utility it increase[*] your satisfaction but that cannot be measured by the gross domestic product. Because the gross domestic product measures anything that can go through the market mechanism. Er, having said that GDP is one of the best measures available of the total economic activity within a country and it is particularly valuable when changes in GDP are used to indicate how economic activity has changed.

C.3

Dr Mormina: Selection, natural selection can act very, very quickly in certain cases and one of the most striking examples of how natural selection can act and can generate diversity is the case of the pigmentation genes. Pigmentation genes the, the genes that, erm, influence our skin colour are known to be under the strong effects of natural selection. And this is the distribution of pigmentation of skin colour across the world and as you can see around the tropics you know is where you find the darkest skin colours and it gets lighter as you move away.

C.4

Dr Mormina: So one of the hypotheses is that, erm, it was that, erm, lighter pigmentations allow the skin to absorb better vitamin D and therefore natural selection in high latitudes where, erm, where vitamin D is deficient has favoured light skin colours that allow more absorption or more efficient absorption of vitamin D. Er, another hypothesis for the distribution of skin colours is that of sexual selection. Basically in these high latitudes people tended to prefer people with light skin colour and therefore that all led to the predominance of light skin colour in high latitudes. Another hypothesis is that, erm, because darker skin colour o- confer protection against UV radiation that it was that effect that favoured the spread of dark skin colour in the tropics where the exposure to UV radiation is bigger.

C.5–C.6

Dr Mormina: But why move? Well, Africa was getting a bit overcrowded. So, moving, reduced competition. It also reduced interbreeding and it reduced overcrowding of course. So around ten hundred thousand years ago we were here. So we had come out of the glacial period so climate had improved. It was again hot or warm so populations were expanding in Africa. And as I said it probably was getting a little bit crowded there. So populations, humans spread out of Africa but when did they spread and how did they spread? And here well there have been several, erm, hypotheses. Some people have suggested that humans spread out of Africa through a northern route through northern Africa through a southern route Ethiopia round there. Some people have proposed that humans spread only once out of Africa. Some people have suggested that they spread in different waves. Some people have proposed some combination of the above and the discussion the debate continues.

C.7

Dr Mormina: There was a northern dispersal and we know that because this fossil here, erm, has been found is the oldest fossil outside Africa ever found and it has been found in the region that is today in the Levant. And it's dated to about ninety thousand years. So at that time I said we were in one of those warm periods so the Sahara as we know it today was a lot smaller. So this northern route was probably plausible. So they didn't have to cross the whole Sahara to get out of Africa. However, as you can see here the Sahara was smaller but it was still the Sahara. But recently palaeoclimatic reconstructions have suggested that despite[*] this area here was a desert there were ancient rivers that could have acted as corridors to facilitate migrations. So this northern exit through Libya probably was quite plausible. However, that exit ninety thousand years ago from Africa from northern Africa probably was unsuccessful, didn't leave any descendants. And we know that because the DNA and probably humans used this corridor and went all the way along the Indian Ocean right into Australia. And we know that this route existed because there are populations living along this corridor today, erm, that point to an African origin. Somewhere here we have the Andaman Islands are a very, very small islands south of India and the populations living in the Andaman Islands look like this. Not like Indians they look like Africans. In the Malay Peninsular we also have populations that have retained their hunter gatherer lifestyle and they don't look like Asian at all. They're short and very very dark. So these populations are likely to represent the descendants of this early migration out of Africa. And of course we have the aboriginal Australians. Again, a very African-like phenotype. But genetics also tells us that we descend from that southern dispersal and we know that because when we look at the again the mitochondrial DNA tree of all known African populations all these lineages, all these DNA lineages join up in a common ancestor that lived around sixty thousand years ago which coincides with this southern dispersal event. So did humans spread once or did humans spread several times out of Africa? And one could argue, well if they found an exit they found a route once, they could have found it several times there's no reason why once they made the move they couldn't keep on migrating. However, the genetic, er, evidence tells us slightly different story. Erm, this is a very simplified version, erm, of what might have happened from the point of view of the, er, genetic diversity that we see today. And these numbers here represent the different genetic mitochondrial lineages that are present in Africa so roughly we

have six major groups. However, when we move out of Africa we only found, we only find three major groups and these three major groups are all descendants of this, this type L3 type. So all these groups are more or less similar in age indicating that they spread at the same time and they have only one common ancestor which is this African type L3 and that indicates that in reality there was only one exit out of Africa. And as I said this was a southern dispersal along the Indian Ocean all the way to East Asia and Australia.

C.8 See transcript on page 96.

C.9

Dr Mormina: ... the evolutionary mechanisms that have generated it, how evolution has acted on, erm, on our human species to create that vast array of, erm, biological forms. And these are exciting times to study human evolution.

C.10

Dr Vlamis: ... er in the fifties and sixties there was an environment of low inflation rate of and low unemployment rate. While in the seventies...

C.11

Dr Vlamis: ... the picture changed. We were in an environment of high unemployment rate and high inflation. That is called 'stagflation'.

C.12 See transcript on page 97.

C.13

Dr Vlamis: What I'm gonna talk about today, I'm gonna just give you a brief introduction of, 'What is macroeconomics?' and, er, 'What are the main questions that macroeconomists are interested, what are the main issues that macroeconomists are interested to address?' [*]Er, so I'm gonna talk about, er, things like inflation rate, er, unemployment, er, the balance of payments, er, economic growth. So that[*] kind of things and I will try to define them, er, properly and also to give you some kind of, er, how we can measure, er, for example economic activity. Er, right OK so what is macroeconomics and, er, why, er, macroeconomists, er, uh what kind of issues, er, macroeconomists are interested in, er, addressing? Er, macroeconomics is about, er, the economy as a whole. OK so it gives us the kind of big picture of how the economy works. We are not that much interested on what is happening in specific sectors of the economy like the primary sector the, er, secondary sector or the or the service sector. Or we are not interested on how individuals are making their decisions. We are mostly interested or on what is happening at the greater scale in the macro scale. OK. So we are interested in macroeconomists are interested in, er, um, er, talking about aggregate, er, phenomena such as the business cycle. How the economic activity fluctuates over time, er, about the living standards whether these are improved as time, er, goes by. Um issues like, er, inflation. OK. We will define properly later, er, what is, er, inflation

but macroeconomists are interested in, er, figuring out, er, what are the costs involved why why we dislike inflation. Why households and, er, companies they both, er, dislike inflation and they want, er, why governments they try to maintain price stability. Why the Bank of England has the main one objective, er, to keep prices um, er, low. Because there are certain costs involved. Er, and what are the policy tools what can governments do in order to combat, er, inflation. These are the kind of questions that, er, as far as it concerns inflation that, er, macroeconomists is interested to address. Or, unemployment. OK. What is unemployment? Why is it important, er, for the economist to address that, er, issue. Um what are the costs involved are there any social costs involved like human misery or, er, psychological depression that they en- the the un- the unemployed encounter. Or um, er, uh o- or are there any financial, er, costs, er, uh involved. And, er, how can we deal with the problem if the unemployment rate is quite high in, in an economy what kind of policy measures can we take in order to combat, er, unemployment. And then, er, is, er, another issue is, er, balance of payment. Er, if for example as a country we, er, import more goods than what we export, er, to other trading partners. Then, er, we it's most, er, probably we will, er, face, er, trade imbalance trade deficit. If there is this trade deficit what kind of policy measures can we make in order to deal with the problem. Um so and also macroeconomists they're interested in, er, finding out what is the optimal policy mix. They the governments they basically have two policy tools in their hands. The monetary tool, er, monetary policy tool f- the fiscal tools and occasionally the exchange rate tool. Monetary policy is um, er, the government can, er, increase or decrease money supply in the econ- in the economy. OK and that's the job of the bank the central bank. Bank of England, European Central Bank or the American Fed. Er, or they can use fiscal policy instruments. Governments can change the tax rates or they can change government spending. OK so these are the tools the fiscal tools that the government can use in order to affect economic, er, activity and help stabilise the, the economy.

Unit 7

7.1

Presentation 1

Maria: Finally, I just want to highlight the most important points in my talk. Essentially, there are three main views on the subject. One is that there will be sufficient supplies of oil to meet demand until about 2040. The second is that new oil supplies will continue to be found, and so we won't run out of oil for another 100 years or so. The third view is that demand will continue to rise rapidly and that supply will be unable to meet demand around 2025. I've tried to show that the third of these is the most likely, and that we need to be making changes now in our use of oil and the development of alternatives to deal with the crisis that we will soon face. ... So, that's it. Thank you. Well, there's some time left, and I'm happy to take any questions or comments you may have.

Presentation 2

Oscar: OK, I'd like to finish by repeating what the main points in my presentation are. First, an increasing proportion of the world's population is elderly, and this is particularly true in the more developed countries. The main reasons for this are that people are living longer because of better health care, and also because birth rates are declining. But this is putting huge pressure on health services and other care for the elderly, and many countries simply can't afford to pay for these any more. As a result, I think we need to change people's working patterns. In the future, more people will need to work beyond normal retirement age, and extend their working lifetime. ... Thanks for coming. If anyone has any questions or comments, we've got a few minutes left.

Presentation 3

Daniela: We're coming to the end of the talk, so let me now summarise the key points. First, air pollution is continuing to increase substantially, particularly as more countries are industrialising. This pollution not only damages the environment, but also has a major impact on human health. I mentioned, for example, the rise in the number of cases of asthma, which may be linked to air pollution. Finally, I went on to argue that we urgently need to reduce air pollution both by tightening up regulations and also by using new technologies. ... Thank you for listening. We've got a few minutes more, and I'll do my best to answer questions if you've got any.

Presentation 4

Gina: Let me end by going over the main points of the talk again. I've tried to show that our attempts to reduce world poverty over the last 30 years have largely failed and that we need to change the emphasis of our approach. First, we need to increase substantially the amount of aid we give to developing countries. Most of this aid should go into improving education and health care. And above all, we need to give developing countries better access to world markets through trade agreements. ... Many thanks for your attention. We've got a bit of time for questions if there are any.

◀)) 7.2

Presentation 1

Maria: Well, there's some time left, and I'm happy to take any questions or comments you may have. Yes, Yann?

Yann: You mentioned that it might be possible to get oil from oil shale. Could you say a bit more about where this is found, please?

Maria: Yeah, erm, most oil shale is in the US – over 60%, I think – and most of the rest is in Russia and Brazil.

Yann: Thanks.

Maria: John.

John: Can I just say that I think you're quite right to warn that we're heading for a crisis? But it's one that governments don't seem to be able to face up to at the moment. ...

Presentation 2

Oscar: If anyone has any questions or comments, we've got a few minutes left. Barbara.

Barbara: You said that people are living longer because of better health care. It's also true that people have better diets nowadays, and that means longer lives.

Oscar: Yes, that's quite right, although it's quite difficult to work out exactly the effect of diet on length of life. Christian, did you have a question?

Christian: You said quite rightly that costs rise as a country's population grows older. But I'm not sure I agree that developed countries can't afford to pay for health services and other care. Isn't it actually the case that they can afford it, but choose to spend money on other things – on defence, for example?

Oscar: Er, well, I suppose that's true to some extent ...

Presentation 3

Daniela: We've got a few minutes more, and I'll do my best to answer questions if you've got any. Yes, Emma?

Emma: I think you're right to say that weak regulation has increased air pollution, but don't you think that more regulation would be unfair on developing countries that are industrialising now?

Daniela: Well, you could argue that. On the other hand, developing countries can take advantage of the cleaner technologies that more developed countries have produced.

Emma: Yes, I suppose so.

Daniela: Johnny.

Johnny: I just wanted to agree with you about the importance of new technology in reducing air pollution. For example, we can use technology to clean emissions from coal-fired power stations, and this means that ...

Presentation 4

Gina: We've got a bit of time for questions if there are any ... Yes?

Danny: You've shown us that reducing world poverty has largely been unsuccessful. I think this is particularly the case in many parts of sub-Saharan Africa.

Gina: Yes, that's certainly true. And parts of south Asia, too, I think. Yes, Haruki.

Haruki: You mentioned trade agreements. I'm not sure I really understood this. Can you explain this in a little more detail, please?

Gina: Well, these are agreements that give

developing countries better trading conditions than other countries. So, for example, ...

◀)) 7.3

should go into improving education
a major impact
and other care for the elderly
around twenty twenty-five
the last thirty years
we need to increase substantially
let me now summarise
what are the main points

◀)) 7.4

1 I've tried to show
2 for example
3 let me end
4 to reduce significantly
5 will be unable to meet demand
6 I'll do my best to answer questions
7 just can't afford to pay for these any more
8 there will be seven parts

Unit 8

◀)) 8.1

Anna: Well, I'm doing a course in Linguistics and, erm, I'm in my first year. We have a tutorial every week, and there's usually about eight or ten students in the group plus the tutor. Basically, we go through one of the lectures that we had earlier in the week. Usually, our tutor didn't give the lecture, but sat in on it so she knows what it's about. So we follow up aspects of that lecture and talk about it. ... Erm, between the lecture and the tutorial we're expected to do some of the recommended reading that's given to us during the lecture. While we're doing that we have to try to identify areas that we don't understand and get some questions ready for the tutorial. And then during the tutorial we ask our questions. Sometimes the tutor just answers directly, or she'll try to guide us, to get us to work out the answers ourselves. Sometimes she'll explain things that we obviously haven't understood, or give some more examples. ... Er, I quite enjoy tutorials, but I find them pretty difficult. There's always one or two people who do most of the talking, and they can dominate things a bit. And it seems to me that all of the other students know more about the subject than I do. I also find it hard to express my ideas clearly enough, so sometimes people don't understand what I'm trying to say. But our tutor's really kind and supportive, and now that I'm getting to know the others in the group a bit more, I think my confidence is growing.

Greg: OK, so, I'm in the third year of my degree in Chemistry. Tutorials vary a bit from year to year, but essentially we have a tutorial every other week where we meet with supervisors. They're usually PhD students, and there are five or six of us students in the group. A few days before the tutorial, our supervisor emails us a problem sheet. The problems are always related to a topic that we've just covered in the course. ... Erm, before the tutorial we have to try to do the problems or calculations on the worksheet, working on our own. That usually involves doing a bit of background reading as well. Then during the tutorial we're supposed to give our answers and explain how we got them. The supervisor asks follow-up questions – I suppose to make us think a bit more deeply about the subject – and we can ask for help if we had particular difficulties in doing certain problems. ... Erm, the tutorial's quite short, just an hour long, and our supervisor keeps things moving pretty quickly. So sometimes I find that by the time I've thought of something to say, someone else has got in first, and that can be a problem for me. It also tends to be that the supervisor asks the more confident students to answer questions. That means that I don't often get asked to speak, so I don't actually say much during our tutorials. It's something I need to work on.

Matt: I'm taking a one-year Master's course in Business Studies. We have a weekly tutorial with one of our lecturers, in a group of about twelve students. We do the same thing more or less every week. We have to discuss a research article on a topic that's related to a lecture we have later that week or early the next. ... Erm, we're given a list of the research articles at the beginning of term. So some time before the tutorial we have to read and try to understand the article for that week in detail. Then during the tutorial we start by asking our lecturer questions about anything we haven't understood. Then in the main part we discuss concepts and theories that are mentioned in the article. We also focus on either the methodology or the findings of the research and try to evaluate it – whether we can think of any improvements in the methods, or perhaps we consider how useful the research is or how it could be applied. The tutorials are challenging, but I feel that I get a lot out of them. The biggest problem I have is trying to take notes and participate in the tutorial at the same time. Mostly I end up just forgetting about notes, and try to follow what's going on and say something when I can. At first I found it quite hard to know when it was my turn to speak – when I could say something without interrupting others in the group – so it can be hard to join in the discussion. But overall, I think I'm getting better at that.

◀)) 8.2

minimum wage
wage bill

◀)) 8.3

bullet point   early retirement   earthquake
gender bias   global warming   health centre
income tax   jet lag   middle management
mixed economy   periodic table   social security

◀)) 8.4

1   A place where people can go to see a doctor
2   The slow rise in the Earth's temperature
3   A system for giving money to people who do not work
4   Unfair treatment of men or women because of their sex
5   Money you pay to the government from your earnings
6   When a country has some businesses controlled by government and others by private companies
7   A sudden movement in the ground
8   An item in a list with a small circle before it
9   When you leave your job before the usual age for stopping work
10 An arrangement of the symbols of chemical elements
11 Tiredness caused by travelling across time zones
12 People who organise a business, but are not the most senior

◀)) 8.5

Frederike: So as far as writing is concerned we had to make, to produce five pieces of work and there were, er, four essays of four thousand words about specific topics. Like, one was about, mine was about gender and development or sustainable livelihoods frameworks or like, erm, stuff related to development basically. And the dissertation was, erm, a topic that we could choose whatever we wanted. So I chose to write about women in Ethiopia. I'd conducted fieldwork over Christmas and New Year in Ethiopian Highlands and I was writing about that. Erm, writing was the most challenging thing this year.

Sabesan: OK. As far as writing is concerned, er, especially being engineer[*] you could write a number of technical report[*] rather than essays like you do in arts or English subject. Er, these technical reports are professional reports: you've got to follow a standard structure as, like, for example, introduction and then methodology and then experiment results and discussion and so on and so forth. So you're pretty much OK with the structures but just need to be, have a good English knowledge to write about the- about the experiments about whatever you use. So normally you pretty much write technical report for whatever you have done in the laboratory.

Anitha: So in my undergraduate days we don't[*] really tend to do a lot of writing for maths. We just have- we g- are given problem sheets by the lecturer and that just involves, you've got twenty questions, short questions and you just answer that based on what was lectured. But, er, for my Masters we had to do a dissertation and that involved summarising two papers. And because the material of these papers was about an application so what I had to do to illustrate that I'd

understood these papers these two papers was to come up with an example that illustrated how the application worked so that's what I did.

Lecture skills D

D.1

Dr Moseley: Why on earth should studying Shakespeare matter? Now, this lecture is an attempt – albeit a very personal attempt – to answer that question. For a long time – for well over a decade and a half – I used to organise this university's, er, summer school in Shakespeare and I've been teaching the plays and the poems in this university and writing about them for getting on for forty years. I could certainly say that I've enjoyed what I've done and enjoyment is very important indeed. And I want especially to think about the place of what that word 'Shakespeare' in quotation marks summarises in our schools and in our universities and in the end in our culture. I don't want to suggest what education is about. That would be foolhardy taking on a task like that let alone presumptuous. I just want to explore with you why I think literature, art and drama matter to us as human beings whatever our cultural background. And that we ought to recognise, far more readily than as a society we currently do, that they are not opposed to but complementary to what the other disciplines and the sciences can offer.

D.2

1   So what's happening here is that when the ball goes around in a circle, the force is at right angles to the velocity. Which means that just like the side wind, it doesn't change how fast I'm going, it changes the direction I'm going.
2   So then we start thinking well what fun experiments can I do? Well what I can do is I can go to the bike shop and I can buy something called a stunt peg and I've got one here I've got a stunt peg with a piece of string attached to it. Stunt pegs are things that kids put onto their, the axles of their bikes so that they can, er, do stunts.
3   Lift on a plane, er, is just a simple thing really, er, people love to make it sound complicated but if air flows over a wing the wing contrives to deflect the air downwards and by Newton's third law of motion every action has an equal opposite reaction: if the air is being pushed downwards, the wing must be being pushed upwards. And we know from lift that the faster you go, the more lift you get. So for instance if you're in a car and you stick your hand out the window and you tilt your hand, we know that if you're going pretty slowly, you don't feel very much but if you're going fast, your hand gets moved around much more. So we know that from experience.
4   If I have backspin on a ball, then the ball comes back towards me. If I have a topspin on a ball, then the ball shoots away from me.
5   Basically in these high latitudes people tended

to prefer people with light skin colour and therefore that all led to the predominance of light skin colour in high latitudes. Another hypothesis is that, erm, because darker skin colour o- confer protection against UV radiation that it was that effect that favoured the spread of dark skin colour in in the tropics where the exposure to UV radiation is bigger.

6 So if you put together all of us, our genetic diversity is much smaller than tha- that of African populations and that indicates that African populations are older. Why? Because they have had more time to evolve.

D.3

Dr Mormina: ... so you can see now that from the initial spread out of Africa populations then had separate evolutionary histories and evolved in different directions. But then between twenty five and fifteen thousand years ago we find ourselves again in a gla- in a, in a cold snap. So we're at the peak of the glaciation. ... But then the weather changes again and at around twelve thousand years we enter into the Holocene. And the Holocene is the period, the epoch we're living in now. We are in the Holocene. And it's characterised far- by a rapid a rapid process of global warming. The temperatures change abruptly and with that all the water that was trapped in the, erm, in the Arctic, in the icecaps, starts to melt starts to- and goes into the oceans. Therefore sea levels rise and as a consequence some of the lowland areas are going to be inundated. So the landmass, the landmasses are reconfigured. And that produced new dispersals so people particularly populations living in in coast lines are going to be affected by, by this event of rapid sea level, er, rise and that's going to spur movement dispersals further migrations. But also around this time we find evidence of the first people crossing Bering Strait and making a move into the Americas. So around twelve thousand, thirteen thousand years we find evidence both in the fossil record but also in the genetic record of the colonisation of the Americas. So I said, erm, the climate changed very, very rapidly at around twelve thousand years. And it was an unprecedented event of climate change. And it certainly had implications for the way humans responded and adapted to the changing climatic conditions.

D.4

1 ... the computer programme required to generate the, the animation does, has nothing more in it than doing addition subtraction multiplication division, er, a couple of square roots and that's about it. Er, OK there's a graphics side of it but that's, er, that's not the physics really ...

2 Means that the water gets trapped in the ice course therefore, erm, the climate in the tropics gets extremely dry. And that means that loads of species are going to struggle.

3 These are a little bit older about s- fifty five

sixty thousand years. When we look at the both ge- genetic and phenotypic diversity today what we see is a very interesting pattern.

4 So all these groups are more or less similar in age indicating that they spread at the same time and they have only one common ancestor which is this African type L3 and that indicates that in reality there was only one exit out of Africa.

5 So if my arms are out, I can move my body around quite a lot but if I bring my arms in then I can put my arms back again and my body doesn't turn much.

6 ... and lo and behold the spin direction is at right angles to the couple which means that I get this gyroscopic procession again. And that's what causes the boomerang to come back and does it roughly like this. And that is gyroscopic procession ...

D.5

Dr Mormina: So. Just to sum up we have between hundred and fifty and two hundred thousand years ago we have evidence of the origins of modern humans in Africa and that evidence is, er, fossil evidence, fossil genetic evidence. Both lines of evidence point to a single origin in Africa at around that time. From then on populations start to expand within Africa. We have in the fossil record the evidence of an early – possibly failed – dispersal through this northern route. Around hundred thousand between hundred thousand and seventy thousand years ago we have an event of glaciation – populations start to contract. A little bit later a slightly, slight improvement in the climate and it's here when we have the first evidence of a successful move out of Africa. Around fifty thousand years humans are spreading into Eurasia. At about twenty thousand years the climate changes again. We enter into the late glacial maximum – very cold populations contract again, erm, there are some extinctions and human groups survive only in tropical refugia. But then the climate changes again and we have Holocene, global warming, populations expand again grow and we have here recolonisation of the northern latitudes and the arrival of modern humans into the Americas. And from eight ten thousand years onwards we have a spread of agriculture – what archaeologists call the Neolithic Period – and the beginnings of civilisation with agriculture communities develop social organisation, erm, stratification and we have the beginnings of what we called modern civilisation.

D.6

Frederike: Erm, I did a lot of preparations. I would just read through the material afterwards and try to y'know to make sense of all of it and then we also exchanged stuff so our class actually set up an email address where we would upload all the things we had. Like all the documents we had created like the, erm, outlines of stuff and and

and extra material we'd found and stuff we would upload and then use all together. ... The lecturers were not involved in that, erm, it was only we were quite an, a class with a high initiative level I'd say like, erm, they were, erm, we just always found new ways of communicating and helping each other. And I must say that everyone was really supporting each other. And that was actually another thing I was surprised about because before I came I was I was kinda concerned that it would all be quite, erm, y'know competitive and that people would y'know wanna be the best and everything. And it was the, the complete opposite. We came from so many different countries. So I guess ten countries within a group of fifteen people. And we were happy to learn about each other's, erm, experiences and lifestyles so. And, erm, the native speakers were always very supportive of us, of the non-native speakers so they were, we were helping, helping each other. Yeah.

Unit 9

9.1

Raquel: ... so that's what I found out about the pros of GM crops. Does anybody want to ask any questions at all?

Nik: Yes Raquel, you used the abbreviation FOE. What does that stand for?

Raquel: Oh, right, that means Friends of the Earth – it's an international environmental organisation. Sorry, I should have explained that.

Elena: You only talked about the advantages of GM crops. So are you saying that there are no disadvantages?

Raquel: Well, no, not at all. What I'm saying is that at the moment there's no actual evidence of health risks, damage to the environment, and that kind of thing. But that doesn't mean they'll never happen. And I think Nik's going to talk about possible problems a bit later.

Richard: Raquel, you talked about 'selective breeding' of plants. What does that mean exactly?

Raquel: Well, what it means is that researchers grow plants that have particular characteristics – their height, leaf shape, their yield, and so on.

Richard: OK, thanks.

Tim: You said that GM foods have better nutritional value. Why is that?

Raquel: To be honest, I don't know. I'll need to check on that.

Tutor: OK, thanks, Raquel. Nik, do you want to tell us about what you found out about potential problems of GM ...

9.2

Elena: So are you saying that there are no disadvantages?

Raquel: Well, no, not at all. What I'm saying is that at the moment there's no actual evidence of health risks ...

Richard: You talked about 'selective breeding' of plants. What does that mean exactly?

Raquel: Well, what it means is that researchers grow plants that have particular characteristics.

◀)9.3

1 **A:** How do you feel about the government's healthy eating campaign?
   B: What I think is that they need to target children more.

2 **A:** What did your survey tell you about motivation levels among students?
   B: What I found was that older students were better motivated than younger ones.

3 **A:** You said that businesses need to spend more on IT. Can you explain that a bit more, please?
   B: What I was talking about was how difficult some websites are to use.

4 **A:** You said that the mobile phone was the most important invention of the 20th century. Why do you think that?
   B: What I actually said was that it was the most important communications device invented.

5 **A:** You mentioned the new vaccination programme. Where can we get more information about that?
   B: What I suggest is that you have a look at the WHO website.

◀)9.4

What I'll be talking about is the GM controversy. What I've done so far is outline the advantages of GM foods.
What I want to do next is discuss some of the potential problems.

Unit 10

◀)10.1

Extract 1

... reduces the costs that individuals and the state would spend on medical treatment. That brings me to the end, so now let me round off by summarising my main points. First, health education improves not only the health of individuals, but also the nation as a whole. Second, it has been shown to reduce the number of premature deaths. Third, ...

Extract 2

... and this will have an impact on how health is promoted; for example, in deciding what features of life style to focus on in health campaigns. OK, let me just recap so far. I've tried to show that although western scientific medicine is dominant in guiding health care around the world, different cultures have different perceptions of health. I'll now say something about how some countries have tried to combine ...

Extract 3

... we talked a bit about health education in poor countries, but overall we thought that there wasn't much point in trying to get people to improve their diets if they didn't have the money to buy better food. People who live in poverty are probably more concerned about surviving from day to day than whether the food they eat will have long term effects on their health ...

Extract 4

... and a lot can be done to improve levels of fitness and stress management in the workplace. OK, I'm running out of time, so I'll finish by giving a brief summary of my talk. I've focused on health education providers in schools, colleges, companies, and healthcare settings, such as hospitals. I've tried to show that ...

Extract 5

... can I just add something here? I want to pick up one of the topics that Zak touched on briefly, and that was the increase in the number of young people in developing countries who smoke. It seems to me that the tobacco companies have a responsibility ...

Extract 6

... although some busy parents may find it difficult to find time to do this. OK, so up to now I've tried to show the importance of health education at home. I now want to give some examples of what's been done in primary schools to introduce young children to the importance of a healthy diet and life style. One example comes from ...

Extract 7

... we went on to talk about health education for children and our general view was that schools could probably do more to make children aware of the importance of healthy eating. None of us could remember being taught much about this at school, and we just ate what our parents cooked for us without thinking about whether it was good for us. Some of the things that schools ...

Extract 8

... and we had something to add about technology. One of the things that Mei mentioned was that people are getting less exercise with more time spent on computers and in front of the TV. But we thought that maybe these could be used more to give health education messages ...

◀)10.2

Olga: Smoking is still one of the main causes of death in a lot of countries. Of course, we should be trying to encourage everyone to give it up. But I think the main focus should be on preventing young people from starting to smoke. So we need better education, campaigns and things, targeting young people.

Maria: If you don't exercise, you have a higher risk of dying from a heart attack, and there's also evidence of a link between exercise and mental health. Everyone knows by now that exercise is important for staying healthy, but people still don't do enough. It's too tempting to sit and watch TV or play computer games.

Ben: It's important for companies to help their employees have a good work–life balance. In other words, to work hard but also to have free time and time with their families. It cuts down on people taking time off work through sickness, and so it's good for the company and also for the employees.

◀)10.3

1 There's a link between exercise and mental health.
2 There's a link between physical and mental health.

◀)10.4

1 human development
2 industrial waste
3 natural science
4 direct object
5 micro-economics
6 economic development
7 municipal waste
8 social science
9 indirect object
10 macro-economics

◀)10.5

1 The UN has come up with an index of human development.
2 Human development is the ultimate aim of economic development.
3 One of the key problems to be overcome is industrial waste.
4 The landfill tax has probably led to industrial waste entering municipal waste.
5 The social sciences include subjects studying the social life of human groups.
6 Some methods from the natural sciences are applied in the social sciences.
7 What's the direct object in this sentence?
8 In English, the indirect object usually precedes the direct object.
9 He was a specialist in micro-economics.
10 The course begins with micro-economics and goes on to macro-economics.

Lecture skills E

 E.1

Larissa: Erm, we have specific topics for each lecture. So it will start and end. Sometimes you have a lot of content inside one lecture so you should prepare a little bit before otherwise you really can get lost because of the amount of, er, information they give you. So, but we should we usually have a reading list, pre-reading list. If you don't, you should ask for[*] the teacher, for the professor something because it really, it's really helpful to have read something before. And, but to be honest it's not really difference[*] we should do the same when we are back home.

Frederike: Yeah, so, erm, my experience with, er, the lectures were like that they were challenging in the beginning because everything was so went so quickly and, er, most of them were native speakers. So, erm, like most of the students and all lecturers of course. So, erm, but really highly interesting so I I really loved going there every morning.

Zaneta: ... we had this lecturer, erm, and he presented his, erm, lecture, er, ... on the PowerPoint. But the vocabulary he was using it wasn't the vocabulary I was familiar with. For me these sophisticated words you know, I would go home and try to translate them into my language because, er, although I, you know, I completed like CAE, FCE exams and, er, courses before I actually went to university I just found that, erm, the language I know it's not actually enough to you know, to go to university. Because, er, depending on what you study for example my, my flatmate she studies psychology and for her it was much even than harder for me because to do psychology in another language you need to learn terminology. So I think that's the problem many students like myself face.

 E.2

Extract 1

What was happening at that time elsewhere? Well Europe, for example, was populated by Neanderthals. Whereas in Asia, we had homo-erectus and more recently we know we also had the hobbits, 'homo floresiensis' but no modern humans, and when I say 'modern humans' I mean people looking like you and me. No modern humans were present outside Africa at around two hundred thousand years.

Extract 2

But what about Europe? Some people have argued that Europe was a separate colonisation event. However, when you look at the genetic diversity of Europe in Europe almost all the mitochondrial lineages belong to two groups. These N and R which are also present in India in Asia and in Australia. So the most parsimonious, the most simple explanation for that is that this southern dispersal this southern route carried these three

major lineages all the way down to Australia, East Asia ...

Extract 3

But what happens if we introduce a barrier? Er, in this case a bunch of hungry cats. If we introduce a barrier, those two individuals are no[t] longer going to be able to freely mate. And they're going to have to mate with individuals from their own group. This is called 'interbreeding' and the result of interbreeding is a reduction of genetic diversity.

E.3

1

Extract 1

It's probably useful to look a little bit at what the environment was[*] around that time. So we were in what palaeoclimatologists call the interglacial, so warm periods, and at around two hundred thousand years we the, the climate changed and got colder so we went into a glacial.

Extract 2

But then but forty between forty and twenty five thousand years ago we find ourselves or we find the, the world into another of these interglacial periods so again the weather the climate was warmer and that favoured populations expansions and these expansions happened independently in the different areas of the world.

E.4

2

Extract 1

But then between twenty five and fifteen thousand years ago we find ourselves again in a gla- in a in a cold snap. So we're at the peak of the glaciation. This is called the 'last glacial maximum'. And what happened here is, erm, populations living in high latitudes start to struggle.

Extract 2

At about twenty thousand years the climate changes again. We enter into the late glacial maximum very cold populations contract again, erm, there are some extinctions and human groups survive only in tropical refugia.

E.5

3

Extract 1

So the fossil record did not give, er, convincing ... conclusive evidence. So that's when back in the early nineties geneticists came to the rescue. And they worked with, erm, the mitochondrial DNA. The mitochondrial DNA is, erm, DNA material that is present in our cells but is not present in the nucleus of our cells it's present outside. And it has a different mode of inheritance. Most of our DNA comes half from our fathers and half from our mothers. The mitochondrial DNA, our mitochondrial DNA comes only from our mothers.

Extract 2

So if you think it works a little bit like surnames. We have one mother. Two grandmothers. Four great-grandmothers. Eight great-great-great-grandmothers and so on but our mitochondrial DNA comes from one of them only so we inherited our mitochondrial DNA from our mothers and our mothers from their mothers and their mothers from their mothers. So it is possible to trace the line of descent very, very clearly.

E.6

1 The difference is that macroeconomists they're looking at the wider picture while microeconomists they are just looking at specific sectors, er, specific products specific individual decisions. And why do we need macroeconomics? Macroeconomics is useful because it enables us to study events that affect the economy as a whole.

2 ... the case also today. Inflation rate, er, is at very, er, moderate levels at about in, in Britain is about two point five percent. Er, in the US it should be around two, to two point seven so, very moderate, er, levels. And in European Union, er, because of the recession, er, is quite low too.

3 While in the seventies the picture changed. We were in an environment of high unemployment rate and high inflation. That is called 'stagflation' OK. Er, the economists used to say, er, in the past that there is a trade-off between inflation and unemployment. That if you want, er, lower unemployment you should be ready to accept higher inflation. Or if you want to disinflate you have to be ready to accept the higher cost in terms of higher unemployment. Er so this is one explanation why unemployment rate increased in the, in the eighties.

4 ... uh you see that, er, growth, er, decelerated. And then again it starting picking up again in the eighties and, er, in, er, the nineties. And as you can see, er, Germany and, er, US they do outperform, er, with the exception of the eighties they do outperform, er, Britain and that might be um, er, it has to do with the structure of the economy ...

5 And the personal disposable income is actually the amount of money that we have in our pockets after we paid our taxes to the government. And we can use that amount of money to spend on goods and services that's why it's called disposable.

6 ...we are talking about investment in machinery or investment in, er, buildings like this one. Um so that has again a positive you sees it is with a plus so that means that has a positive effect on, er, aggregate, er, output.

E.7

Extract 1

So I'm, I'm going to be talking about the role of geography in migrations in human prehistory. Erm, I'm going to be talking a little bit about natural selection and adaptation to different environments and the role of, of culture in, in all this process. Okay, so let's start with this first part.

Extract 2

Today most of the world has a farming economy and there are only small pockets where people have retained the hunter gatherer lifestyle. So I don't have time to go into this now, but one of the things that have interested me most over the years is how did we go from a world of hunter gatherers to a world of farmers?

Extract 3

... macroeconomists, they're interested in finding out what is the optimal policy mix [*]. They, the governments, they basically have two policy tools in their hands: the monetary tool, er, monetary policy tool, the fiscal tools and occasionally the exchange rate tool.

Extract 4

... economists used to say, er, in the past that there is a trade off between inflation and unemployment. That if you want, er, lower unemployment you should be ready to accept higher inflation. Or if you want to disinflate, you have to be ready to accept the higher cost in terms of higher unemployment. Erm, so this is one explanation why unemployment rate increased in the, in the, in the eighties.

E.8

1 Macroeconomics is useful because it enables us to study events that affect the economy as a whole. Without getting into much detail about specific sectors or specific products. So as I said some key issues in macroeconomics: Inflation. What is inflation?

2 ... and then you see since then it decelerated and now inflation rate is around two, two point five percent. Why there was[*] this huge, er, increase in inflation rate in in this country? And as we will see in a minute it wasn't just in this country it was across the industrial, er, the industrialised, er, world.

3 ... a specific measure of output in the market economy and is not a measure of welfare or happiness. OK. So it has certain limitations. We'll get back to that later on to discuss what are the limitations of, of that measure of the gross domestic product.

4 ... just having a look at that statistic is a statistic in fact you get a sense of how your economy is doing. OK. In comparison with other nations, with other economies. So increases in real gross domestic or gross national product I will define in a minute the difference between the two. It's an indication of the expansion of the economy's total output.

E.9

Dr Vlamis: Gross domestic product, er, by just having a look at that statistic (it's a statistic in fact) er, you get a sense of how your economy is doing OK? in comparison with other nations. With other, er, economies. So increases in real gross domestic or gross national product – I will define in a minute the difference between the two – is an indication of the expansion of the economy's total output. And that again that, er, figure, er, that, er, histogram in fact gives you, er, the picture, the relative picture, er, of, er, how the UK the US and Germany, er, were doing growth-wise yeah, er, in sixties, seventies eighties[*] and the nineties. So you see, er, all the three economies, all three economies they were experiencing quite high growth rates in the er, in the sixties. Five percent average annual increase in the, er, in the growth rate in the output growth is a huge number. Er, five percent for Germany about four percent for the US and about three percent for, er, Britain. Because of the oil price shock in the seventies, er, you see that, er, growth, er, decelerated. And then again it starting picking up again in the eighties and, er, in, er, the nineties. And as you can see, er, Germany and, er, US[*] they do outperform, er, – with the exception of the eighties – they do outperform, er, Britain and that might be, er, it has to do with the structure of the economy or, er, there might, er, be different, er, explanations why kind of erm, er, is Britain is, er, outperformed by, the US and Germany. ... Um let me just briefly define, er, the, er, give you the difference between the gross domestic product and the gross national product. Gross domestic product, er, it gives you the output produced by factors, the total output, er, produced by factors of production that are located in the domestic economy. OK? While the gross national product measures the total income earned by domestic citizens. OK? So they they the difference between the two, OK, gross national product is something wider. Er, gross national product is equal to the gross domestic product plus net income from abroad. Example. Erm presumably, er, there are British, er, people that they[*] work for the US embassy in the US. OK. And, er, they live in the US OK, but every month they are sending back to their family, er, an amount of money. OK, because presumably their families are based in Britain. That amount of money is part of the British gross national product because it's not income produced domestically is income produced in the US but is transferred to Britain. OK. Erm so this amount of money is part of the British gross national product but it is also part of the US gross domestic product. OK because it has to do with money produced by factors of production that are located in US[*]. OK? On the other hand if, er, you know nationals from Bulgaria and from Poland and from that er, they work, er, in this country OK, and they get a certain, er, amount of money as a remuneration. Erm that is part of the gross British

gross domestic product. OK. But when they are sending this money, or part of this money, back to their families in Bulgaria or in Poland or in another, erm, Eastern European economies. That is part of the gross national product of these, er, of these countries. Right, so that is basically the difference between the two.

E.10

Dr Vlamis: The next slide that I want to show you is, er, to give you, er, a a relative picture of how Britain, er, used to do, how it was doing in the different decades when compared with the US and Germany. So again here we measure the, er, annual, er, unemployment rate and on the vertical ax- on the horizontal axis we have, er, different decades sixties, seventies, eighties and the nineties. So, er, what can we make of it? Er, in the sixties it was US[*] that was outperforming Germany and, er, and, er, the UK and was that was quite reasonable because as I said UK[*] and, er, Germany they were Germany was completely destroyed and, er, Britain also was in bad shape[*] just after the Second World War so there was huge demand for labour. So unemployment rate was, er, quite low, I mean in Germany in particular it was close to one percent, OK and in Britain about two, two and a half percent. But the trend you see in the seventies and the eighties was for an increase throughout the industrialised world. And that was because of the supply shock, because of the increase in the, er, prices of oil. Remember at that time European economies were much more dependent on oil than they are now. OK? So that's why you see, er, that huge effect in, er, uh unemployment in the seventies and the eighties. And it remained, and you see then in the nineties, it remained at quite a high level.

Appendices

Appendix 1
In-text references

> ➤ *Using in-text references*
> **Unit 3, 10 p48**

1   You may find some alternatives to the in-text referencing conventions you saw in Unit 3. Compare the following styles of referencing:

> … women pay more compliments than men (Herbert 1990; Holmes 1988, 1998; Johnson and Roen 1992).

> … women pay more compliments than men (Herbert, 1990; Holmes, 1988, 1998; Johnson & Roen, 1992).

Both styles are possible. You can see that in the first example the word 'and' is used instead of an ampersand (&), and commas are omitted between author and date.

2   If you include a quotation in your writing, it is usual to give a page number in the reference:

> If the kitten was gently removed a very short distance away from its mother, 'the newborn kitten initiated weight-supported steps to return to its mother's side' (Bradley & Smith, 1988, p. 48).

Alternative in-text references: (Bradley and Smith, 1988, p.48) or (Bradley & Smith, 1988: 48).

Appendix 2
Quotations

> ➤ *Using paraphrases and quotations*
> **Unit 5, 9 pp 77–78, Unit 5, 10 p79**

> ⓘ *Different subjects and different institutions can have different conventions on including quotations in academic writing. In this appendix you will find suggestions on quotations and some examples, but the information you get from your tutor or university may be slightly different.*

1   For *short quotations* continue on the same line and put the quotation in single or double inverted commas (e.g. Extract 1).

    If you need to change a capital letter to a lower-case letter at the beginning of the quotation in order to integrate it with the text that comes before, put the lower-case letter in square brackets.

2   For *long quotations* start a new line and indent the quotation, but don't put it in inverted commas (e.g. Extract 2 and 4).

    What counts as a 'short' and 'long' quotation can vary. If you are not given information about this by your tutor or your university, take short quotations to be up to 30 words.

3   For both *short quotations* and *long quotations* -

   · Give a reference to their source using either the author-date (e.g. Extracts 1, 2 and 3) or the numerical system (e.g. Extract 4). It is usual to give the page number(s) in the reference (e.g. Extracts 1, 2 and 3).
   · Introduce a quotation with a colon if an independent clause comes before (e.g. Extracts 2, 3 and 4).
   · Make sure the quotation supports what you have said (e.g. Extract 3).
   · Make sure you introduce the quotation and, in many cases, add a comment on the quotation after it (e.g. Extracts 2 and 3).
   · Make sure that the quotation is integrated grammatically into the text (e.g. Extract 4).
   · Use an ellipsis (…) to show that you have left a word or more out of the source text (e.g. Extract 1).
   · Put in square brackets any words of explanation that you have inserted into the quotation (e.g. Extract 3).

4   Finally, always check that you use exactly the same words as in the source text.

Extract 1

> As Zygmunt Bauman sums it up, '[t]here are many hardships one needs to suffer for the sake of tourists' freedoms: the impossibility of slowing down, uncertainty wrapping every choice, risks attached to every decision …' (Bauman, 1998b: 98).

Franklin, A (2003). *Tourism: an introduction*. London: Sage.

Extract 2

> Of course the architectural influence arrived earlier as a result of the popularity of the Mediterranean in the early part of the twentieth century. A good example of this is the widespread building of public swimming pools:
>
> > A feature of many of the new European parks of the 1920s and 1930s was the lido – the open-air swimming pool. The word 'lido' was borrowed from the Italian word for coastline, but made famous by the reputation of the Venice Lido, and so the lido became the city's beach. (Worpole, 2000: 113)
>
> After World War II this aesthetic became widely and routinely drawn into modernising fashions and interiors.

Franklin, A (2003). *Tourism: an introduction*. London: Sage.

Extract 3

But just as tourism has become a way of life for a global world, it is, not surprisingly, becoming increasingly difficult to travel anywhere new or different that is in any way free from hazards: '[t]here are only a handful of places left on earth where you can escape all this [global sameness]; as I write there is no McDonald's in Cuba, no Coca Cola in Libya, and no television in Afghanistan. But in order to find real difference you have to travel well outside the political pale' (Simpson, 2001: xxvi). Most people do not travel outside the political pale and so they find themselves increasingly travelling inside the realm of the familiar.

Franklin, A (2003). *Tourism: an introduction*. London: Sage.

Extract 4

The Business Roundtable, which is made up of leading corporate CEOs, issued a report in 1988, *Corporate Ethics: A Prime Business Asset* [43], highlighting the ethics-related programs of ten major US corporations. The Business Roundtable undertook the endeavor because:

> The question of ethics in business conduct has become one of the most challenging issues confronting the corporate community in this era [44].

Epstein, E M (2002). The field of business ethics in the United States: Past, present and future. *Journal of General Management*, 28: 10–11.

Appendix 3
References: other sources

➤ *Giving references*

Unit 6, 8 p91

Type of source	Example reference
An article in a newspaper	Bennett, C. (2010, March 19). *The Guardian Weekly*, p. 21.
An unpublished dissertation	Armstrong, J. (1990). *Farm tourism in Canterbury and the west coast: a geographical analysis*. Unpublished MA dissertation. Canterbury, New Zealand: University of Canterbury, Department of Geography.
A handout from a lecture	White, M. (2008). *Recent trends in strategic management*. MBA lecture notes, 2008/9, Birmingham University, Business School.
An article in an online magazine	Merali, Z. (2007, December 21). Is time slowing down? *New Scientist*. Retrieved November 2, 2001 from http://www.newscientist.com/article/mg19626354.000-is-time-slowing-down.html
An online reference book or encyclopaedia	Kjellberg, A., Ljung, R. & Hallman, D (2008). Recall of words heard in noise. [Electronic Version]. *Applied Cognitive Psychology*, p. 1088.
An article in a journal; originally printed, but found online	Telescope. In *Britannica Concise Encyclopedia Online*. Retrieved 21 May 2010.
Government or other statistics online	Office for National Statistics (UK). (2009). *Smoking-related behaviour and attitudes, 2008/09. Opinions Survey Report No. 40*. Retrieved February 2, 2010 from http://www.statistics.gov.uk/StatBase/Product.asp?vlnk=1638

Appendix 4
Hedges: additional examples

➤ *Language for writing: hedges*
Unit 6, 7 p90

1	Modal verbs indicating possibility	might, could; may, can, would, should
2	Verbs distancing the writer from the claim or showing that the writer is speculating	seem, indicate; assume, appear (to be), believe, indicate, suggest, suspect
3	Adjectives, adverbs and nouns showing the degree of certainty	possible, possibly, possibility; about, apparent(ly), approximate(ly), essentially, (un)likely, perhaps, probable(ly), relatively
4	Other expressions qualifying or limiting a claim	generally, tend to, in most cases; in general, to a certain degree, mainly, to some / a certain extent, normally

Appendix 5
Cause and effect: other expressions

➤ *Language for writing: cause and effect*
Unit 8, 10 p119

verbs	cause, result in, produce, bring about, give rise to; lead to, produce, make is caused by, result from, is produced by, is brought about by; is produced by, is made by
nouns	result (of), consequence (of); cause, effect, result
conjunctions	because, so that, thereby; since, such that
complex prepositions	because of, due to, on account of; as a result of, as a consequence of, by means of, out of
adverbials	therefore, consequently, as a result, as a consequence; accordingly, because of this, in consequence, so, thus

Appendix 6
Passive verb forms

➤ *Passive voice*
Unit 8, G&V 1 p120

Present simple	Literature, it **is argued**, offers knowledge of the world.
Past simple	Neptune **was discovered** in 1846.
Present perfect	The problems **have been solved**.
Past perfect	Several factors **had been identified** in an earlier study by Lowe (1975).
Present continuous	Video conferencing **is being used** extensively by staff.
Past continuous	He wrote the book while he **was being held** prisoner.
Future simple	This **will be discussed** in Section Three.
Future perfect	As the surface of the early Earth cooled, carbon **will have been** one of the first elements to solidify.
With modals	An important limitation **should be noted** here. More funding **would have been needed** if the project had continued.

Other transitive verbs always or usually used in the passive voice in academic writing
be aligned (with), be based (on), be classified (as), be composed of, be coupled (with), be designed, be distributed, be estimated, be intended, be labelled, be linked (to/with), be located (at/in), be positioned, be situated, be subjected (to), be transferred, be viewed (as)

Other transitive verbs rarely or never used in the passive voice in academic writing
belong to, consist of, correspond to, depend on, differ from, resemble, result from/in, undergo

Glossary of grammar terms

abstract noun
A noun that refers to something that can't be observed or measured (e.g. *advice, knowledge*).

adverbial
A word (e.g. *quietly*), phrase (e.g. *through the door*) or clause (e.g. *after she left*) that functions like an adverb.

collocation
Refers to the way words are commonly used together. For example, 'research findings' is a common collocation in academic writing, but 'research opinions' is not.

complex preposition
A preposition made up of more than one word (e.g. *apart from, as well as*).

compound noun
A fixed expression which is made up of more than one word and which has the function of a noun (e.g. *handout, credit card*).

conjunction
A word such as *and, but, if, while, because* and *although* which connects words, phrases or clauses in a sentence. Compare with **sentence connector**.

evaluative adjective/adverb
An adjective or adverb that indicates the writer's opinion of the value, quality or importance of something (e.g. *important, surprising; interestingly, curiously*).

finite verb form
A verb form which indicates tense. Finite verb forms include, for example, *be; she is; he was*. Compare with **non-finite verb form**.

general noun
A type of abstract noun that can only be understood by referring to its context (e.g. *process, argument*). Sometimes referred to as 'signalling nouns'.

hedging
Using words and phrases to state possibilities, to hypothesise and draw tentative conclusions in order to avoid sounding too direct. These words and phrases are referred to as **hedges** and include adverbs (e.g. *perhaps, possibly*) and modal verbs (e.g. *could, may*).

multi-word verb
A verb together with one or more following particles (prepositions or adverbs) that has a single meaning (e.g. *write up, put forward, come up with*).

non-finite relative clause
A type of relative clause, usually beginning with a non-finite verb form, which has a similar meaning to a relative clause (e.g. The steps *outlined* below = The steps which are outlined below).

non-finite verb form
A verb form which does not indicate tense. For example, *to be, being, been*. Compare with **finite verb form**.

noun clause
A type of clause that functions like a noun or noun phrase. Noun clauses are linked to the main clause by the following types of conjunction: *that, if, whether*; *Wh*-words: *how, what, when, where, which, who, whose, why*; *Wh-ever* words: *however, whatever* etc.
For example: *Scientists believe that **the experiment will be completed in 2019**.*
A noun clause can also form part of the main clause, acting as the subject or complement of a verb. For example: ***Whether or not the experiment is a success**, will not be certain until the final results are analysed.*

noun phrase
A group of words where the main word is a noun (e.g. *The research presented in this thesis considers how children acquire language.*).

paraphrase
A report in your own words of what another writer has said.

relative clause
Relative clauses describe or provide information about someone or something that has already been mentioned. For example: *We recently did an experiment **which illustrates how children's knowledge of where an object is determines their behaviour.***

relative pronoun
A pronoun such as *who, which* or *that* which is used at the beginning of a relative clause.

sentence connector
A word or phrase such as *however* and *as a result* that show a connection between two separate sentences. Compare with **conjunction**.

viewpoint adverb
A type of adverb used to say what point of view a subject is being considered from (e.g. *financially, politically*).

wh-cleft
A sentence in which attention is focused on the new information at the end. It most often begins with a *what*-clause which gives old information. For example: *What I recommend is that you read chapters 2 and 3.*

Wordlist

Abbreviations: n = noun / n (pl) = plural noun; v = verb; adj = adjective; adv = adverb; conj = conjunction; phr = phrase; phr v = phrasal verb; T/I = transitive/ intransitive; C/U = countable/uncountable. The numbers indicate the page on which the word first appears.

Academic orientation

abstract *n* [C] (12) a shortened form of a speech, article, book, etc., giving only the most important facts or ideas

analyses *n* [C/U] (12) the plural of *analysis*, which is the process of analysing something

argument *n* [C] (11) a reason or reasons why you support or oppose an idea, action, etc

assumption *n* [C] (11) something that you think is true without having any proof

attribute sth to sth *phr v* [T] (13) to say that something is caused by something else

branch *n* [C] (13) a part of a subject

claim *n* [C] (11) something said to be true, although it has not been proved

connotation *n* [C/U] (13) the feelings or ideas that words give in addition to their meanings

consistently *adv* (11) always behaving or happening in a similar, usually positive, way

critical thinking *n* [U] (11) thinking about thinking; the practise of applying, analysing and evaluating information

debate *n* [C/U] (13) discussion or argument about a subject

determine *v* [T] (12) to discover the facts or truth about something

disparately *adv* (12) in very different ways

dissertation *n* [C] (10) a very long piece of writing done as part of a course of study

distinguish *v* [I/T] (11) to recognise the differences between two people, ideas or things

employ *v* [T] (13) to use something

evidence *n* [U] (11) something that makes you believe that something is true or exists

finding *n* [C] (12) (usually plural) information that has been discovered as a result of an official study

higher education institution *n* [C] (10) a college or university where subjects are studied at an advanced level

impose *v* [T] (11) to force someone to accept a belief or way of living

measure *n* [C] (12) (often plural) a way of achieving something or dealing with a situation

minority *n* [C] (12) a group of people whose race is different from the race of most of the people where they live

phenomenon *n* [C] (11) something that exists or happens, usually something unusual

plagiarism *n* [U] (11) an unacceptable way of using another person's idea or a part of their work and pretending that it is your own words or ideas by not acknowledging their source

proficiency *n* [U] (12) when you can do something very well

significantly *adv* (12) in a way that is easy to see or by a large amount

social sciences *n* [C/U] (13) the discipline which studies society and the way people live

stimulate *v* [T] (13) to make something happen or develop more

summarise *v* [I/T] (10) to express the most important facts or ideas about something or someone in a short and clear form

Unit 1

acknowledge *v* [T] (17) to accept that something is true or exists

adequately *adv* (16) in a satisfactory way; in the amount or to the degree needed

article *n* [C] (14) a piece of writing in a magazine, newspaper, etc

clarification *n* [C/U] (20) an explanation or more details which makes something clear or easier to understand

common knowledge *phr* (14) something that a lot of people know

communicable *adj* (17) able to be given from one person to another

deficit *n* [C] (17) the amount by which the money that you spend is more than the money that you receive

disproportionately *adv* (16) in a way that is too large or too small in comparison to something else

draft *v* [T] (14) to produce a piece of writing or a plan that you intend to change later

extent *n* (20) the size or importance of something

extrinsic *adj* (14) coming from outside, or not related to something

hypothesise *v* [I/T] (25) to give a possible but not yet proved explanation for something

infer *v* [T] (14) to guess that something is true because of the information that you have

influence *v* [T] (20) to affect or change how someone or something develops, behaves or thinks

influence *n* [C/U] (22) the power to affect how someone thinks or behaves, or how something develops, or someone or something that has this effect

interpret *v* [T] (24) to explain or decide what you think a particular phr, performance, action, etc means

intrinsic *adj* (14) an intrinsic quality or thing forms part of the basic character of something or someone

minority *n* [C] (16) a part of a group which is less than half of the whole group, often much less

outcome *n* [C] (17) the final result of an activity or process

peer pressure *n* [U] (14) strong influence on a member of a group to behave the same as the others in the group

progress *n* [U] (16) development and improvement of skills, knowledge, etc

recognition *n* [U] (17) when you accept that something is true or real

remit *n* [U] (17) the things that you are responsible for in your job

scope *n* [U] (17) the range of a subject covered by a book, programme, discussion, class, etc.

social status *n* [U] (14) position or importance in a social group

source *n* [C] (14) where something comes from

statistic *n* [C] (15) (usually plural) a fact in the form of a number that shows information about something

step sth up *phr v* (17) to increase the size, amount or speed of a process that is intended to achieve something

thesis statement *n* [C] (17) a sentence near the start of an essay in which the writer presents their main idea. In this book we refer instead to the *writer's position* on the subject of the essay

unsustainable *adj* (22) something that is unsustainable cannot continue at the same rate

widespread *adj* (17) affecting or including a lot of places, people, etc

Unit 2

consequentially *adv* (28) happening as a result of a particular action or situation

considerably *adv* (28) in a way that is large or important enough to have an effect

constitute *v* [T] (27) to be or form something

cope (with sth) *v* [I] (33) to deal quite successfully with a difficult situation

densely *adv* (27) with a lot of people or things close together

disaster-prone *adj* (33) likely to experience natural disasters more often than is usual

exacerbate *v* [T] (27) to make worse something which is already bad

field studies *n (pl)* [C/U] (27) research carried out in the natural environment, rather than in a laboratory or office

-induced *suffix* (28) caused by the stated person or activity

infrastructure *n* [C] (33) the basic systems, such as transport and communication, that a country or organisation uses in order to work effectively

judgement *n* [C/U] (33) an opinion about someone or something that you decide on after thinking carefully

lead to sth *phr v* (27) to cause something to happen or exist

margin *n* [C] (28) the outer edge of an area

occurrence *n* [U] (27) the fact of something existing, or how much of it exists

originate *v* [I] (27) to come from a particular place, time, situation, etc

prerequisite *n* [C] (37) something which must exist or happen before something else can exist or happen

probability of *n* [C/U] (28) how likely it is that something will happen

quotation *n* [C] (35) a report of the exact words of another writer

relate to sth *phr v* (31) to be connected to, or to be about someone or something

be responsible for sth/doing sth *phr* (27) to cause something to happen, especially something bad

risk management *n* (26) (in business) the forecasting of financial risks with ideas of how to avoid or minimise their impact

superabundance *n* (37) a very large amount of something

sustainable development *n* [U] (26) ways of changing an area that cause little or no damage to the environment

trigger *v* [T] (28) to make something begin to happen

Unit 3

analogous *adj* (49) similar in some ways

carry out sth *phr v* (51) to do or complete something, especially something that you have said you would do or that you have been told to do

catastrophe *n* [C/U] (53) an extremely bad event that causes a lot of suffering or destruction

conceptual *adj* (44) based on ideas

convention *n* [C/U] (50) a usual and accepted way of behaving or doing something

derive sth from sth *phr v* (44) to get something from something else

economical *adj* (53) not using a lot of money, fuel, etc

estimate *v* [T] (52) to guess the cost, size, value, etc of something

evaluate *v* [T] (43) to consider or study something carefully and decide how good or bad it is

extensive *adj* (51) covering a large area; having a great range

genre *n* [C] (50) a style, especially in the arts, that involves a particular set of characteristics

hypothetical *adj* (53) a hypothetical situation or idea has been suggested but does not yet really exist or has not been proved to be true

ideographic *adj* (44) of a written sign or symbol (= an ideogram) used in some writing systems such as Chinese, which represents an idea or object

implicit *adj* (42) suggested but not stated directly

integral *adj* (49) necessary and important as part of something

in-text reference *n* [C] (48) an acknowledgement in the main part of an academic text of a source of information

the literature *n* [U] (48) the information relating to a subject written by specialists

methodology *n* [C/U] (50) the system of methods used for doing, teaching or studying something

microscopic *adj* (53) extremely small and needing a microscope to be seen, or using a microscope to see something

primary source *n* [C] (48) information collected first-hand from historical documents, experiments, interviews, surveys, etc

ranking *n* [C/U] (50) a rank or level, for example in a competition

reference *n* [C] (47) a source of information (book, article, website, etc) that is acknowledged in a text

reference list *n* [C] (48) a list at the end of an academic text of all the books, articles, websites, etc. that have been mentioned in it

referencing convention *n* [C] (48) the accepted way of mentioning sources of information

reinforce *v* [T] (48) if something reinforces an idea or opinion, it provides more proof or support for it and makes it seem true

secondary source *n* [C] (48) a report, summary, interpretation or analysis of a primary source

semantically *adv* (51) in a way that is connected with the meanings of words

skeleton plan *n* [C] (51) a very basic plan

sought *v* [T] (51) past simple and past participle of *seek*: to try to do or get something

symbolic *adj* (44) representing something else

syntactic *adj* (51) the grammatical arrangement of words in a sentence

topic sentence *n* [C] (48) the sentence in a paragraph which summarises what that paragraph is about. In this book we refer instead to the *main idea* of the paragraph

Unit 4

analyse *v* [T] (51) to examine the details of something carefully, in order to understand or explain it

autocratic *adj* (55) having unlimited power and demanding to be obeyed

bureaucracy *n* [U] (56) complicated rules and processes used by an organisation, especially when they do not seem necessary

call for *phr v* (61) to demand that something happens

characterize *v* [T] (54) to describe something by stating its main qualities

classification *n* [C/U] (57) the process of putting people or things into groups by their type, size, etc, or one of these groups

conclude *v* [T] (61) to decide something after studying all the information about it very carefully

conduct *v* [T] (61) to organise or do something

contrast *v* [T] (54) to compare two people or things in order to show the differences between them

diverse *adj* (57) including many different types

embody *v* [T] (54) to represent a quality or an idea exactly

expenditure *n* [C/U] (58) the total amount of money that a government or person spends, or the act of using or spending energy, time or money

hierarchical *adj* (55) of a system in which people or things are arranged according to their importance

ineffectiveness *n* [U] (60) the state of not producing the effects or results that are wanted

insofar as *conj* (64) to the degree that

metaphorically *adv* (60) describes language which contains metaphors (= refers to something that is considered to have similar characteristics to the person or object you are trying to describe)

milestone *n* [C] (54) an important event in the history or development of something or someone

reject *v* [T] (61) to refuse to accept or agree with something

stereotype *n* [C] (54) a fixed idea that people have about what someone or something is like, especially an idea that is wrong

strategic *adj* (53) helping to achieve a plan, usually in business or politics

sustenance *n* [U] (58) the ability of food to provide people and animals with what they need to make them strong and healthy

Unit 5

communicate *v* [I/T] (72) to share information with others by speaking, writing, moving your body, or using other signals

complexity *n* [U] (78) when something is difficult to understand or find an answer to because of having many different parts

comprehensive *adj* (77) complete and including everything that is necessary

consensus *n* [U] (70) when all the people in a group agree about something

dispute *n* [C/U] (79) a disagreement, especially one that lasts a long time

encounter *v* [T] (73) to experience, especially something unpleasant

foundation *n* [C] (77) the idea or principle that something is based on

fundamental *adj* (73) relating to the most important or main part of something

magnitude *n* [U] (78) the large size or importance of something

manipulation *n* [U] (78) controlling someone or something to your own advantage, often unfairly or dishonestly

objectively *adv* (79) in a way that is based on real facts and not influenced by personal beliefs or feelings

observe *v* [T] (74) to watch carefully the way something happens or the way someone does something, especially in order to learn more about it

outline *v* [T] (76) to describe only the most important ideas or facts about something

partially *adv* (74) not completely

qualitative data *n* [U] (117) information relating to what something or someone is like

quantitative data *n* [U] (117) information relating to numbers or amounts

relatively *adv* (74) quite, when compared to other things or people

reliable *adj* (77) able to be trusted or believed

revolutionize *v* [T] (73) to change something in every way so that it is much better

scarce *adj* (77) rare or not available in large amounts

side-effect *n* [C] (76) an unpleasant effect of a drug that happens in addition to the main effect

spatial *adj* (72) relating to the position, area and size of things

transmit *v* [T] (73) to broadcast something, or to send out signals using radio, television, etc

vulnerability *n* [U] (77) when you are able to be easily physically, emotionally or mentally hurt, influenced or attacked

Unit 6

artificial *adj* (92) not natural, but made by people

bias *n* [C/U] (82) when you support or oppose someone or something in an unfair way because you are influenced by your personal opinions

broadly *adv* (87) in a general way and not including everything or everyone

by far *phr* (90) used to emphasise that something is the biggest, the best, etc

clear-cut *adj* (87) very certain or obvious

demonstrably *adv* (84) in a way that is able to be proved

dimension *n* [C] (82) a particular part of a situation, especially something that affects how you think or feel

gender role *n* [C] (85) a position that someone has in a situation based on the physical and/or social condition of being male or female

inextricably *adv* (83) if things are inextricably connected, they are so closely connected that you cannot separate them

interact *v* [I] (83) if two things interact, they have an effect on each other

interplay *n* [U] (83) the effect that two or more things have on each other

interwoven *v* [T] (83) past participle of *interweave*: when two or more things are combined so that they cannot be separated easily

lack *v* [T] (85) to not have something, or not have enough of something

lack of sth *phr* (90) when something is not available or when there is not enough of it

outweigh *v* [T] (89) to be greater or more important than something else

point of view *n* [C] (82) a way of thinking about a situation

prediction *n* [C/U] (82) when you say what you think will happen in the future

be programmed to do sth *phr* [T] (82) to always do or think a particular thing, although you do not try to

prominent *adj* (96) very easy to see or notice

radically *adv* (87) relating to the most important parts of something or someone; completely or extremely

seemingly *adv* (82) appearing to be something without really being that thing

striking *adj* (87) easily noticed

trait *n* [C] (85) a quality, good or bad, in someone's character

Unit 7

abandon *v* [T] (101) to stop doing something before it is finished, or to stop following a plan, idea, etc

anecdote *n* [C] (98) a short story that you tell someone about something that happened to you or someone else

beyond reach *phr* (100) not possible for someone to have

commodity *n* [C] (98) a substance or product that can be traded, bought or sold

discrimination *n* [U] (99) when someone is treated unfairly because of their sex, race, religion, etc

driving force *n* (102) a person who has a powerful influence and causes things to happen

eligible (for sth) *adj* (99) having the necessary qualities or satisfying the necessary conditions

emerging *adj* (100) starting to exist or develop

entrepreneur *n* [C] (100) someone who starts their own business, especially when this involves seeing a new opportunity

eradicate *v* [T] (100) to destroy or completely get rid of something such as a social problem or a disease

found *v* [T] (102) to bring something into existence

fuel *v* [T] (100) if you fuel something you increase or strengthen it

Honorary Professor *n* (98) An honorary professor is a teacher of high rank at a university who does not receive payment

inevitable *adj* (109) if something is inevitable, you cannot avoid or prevent it

influential *adj* (101) having the power to have an effect on people or things

justify *v* [T] (99) to give a good enough reason to make something seem acceptable

meaningful *adj* (100) useful, serious or important

perspective *n* [C] (98) the way you think about something

profoundly *adv* (100) deeply or extremely

proportion *n* [C] (99) the number or amount of a group or part of something when compared to the whole

rise *v* [I] (98) to increase in level

unfold *v* [I] (100) if a situation or story unfolds, it develops or becomes known

unrecognized *adj* (101) if something is unrecognised, people do not generally know about it or accept it as true

virulent *adj* (101) criticising or hating someone or something very much

Unit 8

acknowledgements *n (pl)* (116) a short text at the beginning or end of a book where the writer names people or other works that have helped in writing the book

appendices *n (pl)* [C] (116) plural of *appendix*: a separate part at the end of a book or magazine which gives extra information

axes *n (pl)* [C] (110) plural of *axis*: a line at the side or bottom of a graph

democratic *adj* (111) following or supporting the political system of democracy (= the belief in freedom and equality between people)

exploit *v* [T] (115) to not pay or reward someone enough for something

formulae *n (pl)* [C] (110) plural of *formula*: a set of letters, numbers or symbols that are used to express a mathematical or scientific rule

incentive *n* [C/U] (115) something that encourages you to act in a particular way

literature survey *n* [C] (116) a description of books, articles, essays etc that have been written on a subject

lower-tier grade *n* [C] (112) a less important level in an organisation or place of work

middle management *n* [U] (116) the people within a company who are in charge of departments or groups, but who are below those in charge of the whole company

motivation *n* [C] (117) the need or reason for doing something

negotiate *v* [I/T] (111) to try to make or change an agreement by discussion

outnumber *v* [T] (112) to be greater in number than someone or something

participant *n* [C] (118) someone who is involved in an activity

pervasive *adj* (112) present or noticeable in every part of a thing or place

pilot study *n* [C] (118) a piece of work or research that is used to test how good it is before introducing it properly

progress *v* [I] (111) to improve or develop in skills, knowledge, etc

progress *n* [U] (111) development and improvement of skills, knowledge, etc

tier *n* [C] (112) (in a place of work) one of several levels

transcribe *v* [T] (121) to make a written record of something you hear, such as speech or music

undergo *v* [T] (120) to experience something, especially a change or medical treatment

undertake *v* [T] (121) to start work on something that will take a long time or be difficult

upper-tier grade *n* [C] (112) an important position in a company or other place of work

Unit 9

as a rule *idiom* (128) usually, or in most situations

assimilate *v* [I] (127) to become part of a group, society, etc, or to make someone or something become part of a group, society, etc

compete with *v* [I] (128) to try to be more successful than someone or something else

controversial *adj* (133) causing a lot of disagreement or argument

controversy *n* [C/U] (128) a lot of disagreement and argument about something

cost effective *adj* (128) if an activity is cost effective, it is good value for the amount of money paid.

cultural values *n (pl)* [C] (127) the beliefs people have about what is right and wrong, according to the society they belong to

demographic *adj* (127) relating to the number and characteristics of the people who live in an area

displace *v* [T] (130) to take the place of someone or something

divergent *adj* [I] (129) very different

diversity *n* [U] (127) when many different types of things or people are included in something

illustrate *v* [T] (137) to give more information or examples to explain or prove something

in the long run *idiom* (127) at a time that is far away in the future

be predisposed to/towards sth *phr* (129) to be more likely than other people to have a medical condition or to behave in a particular way

the pros and cons *n (pl)* (127) the advantages and disadvantages of doing something

qualify for sth *v* [I] (127) to have the legal right to have or do something because of the situation you are in

reap benefits *phr* (127) to get good results because of your own actions

reciprocity between *n* [U] (129) behaviour in which two people or groups of people give each other help and advantages

reveal *v* [T] (137) to give someone a piece of information that is surprising or that was previously secret

shrink *v* [I/T] (128) to become smaller, or to make something smaller

subsequently *adv* (130) happening after something else

supporting information *n* [U] (136) additional facts or documents that help to show something to be true

threaten *v* [T] (128) to be likely to cause harm or damage to something or someone

Unit 10

back *v* [T] (140) to give support to someone or something with money or words

chronic *adj* (140) a chronic illness or problem continues for a long time.

consumption *n* [U] (142) the amount of something that someone uses, eats or drinks

criterion *n* [C] (149) a fact or level of quality that you use when making a choice or decision

determinant *n* [C] (139) something that has a strong effect on something else

detrimental *adj* (139) causing harm or damage

dominant *adj* (142) more important, strong or noticeable than anything else of the same type

equate to *phr v* (139) to be the same in amount, number or size

inconsistent *adj* (145) if a reason, idea, opinion, etc. is inconsistent, different parts of it do not agree, or it does not agree with something else

inequality *n* [C] (140) when some groups in a society have more advantages than others

insight into *n* [C] (148) the ability to understand what something is really like, or an example of this

juncture *n* [C] (150) a particular point in an event or period of time

life expectancy *n* [C/U] (139) the number of years that someone is likely to live

mortality *n* [U] (140) the number of deaths within a particular society and within a particular period of time

notion *n* [C] (141) an idea or belief

precede *v* [T] (146) to happen or exist before something else

raise *v* [T] (149) to cause to exist

specifically *adv* (140) exactly or in detail

stance *n* [C] (139) an opinion or belief about something, especially if you say it in public

substantial *adj* (149) large in size, value or importance

symptom *n* [C] (140) a physical feeling or problem which shows that you have a particular illness

to a lesser extent *phr* (150) not as much as something else

to some extent *phr* (148) partly